LIVING OVERSEAS

LIVING OVERSEAS
A Book of Preparations

TED WARD

THE FREE PRESS
A Division of Macmillan, Inc.
NEW YORK

Collier Macmillan Publishers
LONDON

The Free Press
A Division of Macmillan, Inc.
866 Third Avenue, New York, N.Y. 10022

Collier Macmillan Canada, Inc.

Printed in the United States of America

printing number
   5 6 7 8 9 10

Library of Congress Cataloging in Publication Data

Ward, Ted Warren
   Living overseas.

   Includes bibliographical references and index.

   1. Americans—Foreign countries—Handbooks, manuals, etc. I. Title.
E184.2.W37 1984   909′.0413   84–47807
ISBN 0–02–933960–X
ISBN 0–02–933940–5 (pbk.)

For Samuel F. Rowen

*Missionary, educator, theologian, and friend
of each whose life he touches*

*The walk of life is enriched by one's
companions on the trail.*

Contents

Appendixes

Acknowledgments

MANY HANDS, hearts, and minds make the work of an author more responsible, even as they attempt to make it lighter. The people who have helped in substantial ways are too numerous to list, but I'll try to do it, anyway.

The list must begin with Margaret, whose sojourning parallels mine; without her help and companionship this book would have reflected less love. And there are others for whom a special word is in order:

For Alemu Beeftu's care and concern for his people and their relationships with the sojourners from Europe, the United States, and now from Russia.

For Greg Trifonovitch and his witty ways of winning wandering folk to the wonder of culture learning, reflecting the wisdom of Russia, Macedonia, Palestine, Illinois, and now the East-West Center's Institute of Culture and Communication in Honolulu.

For Ricardo and Jennifer Crespo with their bilingual, bicultural insights—a family that lives at home wherever they may be.

For Sarah Ward, medical student and manuscript typist, former Tokyo tour guide and medical sojourner in East Africa. Intense, loyal, and interculturally gifted.

For David and Lisa Ward, sojourners par excellence, of whom a father couldn't be more proud—especially when Lisa's alert ear for language helps weed out the awkwardness from a manuscript!

For Eric Casino's contributions to our culture-learning workshops and especially his happy fusion of theoretical and practical matters.

For Kathy Graham Wilson's assistance in our summers of culture-learning workshops for teachers at East-West Center.

For Eugene Lamoureux's willingness to challenge conventional wisdom and to weed out the unnecessary abstractions in practical culture learning.

For Ruth Hill Useem, departmental colleague at Michigan State University, whose influence on so many of us has always pointed the way to clearer understanding of the world's common family of sojourners.

For the professional team at Missionary Internship, whose capacity to create effective learning has long been an inspiration to many—Sam Rowen, Virgil Newbrander, Duane and Muriel Elmer, Dwight Gradin, and Jack Robinson, to name a few.

For the technical assistance of Judy Hilgenberg, who surely knows her way through a manuscript, and for the expert guidance of my editor at The Free Press, Laura Wolff, for her patience, persistence, and perspective.

For those who have read portions of the manuscript and have shared their experiences, some of which appear in the text: Marion and Anita Way, Rio de Janeiro; Kay and Ken Harder, Nairobi; Chris Brown, Saudi Arabia and Intercultural Technology Associates, East Lansing; Luiz Lima, Rio, Paraiba, and Brattleboro; Margaret and Bryan Truman, Jakarta and East Lansing; Lynn Joesting, Nairobi and Minneapolis. Also for Jim and Lois, Arnie and Cathy, Howard and Edie, Dave and Mary Ann, Joyce, Pat, Maryline, Debbie, Elizabeth, Carol, Nancy, Frank, Marv, Frances, and lots of others, expatriates all.

To those whose professional roles in culture learning workshops and field experiences account for many of the viewpoints I hold: S. Joseph Levine, Jakarta and East Lansing; Dick Arnold, Taipei and Honolulu; Peh-Cheng Ng, Singapore; Sam Oleka, Nigeria; Wayne Shabaz, Teheran and Detroit.

And to end this page, as she has been ending my pages for a dozen years, my secretary and sharer in the way, Geneva Speas.

For all, thanks!

Introduction

AMERICANS ARE going overseas in a steady stream. Many are tourists for whom Paris, Tokyo, and even Bombay are just their latest in a long series of conquests. Like the venerable motive to climb the mountain "because it is there," the urge to see more and more of the world's great sights and cities is compelling and rewarding.

Other Americans will be staying longer. Theirs is the sobering challenge to move into another cultural setting and to establish both home and work in a strange and often perplexing situation.

No one who has lived overseas will tell you that it is easy. All sorts of tasks, many of them not very interesting, are involved. Worse, there are some emotional jolts along the way as you bid goodbye to friends, the familiar, and the handy. It hits hardest when you realize you have to start virtually all over again with many parts of your life: sorting out new people, establishing new friendships, and caring for family members whose own needs have changed.

The veterans of overseas service have their favorite horror stories, and part of the ritual is to pass these along to the newcomer: Sea freight that has been dunked in salt-water. Air shipments that were promised by a certain date (with the supply of baby diapers)— but that was before the airline's employees went on strike. The letter that arrived the day before departure saying that the American

School was already overloaded with third graders; maybe Bethann should stay in Biloxi with Grandma. And you're still in America. Just wait until you see what awaits you in Bangkok!

Before you pull up your roots, you should count the costs. Don't go into this matter blindly. Travel and adventure can be—and usually are—positive and desirable experiences, but for some it will turn out that the anticipation was more delicious than the fulfillment. For weeks and months we look forward to something— maybe with vague misgivings, but generally with bright optimism. Then the great moment arrives. All sorts of snags develop, now and then something comes unglued, the whole thing threatens to jump the track—but we muddle through triumphantly. And in the end we can say, "It was worth it!" Though overseas assignments have become more common, there is still today an aura of glamor and a touch of the exotic about the idea. Few Americans would reject an offer for an overseas assignment without giving it reasonable consideration. The very idea of travel, the challenge to move into the unknown, the chance to "stake out a new territory," the quest for personal accomplishment—these give the overseas assignment its appeal.

Careful thinking about what is involved may raise the flags of caution. Any move is hard; the overseas move is one of the very hardest. Though younger couples with no children may find two or three years overseas to be little more than a ripple on the sea of life, even for them there are some matters to think through very carefully. A mistake about the wisdom of an overseas move can be both costly and embarrassing. And since it usually involves at least a transition or shift in career pattern and lifestyle, it can be the mistake of a lifetime!

Those who want to make the overseas experience the highlight of a lifetime are invited to read, reflect, plan, and prepare. Toward this end, *Living Overseas* offers practical suggestions and illustrates some of the principles underlying the basic skills of culture learning. The capacity to turn the exotic into the meaningful, the strange into the familiar, and the mysterious into the enjoyable takes good intentions, good advice, and lots of practice. There are skills to learn, attitudes to nurture, and ways to get help in the preparation process.

Living Overseas can be useful as a part of one's orientation for expatriate living. It can help intercultural sojourners get off to a good start. One's outlook is more important than a storehouse of information. No matter how much a person knows, there will be surprises. What counts most is being able to learn from experience and to engage in the process of culture learning all the while one is overseas. Being a sojourner—living among others for a time—is a profound exercise in human relationships. Effectiveness as a sojourner is well worth the effort. It can make you a better person and a more valuable neighbor—and employee.

Among those who deal with hiring and firing, it has long been known that interpersonal relationships are the most predictable single source of on-the-job failure. Among those who face tough management decisions about Americans who must be relieved of overseas assignments because they can't handle them, "culture shock" is often used as a glib explanation. In fact, the problems far more frequently relate to interpersonal relationships than to any discernible sort of intercultural issue. Culture shock is quite possibly an overrated excuse for various made-in-America incompetencies.

The reader will discover in this book a reassuring tone that says, "You *can* make it." Scaring people into intercultural competency is out of style; the task today requires development of new skills and attitudes. Cultural difference is all around us, although we may not call it that when it is in our own neighborhoods. Living by one's own standards and values demands intercultural skill anywhere.

But make no mistake about it. An assignment in Toledo, Spain, is very different from one in Toledo, Ohio. There are skills to be learned that will make a difference, and there are ways to learn that will make a difference. The experience can be made more enjoyable, more understandable, and, ultimately, more rewarding in terms of both the purposes of the mission or industry and one's own fulfillment as a human being.

The purpose of this book, simply stated, is to explore the most important topics that relate to preparation for overseas living, and to alert the reader to the major matters that can make the difference between success and failure for the overseas family. Suggesting and illustrating a constructive approach to these matters is the practical side of this concern.

Living Overseas can be used in various ways: as an "assigned reader" for preparational workshops and training programs and also, more informally, for the self-directed reader who seeks a clearer understanding of what the overseas experience will offer and require. Every reader should find useful ideas and, above all, gain a clearer view of what the intercultural situation requires of tourist and resident alike.

Those who have studied this field are aware that two major weaknesses infect many of the intercultural preparation programs and much of the available literature. The first weakness is the assumption that orientation is more a matter of information than of outlook. The second is the tendency to make "orientation," whether in training programs or in literature, a matter of warnings—don't do this, avoid that, beware of this, and so on.

The predictable outcome of the first of these errors is the learned fool—a person who knows far more than he or she can possible use, but who lacks the rudiments of competency to *do* that which is purposeful and functionally sound. The remedy for this is to focus on the more generic skills, competencies, and understandings that add up to an open-ended capability to "learn by doing." It is simply out of the question to provide people, in advance, with all the facts and figures that they will need. A far better use of time is fulfilled in preparation—whether through individual reading or group experiences—that focuses on the way to look at a "foreign" experience. What should you look for? How can you accept the difference? How do you make meaning out of it? What do you *do* when it is clearly not the sort of context in which you feel comfortable?

The outcome of the second error, listing a forbidding set of warnings, is even more predictable. It raises the level of anxiety or creates a false confidence that is readily shattered on the field. Part of the problem is that the sheer mass of supposedly necessary warnings is beyond a reasonable capacity to list. But in addition, giving a person a list of warnings, especially when he or she is convinced that the warnings are important, encourages a sense of false security. As likely as not, the problems that actually will be encountered aren't even on the list!

Certainly there are some things you had better know before you try to get into Mecca, attempt to visit any mosque, or pat a child on the head with your left hand. But whatever warnings may be necessary are more appropriate if put in the forms of useful suggestions—advice about *what to do*, not what *not* to do.

Since these weaknesses—too much information and excessive warnings—are neither necessary nor satisfying, this book carefully avoids them. As a consequence, I have run the risk of making the tasks of intercultural living sound too easy and too much a matter of outlook and personal orientation. The alert reader will see that such oversimplifications are also invalid. An overseas move is a serious matter. In personal terms, the experience can be full of social enrichment, intellectual stretching, and a heightened consciousness of self and others; or it can be a disaster. Though the intercultural "disasters" get more attention, those who live in an intercultural limbo are even more to be pitied. Some Americans simply transfer their dull, humdrum lifestyle to an overseas location; they seem not to have noticed that they are living in a different country. They take their aches and pains with them; they continue to center their lives on the mundane, avoid new experiences, and resist friendships with people of the host nation. Their conversations are petty and they lack a passion for life.

At the institutional or corporate level, the overseas American is a highly visible representative for his or her sponsor. Whether missionary, relief worker, diplomat, or corporation manager, the overseas American represents a huge gamble for the sponsoring agency or corporation.

Some personnel people in such organizations believe that the agency or company would be better off if it didn't have to send anyone overseas. If only there were enough nationals who really understood the mission and were trained to do the job! But everyone knows this is wishful thinking. The shrinking world demands that the people of this nation must learn to work with the people of other nations, and to some extent this means—and will increasingly demand as time goes on—that *some* of the people in each nation will need to spend weeks, months, and years in the nations of the others.

Early in the century, when the shrinking world was first recognized as an important socio-cultural problem, all sorts of propositions were made about how to deal with it. Certain of these propositions were based on very naive assumptions. It is tempting today to call them silly. For example, there were the "one-world" advocates who saw the trend toward world-wide "closeness" as equivalent to coziness. "Since modern travel and communication put us all in close touch, we will know each other better and thus trust each other more," they said. Test this theory by putting a family of five or six in a mobile camper for a two-week cross-country tour. The underlying fallacy will emerge promptly. Closeness does *not*, of itself, lead to better understanding and improved relationships.

Fantasies persist. Today's favorite is that "*anyone* can do the overseas job." It hasn't appeared in serious print, but it has taken root here and there, especially in new high technology corporations that seek rapid expansion of international sales and among rapidly expanding relief and development agencies. The common factor here, rapid expansion, is a clue. After all, the reasoning suggests, the important thing is the product. People will want the product, we need to get it to them, it will help them, they will come to us. Thus it follows that our "reps" can get all the help they need after they get there—after all, plenty of people speak English. This reasoning leads too easily toward an underestimation of the complexities of the intercultural task.

When a military commander sends untrained troops into battle, the cause is jeopardized. Brash organizations do it all the time, and some even get away with it. But their people are badly wounded in the process. It is immoral to send unprepared people into intercultural assignments. In recognition of this problem, *Living Overseas* was written as a contribution to higher moral and ethical standards in American intercultural activities. To the extent that the reader is alerted to the realities, encouraged and specifically guided into sound preparation, and motivated to persist overseas as an effective learner of a second culture and its language, this contribution will have become a worthy investment.

To pursue this purpose it was necessary to bring together three types of literature. The matter of adaptation to cultural difference has long been a sort of side exercise for scientists of many varieties. Since the seventeenth and eighteenth centuries when aristocrats opened up the tradition of studying human variation, the ways that people relate to "foreigners" have been of interest. Much of the early literature of this sort tells us more about the idiosyncracies of the traveler than about the cultures visited, but it is worthy of attention nonetheless.

The aftermath of World War II, and specifically President John F. Kennedy's founding of the Peace Corps, opened the latest and most intensive period of research on intercultural adaptation. Once it became clear that there were pragmatic values in better preparing people to go into overseas service, the idea of studying what they need, how they perform, and how to train them became quite acceptable.

The major intercultural groups of the past had been somewhat "above" such questions since they played by the mandates of their own subcultures. Diplomats, since ancient times, have related almost exclusively with their diplomatic counterparts. Royal and imperial courts, for all of their variations across space and time, have shown more acceptance from culture to culture than have their subjects. For example, King Kamehameha IV of Hawaii was able to handle the stylistic demands of Queen Victoria's court. And Queen Elizabeth II seems to handle herself well enough in the court of Tonga. The differences—surely they are great—are willingly over-looked out of respect for the honorable status of each other. Would that all human beings could see the honorableness of their intercul-tural counterparts!

Missionaries usually lack a counterpart group until they build one. Too often, the formation of such groups depends on transform-ing and reshaping other peoples and cultures into American or Eu-ropean models in order to be able to relate to them.

Military people, of course, have fewer problems because they are expected to keep to themselves and because—it is always fer-vently hoped—they won't be there very long. (The military fiascoes in Vietnam and Afghanistan have provided everlasting reminders of the folly of this thinking.) Indeed, whether missionary or military, the fact that an intercultural undertaking has an explicit and lim-ited purpose does not reduce the need for intercultural compe-tency—not in the slightest.

The Peace Corps, professional exchange programs, and all sorts of international assistance programs have ushered in an era wherein many people need to be able to function well overseas—to be able to "hit the ground running." Research has been undertaken by Ameri-cans, Canadians, Europeans, and others in order to shed light on the personal and interpersonal skills needed for coping with inter-cultural difference.

Unfortunately, much of this research is out of reach, limited to technical reports in obscure journals and esoteric conferences.[1] It is not easy to "popularize" the research literature in this field. Rarely does it produce sensational findings; indeed, some of the basic find-ings sound distressingly like common sense. *Living Overseas* is based, in part, upon selected recent findings from this literature.

The literature of intercultural training has also been tapped. As the need for competent international workers has increased, the persons, teams, and agencies available to carry out training pro-grams have increased. Much of the literature that these people cre-ate is intended for use by other professionals. It consists mostly of manuals for the conducting of intercultural orientation workshops.[2] The major source of the materials that circulate within and among the networks of professionals engaged in the development and eval-uation of intercultural training is the Society for Intercultural Edu-cation Training and Research.[3]

The venerable and widely popular field of travel literature is a third source for this book. No survey or summary of that literature is included here, but the influence nevertheless is real. As can be seen in the great landmarks of this literature—Charles M. Doughty's *Travels in Arabia Deserta*; Robert Louis Stevenson's *Travels with a Donkey*; Mark Twain's *A Tramp Abroad*; Sir Richard Francis Burton's *Personal Narrative of a Pilgrimage to El-Medinah and Meccah*, *City of the Saints*, and *Exploration of the Highlands of Brazil*; and, of recent years, John Steinbeck's *Travels with Charley in Search of America*—the key to good travel literature is that it can be interpreted at two or more levels. People, places, and incidents are described in the narrative. The reader is expected to ponder the meaning—to consider the truth underlying the incidents. The author interprets and shades meaning, of course, but the reader is invited along on the journey as a full participant.

The literature of modern anthropology has its roots in this persistent tradition. The remarkable books of Franz Boas, Ruth Benedict, and Margaret Mead owe their style, the overcoming of scientific pedantry with the joy of discovery of people, to their predecessors in the travel books.

Living Overseas is intended to teach rather than to entertain, but in the manner of travel literature it uses illustrations and reflections in the first person. Lessons are shared as living encounters, each drawn from the experiences of the international circle of friendships which enrich my life. Each of the stories told here has the obligatory "moral." The reader may have to search to find it now and then, but there is at least one level of meaning beyond the entertainment itself—sometimes two.

1

An Invitation to Experience

AMERICANS ARE mobile people. Not nomadic—we don't move as huge extended families or as tribes—we just move, as individuals and as nuclear families. We move in this direction and that; to the summer cottage, to Florida for the winter, to the West for a new lifestyle, to the Sunbelt for a new job, from the unprofitable farm to the city, from the city to the suburb. Perhaps it is to benefit the kids, but whatever the reason, we move. Never mind where grandma and grandpa are, never mind the family cemetery plot, never mind that great-grandad's name is fading on the end of the old barn, the scavengers are stealing the barn-siding piece by piece, anyway; just move.

A NATION OF MOVERS

Our roots are shallow. Few of us live now where we lived as children. Few of our children will live near us after they grow up. It is easy enough for us to move. Americans have been doing it since the Mayflower. Our ancestors left the "old country" behind. Then they left the eastern ports and plantations behind. They moved westward. They slowly but surely filled up the livable spaces in a vast continent, but that wasn't the end of it; even today moving is a matter of typical American lifestyle.

As the technologies of transportation and communication have made the world smaller, the whole globe has become part of the swirling pattern of American movement. Americans come and go as tourists wherever they aren't locked out. Americans take jobs anywhere they can get work permits. Even where they can't, they often show up anyway, employed by "outside" agencies as missionaries, as relief and development assistance workers, as representatives of the government of the United States.

Americans retire overseas, taking advantage of any country that provides a lower tax structure or—depending on cleverness or affluence—even retiring to countries that have higher taxes. You find these senior citizens on Warsaw park benches in the summer, in Acapulco, in Costa Rica, in Guatemala, Puerto Rico, Canada, Italy, Greece, England, Bermuda, and in lesser numbers almost anywhere.

For people who take movement for granted, the idea of going overseas is very much within reason. For those who want to deepen the experience and gain the insights and human qualities that can come from learning a new culture, preparation is in order.

STRETCHING

An overseas assignment is an enviable opportunity for expanding yourself as a human being. You can look at the experience in terms of what it will ask of you—and it will ask much—or you can see it in terms of what you will gain. Given the right sort of preparation and a dedicated intention to learn and broaden your horizons, the time you spend overseas will stretch you in significant ways.

Intercultural encounter puts a person into potential tension and conflict with people whose outlooks and values are so different as to seem incomprehensible. Fortunately, no one needs to remain baffled. Even the unprepared person will pick up some culture learning skills—the hard way. How much better it is to let go of some of one's narrowness *in advance* and to stretch oneself into the basic understanding and skills of culture learning. It can begin now. To do so is to reduce the likelihood of pain and injury later.

Becoming more "experienced" is at the heart of the overseas sojourn. People who live and work in countries outside their own— they are called "expatriates"—are sure to see, hear, taste, smell, or touch things that their stay-at-home American cousins will never experience. It is this certainty of the new, the unknown, and the mind-expanding experiences that gives the overseas assignment its "good news and bad news" reputation. The good news is that it will be sure to stimulate and fulfill several vital human needs: curiosity, for one, and also the need for variety and the drive for conquest that springs from the human abhorrence of confinement. The bad news is that unless it is handled well, and especially if the expatriate is inadequately prepared, the overseas assignment can turn out to be confining, restrictive, and so loaded with anxiety that it will destroy self-confidence and reduce consciousness rather than expand and increase them.

Preparation should be keyed to what you want to experience rather than what you want to avoid. A defensive approach is a waste of time. Almost any intelligent adult can walk at the edge of the road and decide when to step aside when oncoming traffic approaches. It doesn't take a ten-hour learning workshop to learn rudimentary defensive tactics. What is needed far more is a commitment to get out and walk in the first place!

Preparation for the intercultural experience should lead to this commitment to get out and walk—and to walk briskly, knowledgeably, and expectantly. Perhaps a good place to begin is to become aware of what good it will do to invest several years of your life in an overseas assignment. Richard Brislin, one of the outstanding research reviewers in this field, has listed four categories of outcomes which he sees as thoroughly predictable and another dozen which are more or less sure, depending on the situation.

Beginning with the matters in which Brislin indicates highest confidence, you may wish to consider whether or not such stretching of mind and spirit would lead toward fulfillment for you.

Stretching Your World-mindedness

Keyed specifically to the awareness, tolerance, and acceptance of people of other cultures, world-mindedness is the opposite of narrowness, chauvinism, and bigotry. At the personal level it is represented by friendliness and willingness to appreciate differences of habit and viewpoint. At the philosophical level it is embedded in the conviction that all human beings have worth and dignity.

People with deeply held religious values tend to be ambivalent about world-mindedness. If world-mindedness is confused with "worldliness," it is viewed with suspicion. To be worldly implies being motivated by material things and unconcerned about spiritual matters. Indeed, it should be freely admitted that world-mindedness can be seen this way. But by no means is this the only way for a person strongly committed to a religious orientation to see world-mindedness.

A very old and substantial thread running through Judaism, Christianity, and other religious traditions as well is the exaltation of God the Creator through respect for and responsible stewardship of the creation. The reverence for life reflects this sort of world-mindedness. To be world-minded is to become more aware, more sensitive, better informed, and to be a participant in the joys and sorrows of humankind.

World-mindedness is a state of consciousness, of alertness to the mutual dependency of the family of humankind. To use Buckminster Fuller's metaphor, "spaceship earth" has many diverse passengers. Somehow they must see one another as worthy fellow inhabitants of the single vehicle. Whatever one traveler does affects the well-being of all. This abstraction summarizes a wealth of concrete facts that are of concern to the world-minded person. Wherever I sit, whatever I am doing, I see things about me that remind me of my indebtedness to others. My Brazilian coffee (the packager has blended it with portions of Kenyan and Colombian), my pen with its Zaire chromium, my clothing with Asian workmanship, my cat standing guard over her Japanese-netted tuna scraps: these things serve as constant reminders that there are "foreign" people to whom I am indebted and whose lives are touched by my life, even if I never leave home.

Their conflicts are barely under the surface: the struggles for decent wages of the African miner, the coffee worker, the Asian garment piece-worker; the battle at sea for access to the dwindling reserves of tuna. These are the realities of human conflict: Am I exempt? Do I share no responsibility? Am I fully human if I pretend that they are of no concern to me?

Christians, for example, believe in praying for other people. How can I pray responsibly for those whose experiences are frozen out of my life? For those of whom I have no consciousness? For those for whom I have no sensitive feelings? World-mindedness is an aid to responsible religious experience. One of the most effective ways to gain this valuable social consciousness is to spend time outside the United States living, working, and adapting one's lifestyle to the realities of another culture. One need not live in every culture to make these gains; indeed, there is a point of diminishing returns. What is most important is one's first substantial immersion in a frame of reference that is different—that is when the narrow boundaries of one's single culture are discovered and, potentially, broken open once and for all.

Stretching Your Humane Acceptance of Others

Brislin describes this second form of stretching as a "decline in authoritarianism." But instead of thinking of it as a reduction or decline, think of it as an increased capacity to accept others' viewpoints and a consequent willingness to share one's own autonomy. In one of the earliest studies that identified this factor, Watson and Lippitt found that returning sojourners tended to become less authoritarian and more accepting of others—even in their own culture. Moreover, this change persisted and matured even two years after their return to the home country.[1]

Measurement of tendencies toward authoritarianism has long been a favorite procedure of social psychologists, and sound tests of the trait have been available for many years. These tests measure the tendency toward black-and-white judgments (something is seen as either all good or all bad), the tendency to be suspicious or negative about anyone who is different, the insistence on systems of absolute obedience, and the presumption that one set of standards is or would be best for everything, everywhere, for everyone.

When confined to one culture—the culture of one's own childhood and youth—it is possible to maintain and even to entrench such authoritarian tendencies across a whole lifetime. The sojourner's experiences in another culture serve to knock loose the rigidities. If the tendency toward authoritarianism is very strong, the intercultural encounter can be very painful—for some, in fact, it can be so threatening that they may retreat into an isolated cocoon of their own making, or even return home prematurely. But if there is any adaptive flexibility that is not being suppressed by some extreme of bias and bigotry, the "breaking loose" has long-range positive effects, even if it begins with conflict and tension. Kagitcibasi's study of Turkish students in the United States supports the view that the lengthy sojourn in a second culture requires tolerance, flexibility, and open-mindedness. As these characteristics expand, one's tend-

sounds like ethnocentrism

ency toward authoritarianism decreases.[2] As the reminiscence and
reflection on the meaning of the intercultural sojourn find place in
the person's own history and perceptual background, their impact
on outlook and attitude toward others continues to grow.

Another way to explain these findings might be to consider the
sojourner's "return home" as yet one more intercultural experience,
presenting its own additional experiences and opportunities to reflect on circumstance and habits that once were taken for granted.
All these things work together to continue the stretching process.
People become more important in one's life. Accepting, trusting,
and affiliating become easier. One becomes more "at home" with
the family of humankind, wherever and whomever.

Stretching Your Capacity for Internal Control

Psychologists like to draw a line between internal and external control. The issue is relatively simple: a person is largely controlled either by standards and values that he or she has internalized or by
other people's commands, beliefs, or wishes. Think of it in terms of
normal childhood development—a child's life is largely a response
to outside schedules, standards, and expectations. As a child matures, a wise parent will allow increasing autonomy, encouraging
the child to make decisions and face the consequences. Thus as a
person matures, self-direction becomes more feasible and necessary.

Now and then we see a person who has never grown up. Though
physically an adult, this person always places responsibility and
blame on others. Such a person takes little or no initiative but is
highly responsive to outside influences, blown this way and that according to the "prevailing wind" of other persons who are seen as
the ones who really count.

The extreme of this syndrome is, of course, a serious form of
mental illness, but in its more subtle ways it can affect everyone
now and then. The argument can thus be made that intercultural
encounters have a mental health value since the very necessity to
cope with new and changing situations stimulates the development
of internal control.

Research on intercultural coping shows that most people cope
successfully most of the time. Successful coping gives a conscious
feeling of increased self-reliance and confidence. Thus it follows
that the increase in satisfaction that accompanies the exercise of internal control is one likely outcome of the intercultural experience.[3]

Research on internal and external control almost always includes a look at religious values and particularly "religiosity"—the dependency on the external patterns and standards of one's claimed religion. Religiosity should not be confused with the essence of one's religious convictions and internalized principles. It is concerned with the "for display purposes" aspects of religious affiliation. These externals of religiousness tend to decline as internal control increases.[4] In other words, intercultural experiences can tend to strip one's religiousness down to its basics. If there is no substance underlying the externals, it could be said that such a person might lose his or her religion as a consequence of the overseas experience; but by no means is this sure to happen. Habits die slowly.

For most people who value taking responsibility, being accountable, and being self-directing, the stretching of capacity for internal control is likely to be seen as an important plus. Thus the intercultural sojourn and its stretching of one's internal control tendency and capability are eagerly to be desired.

Stretching Your Achievement Values

Achievement involves goal setting, effort, and ability to make realistic assessments. These qualities and skills are not in any way unique to the intercultural experience. What, then, is the connection? The studies of returning sojourners and the follow-up research on those who have had extensive overseas assignments reveal a persistence of the increased internal control that affects achievement. These findings are especially important because a more simplistic view might hold that becoming an "internationalist" could work against the achievement values so essential for survival—or at least for career advancement—in the United States.

Apparently the intercultural experience increases one's abilities to set goals, to exert effort, and to make realistic assessments. These abilities are predictably gained or increased by a majority of expatriates, especially those who work in international agencies. Thus the outcome is a stretching of one's achievement values and related work performance.[5]

More Stretching

Beyond the four highly predictable consequences of intercultural experience identified by Brislin, there are other possible outcomes. In summarizing the clues for which his interview data did not provide solid predictive evidence, Kagitcibasi suggests trends toward

> less emphasis on social, national, and religious differences, greater tolerance and understanding of people; greater skill, ease and initiative in interpersonal relations; greater sense of responsibility; more self-control and self-knowledge; greater objectivity and flexibility in thinking, and tolerance of different points of view.[6]

One's _creativity_ is likely to be stretched by the intercultural sojourn. In the arts and literature one sees that many of the masterworks and "great periods" of highly creative individuals have been associated with one or another intercultural sojourn. The travel literature, for example, is rich with evidence that cultural contrast "turns on" the creative processes.

BECOMING A CULTURE MEDIATOR

The capacity and tendency to be a _culture mediator_ is another of the likely outcomes of the intercultural experience. The career patterns of many former sojourners reveal a tendency to volunteer or to be enlisted for roles or sideline activities as "culture interpreters or mediators." Knowledgeable sensitivity to cultural variations, skill in communication, and the attitude of reconciliation all persist and become the available bases for playing the role of mediator in intercultural or subcultural tensions in the work place or neighborhood.

Peter Adler[7] and Marvin Mayers[8] suggest that a new type of person and personality can come from the intercultural sojourn. Their arguments for a _bicultural_ or _multicultural person_ are well summarized in the following:

> Whatever the terminology, the definitions and metaphors allude to a person whose essential identity is inclusive of life patterns different from his own and who has psychologically and socially come to grips with a multiplicity of realities. We can call this new type of person multicultural because he embodies a core process of self verification that is grounded in both the universality of the human condition and in the diversity of man's cultural forms. We are speaking, then, of a social-psychological style of self process that differs from others. Multicultural man is the person who is intellectually and emotionally committed to the fundamental unity of all human beings while at the same time he recognizes, legitimizes, accepts, and appreciates the fundamental differences that lie between people of different cultures. This

new kind of man cannot be defined by the languages he speaks, the countries he has visited, or the number of international contacts he has made. Nor is he defined by his profession, his place of residence, or his cognitive sophistication. Instead, multicultural man is recognized by the configuration of his outlooks and world view, by the way he incorporates the universe as a dynamically moving process, by the way he reflects the interconnectedness of life in his thoughts and his actions, and by the way he remains open to the imminence experience.[9]

THE PITCH

Here's the way overseas experience is often advertised nowadays:

> If you're looking for adventurous living in a foreign land . . . the chance to travel to exotic places . . . and substantial financial rewards, we're looking for you. For many it's a daydream come true . . . foreign service in Saudi Arabia and the opportunity to put what you've learned to work for a top aerospace company.

The "exotic places" and "adventurous living" may turn out to be a bit sandy and dry, but the idea is the same as ever: exotic adventure is still appealing. Long-term employment overseas, especially because it involves moving one's family and making major changes in one's lifestyle, usually does not reflect the glamour suggested in this employment advertisement.

More to the point is another paragraph in the same ad:

> We offer a good base pay with a foreign service additive, a cost of living differential, and a completion bonus. An employee can accumulate substantial savings during his stay. In addition, housing, utilities, furnishings, local transportation, and educational expenses for dependent children are provided at no cost.

Whether actually necessary or not, the long-standing assumption in business, industry, and government is that it takes extra pay and extra fringe benefits to get the right people to take overseas assignments. In the example cited above, this may be true, because doing shop maintenance and servicing American-built jets in the Royal Saudi Air Force will probably turn out to be a bit less than an exotic adventure, except in the technical sense of the words.

The combination of glamor-loaded recruitment and the throwing of extra money into the hands of overseas employees accounts for some of the tensions among overseas Americans. Within the expatriate community there is a very wide span of salaries—even

greater than among comparable people and jobs "back home."
Thus social distances are exaggerated and resentments often flare.
The missionaries, at the one extreme, and the American executives
of multinational corporations, at the other, are worlds apart in so-
cio-economic terms, although in other ways they are part of the
same "minority."

Money can't buy happiness, whether at home or abroad. But we
can make some valid claims about preparation and its relationship
to satisfaction, achievement, and happiness. The chapters ahead are
concerned with practical steps to increase the probability that you
will have a satisfying and stretching experience in your sojourn
overseas.

With apologies to Professor Harold Hill, here is another way to
compose the advertisement:

> Step right up! You are about to enter into one of life's most intriguing
> adventures. You will never be the same after your very own discovery
> of the wider horizons that await you. Now friends, you wouldn't ex-
> pect to find that a thrill of this magnitude, an experience of such life-
> changing potential, and an encounter of this kind would be without its
> costs. Nosiree. There's a price to pay.
>
> But gather round close: The good news is that the cost isn't any-
> where near as much as you might have feared. Just for you and on this
> special occasion I'm offering a chance to enter into this most stretching
> of all life's experiences so very well prepared that the cost to you will be
> minimal. Minimal, I repeat; you can bear in mind that I didn't say
> "free."

A pitch of this sort is sure to make a sophisticated person suspicious. We learn quickly in life to put up our guard against anything
that sounds too good to be true, and we associate extravagant claims
with deception. So keep yourself alert. Ask what the following ideas
mean in terms of *your* understanding and experience. Don't take
anything for granted. After all, it's *your* life overseas that you
should be concerned about.

DEVELOPING A THREE-DIMENSIONAL VIEWPOINT

The overseas experience, at least its contribution to your maturing,
begins before you go. In the processes of preparation and orientation, things begin to happen. Far more than just anticipation, eagerness, and curiosity, what begins this enrichment process is the
orientation that awaits you. Whether your orientation is largely
through reading or through participation in an organized program,

you owe it to yourself and to the quality of the overseas experience to take it seriously.

Orientation is concerned with how you look at things. It's a matter of where you stand, where you direct your attention, and what you are expecting to see. The names of many landmarks, even some towns and cities, give evidence of this combination of concerns. Hiking on a mountain trail with an experienced guide, your party rounds a sharp bend and a new vista appears. "See it?" the guide asks.

"See what?"

"The Indian—Indian Rock!"

And you see it—for the first time—that nose, the headdress with the barest hint of a feather. Sure enough, from right here, perhaps nowhere else, the rock outcropping looks like the profile of an Indian.

"So that's why this mountain is called Brave's Point—I'd never realized that!" you exclaim. Ten steps later the profile fades back into its reality—a tumble of mighty boulders perched helter-skelter on the rugged mountainside. All over the world, well-oriented local folks can show you such spots: Castle Rock, the Citadel, Sheep's Nose Point, Indian Point, Washington's Profile, Lincoln's Rock, the Camelback, and so forth. The reason for the name isn't clear until you get into the right position, look in the right direction, and exercise a little imagination!

You learn to appreciate another culture in much the same way. The same three criteria are the ones that most need attention: where you stand, where you direct your attention, and what you are expecting to see. In the value system represented in this book, being well-oriented is a matter of actively learning a new culture by continuously cultivating an open and accepting attitude and outlook. A well-oriented person welcomes clues and suggestions about where to stand, where to look, and what to look for; but such a person doesn't want secondhand experience. As you get proper guidance and encouragement, you too will want to find out for yourself. You will come to value the exhilaration of search and discovery. Guided discovery is the name of the game—not naive wandering.

Where You Stand

Class consciousness and an "air of superiority" are ever so tempting for the expatriate. Pride and awareness of one's superior advantages and privileges in life can work toward a look-down-from-above stance. It is not unusual to hear Americans overseas tell of this temptation even if it had never been a problem for them before going overseas.

Perhaps it is the necessity of seeking housing with the other expatriates—often among the wealthy. Perhaps it is the staggering exposure to the destitution of the have-nots who crowd the *barrios* and the street corners in so many districts; perhaps even the heightened awareness of one's privileges in being an American citizen and having a job with a prestigious organization. Perhaps it is all of these and more, but whatever the cause, relating to others can so easily take on a tone of patronage and superiority.

In some ways, the local people play into this. In many situations it works to their advantage to feed the ego of the Americans. Thus, far from helping to develop a sense of comradeship, one's local associates become the perpetuators of the myth of American superiority. Especially for those who have "local-hire" subordinates and house servants, this posture—standing above and looking down—is hard to escape. Some even find that they enjoy it.

Standing at the shoulder-to-shoulder height of friendships and honest peer relationships is usually worth the effort, if it is allowable in the culture. Lasting friendships and the insight-producing heart-to-heart talks that can occur interculturally await those who find a humble and humane stance.

Where You Direct Your Attention

It never fails: a person can sense what you are looking at, whether you stare or glance. Acceptance is based on an open and non-judgmental appreciation of the other person's right to be different. A well-oriented person knows where to focus attention, and this refers to eyes and more than eyes. To match the host-country person's tendency to look at your eyes (or not) while conversing is a good first step, but to be aware of the sensitivities and preferences of one's colleagues is the foundation for the next dozen steps. You don't want to cause embarrassment by showing too much curiosity, nor do you want to ignore the interest or curiosity of others.

In every culture different sorts of things are acceptable to be talked about. In our experience in the United States it would be expected that a person would show sincere interest by asking about a friend's spouse: "How's Margaret?" But we would not compliment a friend by saying: "What a nice new watch! How much did it cost?" Yet there are other places on this earth where the exact opposite would be true: it is permissible (even expected) to ask about cost, wealth, income, and other such "personal" matters, but not accept-able to ask the *really* personal questions such as "How is your spouse?"

How to direct your attention so as to build and encourage trust is one of the first things to discover as you move into a new culture. Levels of formality, for example, can play a vital part. If the oral use of first names is common among newly made friends, then use the current American style. But if, as in Germany, Switzerland, much of England, and many many other places, first names are *rarely* used in any public situation or among business colleagues, be careful not to misdirect your attention—and theirs—by being too casual. Far from encouraging trust, it will build suspicion and hos-tility. Remember, whether you think of an act as trust-building is less important than whether the *other* person thinks of it as trust-building. Where you direct your attention must become quickly regulated by the new culture's standards and practices. When you are the outsider, it is up to you to adapt.

Accepting different viewpoints and values is among the hardest tasks in intercultural orientation. Be patient with yourself if it doesn't come easily.

What You Expect to See

Expectation is almost impossible to fake. If you are convinced all along that others are going to let you down, you have little if any faith and trust in fact, and this is very likely to show through. "I keep trying, but everyone knows these Africans just can't be trusted."

Really trying means accepting the risk of being let down, not simply guarding against it. Trust is more than an attitude; it is a whole system of investment. Lack of trust is like putting all one's money in the mattress. You may be able to sleep on it, but it won't do much growing. Trust is like an investment; there may be risk as-sociated with it, but you don't *expect* it to go bad. You expect it to grow. And, within reason, a well-made investment *will* grow. So it is with trust; you don't expect it to be violated, though once in a while it may go sour. You expect it to grow, and it usually does.

One should not be naive or overly incautious, especially in matters of health and safety, but risk-taking is necessary in intercultural relationships. One simply cannot wait until everything is raised to the level of confident certainty before acting. And even beyond this pragmatic aspect there is the satisfaction—even joy—that comes from a trust relationship with another person.

2

Who Are We?

Americans are everywhere. Some are enjoying their overseas careers; some are not.

Americans, more than any other national group, have opportunities to take up short and long assignments in various countries. The opportunities arise out of the particular social and economic realities of the American dominance in the free world today. It would be a mistake to assume that the opportunities come to Americans because they are extraordinarily gifted in the skills of intercultural relationships. Indeed, this is hardly the case. It may be more realistic to say that much of this "internationalism" is a by-product of affluence.

Of the purposes stated on passport applications by U.S. citizens, "pleasure" accounts for 26.8 percent, "personal reasons" for another 43.5 percent, while business, religion, health, and government together account for just over 9 percent.[1] These statistics indicate that Americans employed overseas are substantially outnumbered by American tourists, possibly by five or even more to one. The perceptions and opinions about Americans that are formed in the minds of host-country persons are shaped much more by the tourists than by the long-term sojourners. Our wealth—middle-class Americans avoid this word, but on the world standard it is an appropriate term—puts us in other people's neighborhoods virtually whenever and wherever we choose to go.

Long-term overseas assignments are less common than a rotation of two to five years within the span of a career. Even religious missionaries, whose overseas careers are generally the longest, are more apt to be two-to-ten-year people than ten-years-and-up. The concern of preparation for overseas living is not transplantation so much as temporary accommodation. The goal for the sojourner-in-preparation should be to become ready to make the very most of the overseas assignment and the opportunities that it will provide for development as a human being and a competent worker.

In the view of many who study this matter of intercultural competency, the preparation best begins with a clearer view of oneself. What influences and circumstances have shaped one's life and outlook to this point?

No one goes into an intercultural experience as a blank slate to be written upon by the events and people of that place and time. Each of us carries along a culture. We are what we are—whether or not we are conscious of it. What we are determines, to a large extent, how we will relate to others and how they will relate to us. Our culture interacts with their culture through day-by-day encounters.

Preparation will enable us to see ourselves more clearly and to be more in command in encounters with others.

Clarified personal, social, and historical perspective. Who am I and what makes me the way I am? Especially in the cultural and historical sense, what is an American?

Refined anticipation of what can be expected in the intercultural experience. What will it be? What will it demand? Of what value will it be?

Refinement of skills of intercultural encounter. How should I act? What can I do to communicate my interest and concern for others? How can I open myself to accept and trust people whose ways are substantially different from mine?

Self-assessment of readiness to enter into the challenges and stress of an intercultural assignment. How can I decide if I am ready? Can I anticipate and correct my liabilities before it is too late? What personal strengths do I have which will help me be competent and confident?

Honest assessment of one's intentions in undertaking the intercultural assignment. What am I intending to do? Are my motives responsible in light of humane concerns for the worth of people? How can I reconcile my intentions with the cultural values and circumstances I will find?

Development of a vision of the completion of the overseas experience and the return to the homeland. In what ways will I be different? How can I work toward a pleasant re-entry?

Becoming an effective sojourner begins with increasing your consciousness of who you are and how you got that way. Objectivity and a sense of humor help. Defensiveness and self-centered stubbornness are the most important enemies.

7–4–76

We are the people of 7–4–76. Nothing more succinctly illustrates the fact of our cultural peculiarity. On the fourth day of July in the year 1776, a dangerous step was taken by a somewhat representative body of fed-up colonial subjects. They were weary of British authority. Thus these Americans, on that date, chose to break with their own heritage and with the structures that had established and maintained the world that they had known.

They based their action on "the Laws of Nature and Nature's God" as well as "a decent respect to the opinions of mankind." Brave, bold, and from our own historical perspective, admirable. But one wonders about the possibility that the particular "mankind" whose "opinions" were "respected" might not have included the loyal subjects of King George III. Americans ever since have been in the habit of overgeneralizing their reasons for doing virtually anything of importance. If we see that something needs to be done, then it must be done—not simply because we think so but because nature and God so ordain and the opinions of mankind cannot be far behind. Dangerous logic, at best, but less well-justified in many subsequent decisions than it was in 1776.

> We hold these truths to be self-evident, that all men are created equal, that they are endowed by their Creator with certain unalienable Rights, that among these are Life, Liberty and the pursuit of Happiness.

Who are we? We are the people of 7–4–76, free to respect and, at the same time, to criticize our intellectual, moral, and political foundations. We are the people of open debates. We exalt the ideas and language of Thomas Jefferson's committee as represented in the

Declaration of Independence. But at the same time we are not ancestor worshippers. We freely acknowledge that Jefferson's and Franklin's appeal to the "Creator" was fuzzy and shallow at best, and that "all men are created equal" was believed only as an idealistic generalization. But the words reflect a foresight and integrity which continue to underlie the nation's highest ideals.

In modern America's craze for personal liberty—valued even above a free *society*—one sees life's liberty denigrated to the license to selfishly pursue the *things* of happiness. Our aspirations as individuals so often come from those values that inspire competition more than cooperation, achievement more than worthiness of purpose, and the material goods of an acquisitive lifestyle more than spiritual peace. Where do we learn that rights, of whatever sort, must be grounded in a quest for justice? That's a lesson so many Americans seem never to have learned.

Americans tend to be self-centered and to obtain security and a sense of worth from power. We are not alone; there are others almost like us in every nation on earth. But the discovery that our counterparts in many another nation are the rich and the powerful comes to many as a shock. We choose not to talk about it. Few have the courage to write about it: The American middle class is much the same as the aristocracy and the ruling classes in other countries. Our counterparts are the controllers of land and money, the people of bureaucratic authority.

As hard as it may be for affluent Americans to accept, even those of us with genuine concern and compassion are more like the rulers than the ruled. Our personal and social values, awash as they are in American materialism, brand us as rich.

Where do most overseas Americans live? In the neighborhoods of the wealthy. We simply do not "fit" in the *barrio* or the *favela*.

Where do most overseas Americans work? In the tall buildings of the cities. We simply are not overseas to slosh about in the rice paddies.

Where do most overseas Americans ride when they travel? In our own cars—rarely in local buses or trains. And regionally or internationally, we travel in airplanes—something as far from the life of the masses as the Land of Oz.

Yes, there is such a thing as "the masses." Yes, there is such a thing as a "peasant." The background of middle-class Americans causes most of us to see ourselves as neither rich nor poor—just "typical." But the hard fact is that *typical* in North America is *elegant* in much of the world. The gap between "the majority" in our country and the masses of Uganda, India, Brazil, China, Mexico—or even of Bulgaria, Poland, Spain, Greece, and Italy—is enormous.

Who are we? We are different, that's for sure. And the sooner we understand this, the better. We are the people of 7–4–76. The very sequence of those numbers is significant. The rest of the world, almost all, would write it 4–7–76. In our habit of speech, we say January first, June thirtieth, or September fifth, with the day following the month. Ironically, for our special national day we say, "Fourth of July." But when we write it or print it, it's still 7–4–76, July 4th, '76. When you get a letter from France, Brazil, or Japan dated "4.7.85," how do you read this? "April seventh" of course. Watch out! The rest of the world does it "backwards." So you have to remember the sequence: day, month, year. To any logical mind, this sequence has a reasonable appeal: from smaller unit of time toward larger units. But no. *Our* way is the norm. We are the people of 7–4–76; month-day-year, whether it's logical or not. So what is wrong with doing it the way we want to do it? Nothing. It's *wrong* when we think of *our* way as *the* way. It is wrong for us to presume that our way is the world-wide norm by which all other techniques and styles must be judged. The Japanese, like the British, drive on the "wrong" side of the road. Who is to say that the left side is the wrong side or that our way is the best way?

THE TYPICAL AMERICAN

A person may be every ounce an American—with every word and act fulfilling and demonstrating the accumulated essence of Americanness—and still not be self-conscious of it at all. Indeed, if the person on the street were asked, "Do you see yourself as a typical American?" the reply would probably be evasive or vague. Few of us have any particular consciousness of what makes us unique among the world's human family.

The ability to comprehend and accept uniqueness requires three characteristics that are not readily found in the typical American:

A person must have an intellectual awareness of the ways in which cultures can differ. If, for example, a person assumes that since all Americans seem to want to own cars, all people in the world would want to own cars, that person lacks awareness that cultures can differ in matters of values. If a person presumes that because Americans prefer steak to raw fish, all human beings must disdain raw fish, that person lacks awareness that cultures can differ in terms of dietary choices.

A person must be emotionally able to accept that his or her own values and outlook do not necessarily constitute valid world-wide norms and standards. The tendency to see difference merely as deviation from one's own norms is not unusual among human beings. Those who are different are seen as being in need of help to get closer to the norms. Such a view is the very antithesis of acceptance of the uniqueness of others. Accepting uniqueness implies that one believes there are contrasting norms in the world and that these represent fundamentally different starting places for comprehending oneself and others.

A person must creatively seek opportunities for exchanges and sharings across cultural lines. Lacking this qualification, a person will inevitably assume the role of giver and sharer, seeing oneself as having something that others need. The compulsion to give, to tell, to show, to explain, to help, and to provide creates a one-sided relationship, and it ultimately undermines whatever potentiality may have existed for mutual trust and sound human relationship.

Certainly chauvinism and cultural naiveté are neither uniquely American nor characteristic of all Americans. It isn't necessary for Americans to "put themselves down" in order to move forward into intercultural competency. But personal humility surely helps. Our single-minded notions of national unity, our tendency to glorify our past and exalt our heroes, our presumptions of supremacy and our view of ourselves as God's great gift to the world need to be held in check lest they dominate our relationships with others and blind us to realities of cultural difference and the validity of cultural uniqueness.

In sum, we Americans are people of an ascendant culture, tending to be proud of ourselves and of our culture and somewhat blind to those around us. The worst of it is that we tend not to see ourselves very clearly. If asked to describe the typical American, how would you answer?

CULTURAL CAPSULES

Automobiles, for Americans, serve as cultural capsules. They provide a way to enter and observe a foreign environment without risking the dangers of becoming part of it.

Not long ago I was eating breakfast at the non-com mess at an American Army post in Japan. This post, like several others on the outskirts of overpopulated Asian cities, is surrounded on all sides by the "teeming Orient." If ever there was a "forbidding" cultural challenge it is to the residents of such an island of foreignness.

A private, a tall Oklahoma youngster, was talking to a sergeant across the table, a woman who had evidently been in Japan long enough to gain some useful intercultural skills. I picked up on the conversation as the younger American was saying, "But I'd have to ride the trains to do that and I'm scared to death of this train system." "It's easy," the woman answered with the exaggeration that comes of wanting to forget that she too once had to learn how to transform the seemingly difficult into the easy and routine.

"I'd never learn to use them. Their signs are all in Japanese and you have to change trains so often. I'd be lost after the first stop."

"No, you'd catch on. Get someone to show you just once. Take an hour or two on Saturday and learn how."

"It would take me all weekend and likely ten thousand yen just to find my way back home. No. I'm just going to stay on post and go to a movie."

One more passive tragedy of the "American in Japan," I thought. It isn't unusual for people to become thoroughly intimidated by the combination of a nonromanized language, a location away from tourist-style resources and bilingual shopkeepers, a secure home base among English-speaking friends, and a growing conviction that one really shouldn't venture out for any reasons other than sheer necessity.

As the conversation went on, I caught bits and pieces between my cheese omelet, bacon, and grits (yes, Army grits on the Kanto Plains of Honshu). I heard one, then another clue that this young soldier with his fear of the Japanese train system (one of the finest in the world) owned a car and was driving all over the place. He was apparently willing and eager to go any place his car would take him, but he would turn down any excursions that required going by train.

Driving a car in metropolitan Tokyo? He was willing to do *that* but not to trust himself on a Japanese train? A real American! The car as capsule—his own private world, his foot on the controls, his hands doing the steering, his air conditioner, his stereo, his own selection of tapes. His America—afloat in the overworked, narrow, crooked streets of one of the world's most massive and complex cit-

ies. That he could handle. But the much faster, safer, more efficient
(and cheaper) Japanese train system? No, too scary.

What is the real problem here? American individualism? Infatu-
ation with the automobile? Fear of the unknown language? Unwillingness to take the risks involved in learning something new? Lack
of motivation to experience the particulars of a different culture?
Yes, I believe, all of the above.

RED TAPE AND BUMPER STICKERS

Bureaucracy, especially in the form of red tape and officious persons, tends to rub Americans the wrong way. In our own country
we grumble and complain, often trying to make shortcuts around
the red tape and avoid the self-important gate-keepers if at all possible.

Overseas, especially in the postcolonial nations, one can run into
red tape and officious persons in quantities never imagined even in
one's nightmares.

One common feature makes it slightly more tolerable: petty bureaucrats in many situations have some sort of "badge of office,"
worn proudly to signify that the wearer is a person of importance.
Many of these little semi-uniforms are selected and provided by the
wearer. Some Americans find it laughable; others are angered by
what they interpret as phony pretension. Instead of laughing or being offended, it might help to make a mental list of these little symbols of status, and recognize them for what they are, a human statement of self-worth.

My list includes a Bolivian customs man with a New York City
Police Department cap, an African parking supervisor with a London bobby's hat, a car rental station manager at a sweltering Southeast Asian airport with a very tired yellow raincoat emblazoned
with the logo of an American airline. Not to mention the little
touches: a shirt pocket absolutely jammed with pencils of many colors, a U.S. Marine sergeant's stripes sewn upside down on the sleeves
of a tee shirt, and a matched set of old blue-on-yellow LBJ buttons
neatly aligned over the breast pocket. I save my sympathy for the fellows who are required to wear ties in the tropics, especially those
whose ties show every evidence of never being untied—the knots are
loosened, pulled up over the head, and on again in the morning.

The overseas American will likely encounter such things and
laugh—at least inside. What right have we to laugh? These little

shreds of pride are, in many cases, the best claim to dignity that such folk can hold. All human beings have little ways to establish and communicate identity and purpose. Take a look at the Americans you encounter here or overseas: individualistic hair styles, clothes, shoes, baggage tags, bumper stickers, imprinted tee shirts, briefcases, and—especially—glasses. We have our little badges, too. And, on a per capita basis, more of us are bureaucrats!

DRESS CODES

Overseas Americans seem to take their dress codes more from each other than from the nationals they deal with. I shall never forget the insanity of wearing a tie while on duty in the U.S. Agency for International Development (USAID) office in Indonesia—a tropical among tropical countries, and one where the citizens are inclined toward casual dress. We Americans, even those on contract projects, had to take our cues from the Department of State civil servants whose grounds we shared. And so ties were worn, never mind the heat.

On the other hand, Tokyo is also hot and sticky in the summer. The American military uniform and off-duty garment in hot weather was the predictable "G.I. sloppy." As everyone familiar with Japan knows, the dark suit and tie are the order of the day— *every* day—among Japanese men. This "strange" habit *can* be found here and there in the tropics, especially in postcolonial East Africa.

Thus in Jakarta, where making appearances and showing off aren't really very important, the official Americans are laughed at behind their backs for their masochistic choice of stuffy costumes. Yet in Tokyo and postcolonial Africa, where appearances mean so much, Americans, even Army and Air Force officers who are being interviewed on television, often look as if they have just come in from mowing the lawn.

WAITING . . . WAITING . . .

Rare indeed is the American who enjoys waiting. Even in the United States waiting accounts for a significant chunk of time for most of us, but when overseas one tends to notice more and resent more the time and frustrations of waiting. Overseas it becomes easier to blame the waiting on distinctive others: *them*.

In any situation where the demand is greater than the supply, the flow tends to get slower . . . and slower. When a whole plane-load of people must line up at the ticket counter to seek alternatives for a canceled flight, things go from slow to slower. Complaining seems to make it go even slower.

Much of the slowness and "inefficiency" that is attributed to third world people (and to many others that Americans encounter overseas) can be traced to the simple fact of greater demand than supply. Shortages of all sorts are a continuing problem in many places.

In our own country we know where the shortages are at any given time and we are less inclined to be angry because we expect them. In our local hospital, for example, the emergency room can be counted on to be slow. It takes anywhere from ten to twenty minutes for the overworked clerk to get the questionnaire filled out. The demands for service are greater than the available resources. Workers get so accustomed to being a part of a slow system that even when there isn't an overload of demand, they can be counted on to be slow.

If we get used to a particular system being slow, we don't pay much attention; we simply adjust. But when we encounter an unex-pected slowdown in some system, we remember it, talk about it, and sooner or later we create a critical stereotype.

It is important to remember that there are far more shortages of trained personnel and specific commodities overseas than there are in the United States. Thus there are more slow systems. When you are tempted to complain and call down the wrath of heaven upon the heads of the people who seem determined to make you wait, re-member that we have our share of slow systems "back home" even with the comparative abundance with which the United States is endowed.

LOCKED UP WITH MR. HALLIBURTON

They threw Richard Halliburton out of some of the finest tourist spots of the world. To increase his own enjoyment of things "for-eign," this popular adventurer-author of a half-century ago insisted on showing up after hours, climbing fences, hiding until guards had closed up, and then indulging in one or another of his blanket-wrapped chilling nights which would assure a fresh and sparkling tidbit for his lectures back home in the States.

Halliburton was an American, and his audiences, with whom he was indeed *very* popular, were also Americans. They could identify with him every step of the way, especially with his compulsion to do things no one else had yet claimed to do. Born in 1900 in western Tennessee, he accomplished his feats in that period of deceptive calm between the two "Great Wars."

Paying his dues to the American ideal of the self-made man, Halliburton "worked his way" around the world, though his family's financial resources could have been tapped more easily. As a promising graduate of Princeton, he sold journalistic writings about his travels as he went, now and then taking work as a shipboard crewman, but always doing the unusual: crossing the Alps on an elephant (in the manner of Hannibal), flying from England to France in a little airplane (several years before Lindberg), climbing the Matterhorn the hard way—in winter, swimming across the Hellespont and from end to end of the Panama Canal—in stages, of course—"locked through" like any other ocean-going vessel and paying the fee on the per-ton basis, prorated to his 154 pounds. He was a traveler with an eye for the fantastic. His capacity to capture the commonplace and convert it into romantic images has inspired every travel writer since, and at least two generations of Americans overseas have sought the romance he glorified.[2]

Halliburton was a "places and things" person far more than a "person" person. He did heap praise on people of various cultures for their friendliness and kindness. But he seemed less motivated by concern for people than by his own curiosity and personal ambition to do the unusual. He assumed that his readers would be more interested in the adventures of going and seeing than they would in the interacting with other human beings. Overseas workers or travelers should be aware of the hazard of being locked up with Halliburton in this soulless compulsion for "going places" to "do things." For Americans, today, as for Halliburton, three problems combine to lock us out of an intimacy with people—and without intimacy there is no satisfying purpose in culture learning.

The first of Halliburton's problems was too much movement in short time periods. He simply tried too hard to do too much. Far better, of course, than lying in bed, but he moved *constantly*. In the complicated maze that was and is Cairo, he made a point of walking every street and lane. How much better a sense of the Egyptian people he would have had if he had cut out half the street hikes and spent the time sitting in two or three coffee shops talking to the

Egyptians, to the British military folks, and to the various expatriate families represented in that Arab-African metropolis.

Halliburton's second problem was one shared by most of his fellow Americans, even today: language barriers. Short-term visitors have an excuse for their linguistic shortcomings, but those shortcomings are very real and they do have their unfortunate consequences, alibi or not. To be able to converse only with those who speak English narrows the available sources of information down to those most likely to have opinions and outlooks substantially different from the rank and file: the travel agency and tour system employees, the wealthier folk who come and go in international travel, the better-educated minority (the privileged class), merchants selling their wares to tourists, and other expatriates. Halliburton made the best of these limitations and his example is sound. But, make no mistake, linguistic limitation is *real* limitation. Halliburton did far better when he described the British and the Germans (despite the apparent limitations of his schoolboy German) than he did with the Greeks or the Egyptians.

His third problem was his greatest handicap. Perhaps it is unfair to come down hard in judgment of him because he did not present himself as a true "culture learner," but it is necessary, nonetheless. Halliburton is, in so many ways, a paradigm of all Americans overseas; he is a mirror in which we can assess ourselves. His greatest weakness was in his purpose. He had come to exploit. No, he didn't think of it that way, and surely he would have contested this criticism. But his eye was always on what his exploits would mean back home. What difference his presence might make in terms of the health and welfare of the local folk seemed remote from his thinking. He wasn't out to hurt anyone, and one would hardly assert that Richard Halliburton did any sort of damage to international understanding, but his purposes were excessively restricted to his own capacity to entertain and inspire his own countrymen.[3]

Unfortunately, there are plenty of Americans overseas who are just putting in time to their own advantage and toward the advancement of their careers and their earning power. They are altogether locked into the narrowest of Halliburton's prisons. Making an effort to learn about the host culture might be a good way to escape that prison.

Then there was Gibraltar in 1922, and the camera. Halliburton had been explicitly warned that the British were very sensitive about photography from the heights of the great Rock, but like many Americans before and since, getting that "one more shot" was an all-consuming passion. In the words of an American adage, "rules were made to be broken," and up he went with his camera. He got away with it—the first time—and the second. But then thunder came down in the uniform of the British Army, and he spent several days thinking it over in a military prison.

Some of the most ridiculous things we Americans do overseas are done for the sake of that "one more shot." I've run the risk of getting stoned by photographing sensitive crowd scenes and riots from inside a closed car. I've dangled from precarious heights while local folks shouted out the dangers in three languages. I've waded in quicksand for the "perfect" angle of Mont-Saint-Michel. I've been held at gunpoint in Beirut and Tel Aviv. I've been chased by security officers in East Germany and taken to jail in Brazil—all for that one more shot. Is it worth it? . . . Would you like to see my slides?

In one way or another, we are all locked up with Richard Halliburton. Adventuring isn't dead yet!

AGGRESSION

Ours is an aggressive society. Our advertising, our television, our literature, even our children reflect this tendency in many ways. Given a bucket of Tinker-Toy parts, four-year-olds will, more often than not, put two or three pieces together to form a gun and then blaze away at each other, accompanying themselves with appropriate sound effects.

Aside from the moral consequences and the undermining of the quality of life in our own nation, this aggressive tendency has consequences in terms of how Americans are perceived overseas. Others develop stereotypes of Americans, whether or not deserved, and act upon them in their dealings with us. If you are from Chicago or New Jersey, be prepared to be asked how many gangsters you know. If you are alert, you will often detect a sort of "bracing against the blows" when people of other nationalities are approached by Americans, even in business relationships.

Among ourselves, we relegate the Western gun-slingers to a bygone period of history and recognize the shoot-first-and-ask-questions-later style as a caricature. For us it is a matter of simplistic tradition: good against evil, action rather than inaction, individualism, rights, and pride. But in societies where activism, individualism, and rights-claiming are less important to "the good life," Americans are seen as pushy, selfish, and conquest-minded. Many of our hosts overseas have learned to be "on guard" when dealing with Americans.

Since Americans are also rather good at spotting people who are "on guard," the plot thickens. Nothing brings out American pushiness quicker than an aloof, defensive, and slightly "fists up" stance of the opponent. The Western code of honor says you don't draw until the other fellow reaches for his gun, but even to have a defensive finger on one's weapon can be interpreted as the signal to attack. The very stance of the host national, no matter how peaceful and non-aggressive his intentions and hopes, is often interpreted as "spoiling for a fight" and the American lets him have it with guns from both holsters.

The tendency to shoot first and ask questions later is a deplorable consequence of being swept up in a culture of aggression and hostility. As Americans, we don't like to think of ourselves this way, but for many of us gentleness is a lost art. The overseas American needs to recover it.

REASONING DEMANDS REASONS

Is there an American with soul so dead who never to himself hath said, "Why? Please tell me why?"

Whether it is a police roadblock or a gardener who shows up on the wrong day, the American question is "why?" The reason for this concern about *why* is the concern for reasoning itself. Much of our intellectual life is wrapped up in a quest for connecting events to their causes. The linkage between cause and effect is a matter of concern dominant among people of Western societies. For Americans it is elevated to the level of a sort of basic right—the right to know why. When Americans push their *why* questions with such vigor and insistence, they become obnoxious to others.

In many of the world's venerable religious and philosophical systems, it is not expected that every experience or event will have apparent or even rational causes. Things simply occur—events just *are*. What do you mean "why?" Maybe there is no *why*—maybe these things are just the unfolding of destiny. *Que será será . . .* What will be will be.

Compounding this problem is another American assumption: the right to ask. It is best illustrated in practical situations. Consider the following situation:

At the Rio airport to pick up your colleagues returning from furlough, you discover that the plane from Miami is posted as being two hours late. "Why didn't they tell us it was late when I called just an hour ago? Now we have to sit here and kill two hours." Looking around, you discover many other people who are going to have to wait two extra hours. But it is the Americans who are "killing" the time; the Brazilians seem to be making some sort of jolly social event out of the unexpected good news that there will be two extra hours to talk, drink *cafezinha*, and perhaps make some new friends.

The Americans are more likely to congregate at the VARIG counter to ask *why* questions. "Why didn't they tell us the plane was going to be late?" The VARIG agent politely answers, "I don't know." He seems to find this answer more satisfactory than his American interrogators do. Indeed, he seems not even to care to know why this momentous news was not transmitted to these irate callers. He is thinking, "What difference does it make why they didn't tell you? Knowing the answer now won't change things for any of us." In his cultural perspective the answer to *why* seems trivial; but his life would indeed be simpler if he could give an answer to these Americans. Knowing *why* is important to their sense of well-being. What this Brazilian doesn't comprehend is that Americans see themselves as having a right to ask, and they are doubly distressed to discover that he doesn't share their curiosity. Why doesn't he call somebody and ask, "Why weren't these people told the plane would be two hours late?" As he sees it, not even he himself has the need to know. His duty is to pass along what he has been told: that the plane is two hours late. What else is there to say? And surely, the inquirers have no business pushing him to ask someone else; it would be beyond his proper role.

Sooner or later the Americans, having satisfied their cultural ritual of pushing and shoving on behalf of their "right to know," will have increased their stress levels and blood pressure as is common "back home." Then they will leave the counter, discover that lounge seats are hard to find because of all the convivial Brazilian parties, and thus cluster themselves in little angry circles, telling grim VARIG jokes and questioning the right of Brazil to have a seat in the United Nations.

Before long, it occurs to one of the more anxious Americans that a two-hour delay could mean something more serious than a stewardess who overslept in Miami. "Why is the plane late?" And the game is on again. Emissaries from the little angry groups are sent back to the VARIG desk and the pressure is cranked up even higher this time. The "right to know why" that Americans take most seriously is the right to know why the welfare of one's friends and relatives is in jeopardy. The new question "Why is the plane late?" can be asked with histrionic pathos and a sense of moral indignation that will drive the Brazilians to panic.

But Brazilians usually elect to sit on the bench while the Americans go on the offensive. Soon it is clear that the answer is, "I don't know." Americans then use the old end run: "We insist on talking to the supervisor." So at a higher level the attack is redoubled: "We insist on an answer—why is flight 605 from Miami late?"

The instincts of polite Brazilian personnel at the managerial level seem to include tactics of dealing with "Americans who irrationally insist on being rational." The supervisor graciously promises to find an answer, picks up a nearby telephone and dials three or four digits. (At random?)

"Yes, Control? Can you tell me about 605 from Miami. I have several people here who want to know why it is two hours late. . . . Yes, . . . oh, I see . . . yes, I will tell them. Tchau."[4] (Was he really talking to Control?)

"Ladies and gentlemen, thank you for being so patient. Weather over North Brazil has apparently required a slight diversion in order to assure a comfortable flight for your friends. All is well."

The triumphant Americans, now in command of the situation because they have the information, return to their little clusters of friends and relax a bit—but not much.

A variation on this rather common routine can occur in very large terminals when two separate supervisors, out of sight of each other, simultaneously go into their telephone act (or one of the other ploys used to make Americans more comfortable). Invariably, two different answers to the *why* question get into circulation and American tempers explode once again.

A second right that Americans claim at even a higher level than the right to know why is *the right to know whatever someone else has been told*. When two emissaries return to the same group to compare notes on what they found out, their stories are different. "That fellow over there told me it was a weather problem." "Well, the woman I talked to said she understood they landed in Belém for refueling."

When stories from two sources in the same organization aren't exactly the same, a third presumed American right comes into play: *the right to call other people liars.* So, it's back to the counter to start over, this time with all the meanness that can be mustered. After all, Brazilians *must* learn that you can't push Americans around, much less lie to them.

This type of experience, with all the hostilities and mistrust it engenders, is repeated in thousands of settings. One of the first lessons that Americans must learn in order to find peace and contentment is that there are some things best left unexplained. You really don't have to know the reason for everything.

Further, it helps to discover that there are lots of things we take for granted that really can't be explained in terms of *why*. Wait until you try to teach English spelling to someone with a phonetic-language background: Why is "sent" spelled three different ways? Why does "won" sound like "one"?

Before we leave the incident at the airport, take another look around. The Brazilians are having so much fun they'll be able to accept easily the change that just flashed onto the VARIG display: 605 from Miami is now posted *three* hours late.

PORTABLE CULTURE

Americans tend to take their culture with them. Perhaps it would be more fair to say that all human beings do, but Americans generally do a more thorough job of it because they can afford it. To see this phenomenon at work, one need look no further than one's own neighborhood. Even the decorations on a house, the way one grooms the lawn, or the type of decoration on an apartment door can tell something of the cultural history of the occupants. Note the decorations for a holiday—Christmas in particular.

On a much larger scale one sees the lawn-habit, born and nurtured in the eastern states and now consuming vast quantities of the Southwest's scarcest natural resource, water. To the expanding towns and cities of Arizona, New Mexico, and Southern California where hundreds of thousands of new immigrants have gone to search for jobs and warmer climates, they bring their culture from the East and Midwest; that culture includes lawns. And so they struggle. There goes the water.

The same thing can be seen overseas. Toilet paper, for instance, is a basic rudiment of American culture. Nowhere on earth do they make toilet paper as elegant as in America. So even if it costs an arm and a leg, expatriates will pay dearly for it, if and when they can find it.

The American culture now embraces convenience foods as a staple item. It can be amazing to behold the American buying frozen Birds Eye and La Choy oriental-style prepared foods in the commissaries at three times the price of the real thing in the markets and food stalls of the surrounding oriental communities. So deep are cultural habits that they are rarely questioned. How can such strange habits be explained? The answer is culture—ours.

McDONALD'S IN STOCKHOLM
AND OTHER TEMPTATIONS

The day McDonald's opened in Stockholm wasn't a good day for an American in Sweden. Swedes are especially sensitive to foreign influences that reduce their Scandinavian uniqueness.

In came McDonald's. Over 40 billion sold or whatever it was by then—largely sold on the everlasting promise that the next one will be predictably like the last one. Why not? Who wants a surprise in every hamburger? That idea went out with Cracker Jack.

Two issues came together in the riot of St. McDonald's Day in Stockholm: displeasure over the American involvement in Vietnam and anger over the audacity of American entrepreneurs to put up a McDonald's-type building and its customary advertising smack in the center of Stockholm's unique blend of the ancient and the ultramodern. Hardly anyone would have defended the architectural insult it represented, but it probably wouldn't have come to such a bad end—broken glass and all sorts of other wreckage—if it hadn't been for the deeper resentment of the pacifistic Swedes against the seemingly pointless American militarism in Southeast Asia.

Symbols draw fire. To understand tension in the various flashpoints of this troubled world, you need to be sensitive to *symbols*. A large car is a symbol of affluence. If people are angry about their oppressed condition and the contrast they see between themselves and the rich, they may lash out at a big car. A large house can be a symbol. Any sign of personal wealth can draw fire in a tense moment. But it goes beyond these personal things. A hospital or

church can be a symbol. To those who provide such good and
needed things, it may seem incredible that there isn't more universal
appreciation. "After all, you just can't help some people," one mut-
ters. People everywhere will accept only so much from the outside
before they begin to resent it. Consider what has happened to the
attitude in America toward Japanese cars. People feel dominated by
things that rain down unsolicited from some domineering source.
Their resentment becomes a cause and symbols of the intrusion become targets of mounting hostility.

Symbols—American and other—can sometimes be huge and the
waste they represent catastrophic.

One of the worst I ever saw was a huge and empty hospital in
Addis Ababa, Ethiopia. During the fascist expansion prior to World
War II, Mussolini had sent an occupation army into Ethiopia. All
sorts of evil resulted. The postwar Italian government wanted to
make a great display of its contrition and good will toward the Ethiopian people, and a huge hospital for the capital city seemed just the
answer. But the Ethiopians would not be so easily appeased. The
hospital, which had been built and presented with great fanfare,
was allowed to sit and fall into ruins. The Ethiopian government
stubbornly refused to outfit it, staff it, and use it. It became a symbol—a memorial not to Italian compassion but to Ethiopian disdain
for the Italians and their humiliation of a generation before. After
several years of making their point, the Ethiopians completed it as
theirs.

Americans sometimes identify themselves warmly and unthink-
ingly with the very symbols that focus people's antagonism toward
America. McDonald's should not be seen as either the root cause of
world tension nor as the most callous and offensive of the multinational corporations, but overseas Americans should think twice before becoming habitual patrons of such establishments as Mc-
Donald's, Kentucky Fried Chicken, Denny's, Bresler's Ice Cream,
Sara Lee, and the others moving steadily into overseas cities. To be
too close to them is to run the risk of being caught in the emotional
cross-fire. Make no mistake about it, some people resent these things
as symbols of American decadence, just as surely as they are accepted as evidence of "progress" and "development" by others.

For the "touch of home" and the occasional self-reward to which
overseas Americans like to treat themselves, these establishments
will always be popular. But it does seem sad to find them being used
by poorly adjusted expatriates to bolster their courage and fill the

needs caused by resistance to local restaurants and local tastes in food.

MUST WE BE NUMBER ONE?

Americans have become very conscious of chauvinism. The epithet "chauvinist" is used frequently. Minorities use the term to criticize those they see as their oppressors. In turn, in their search for dignity, the same minorities will themselves become chauvinistic in matters of ethnic power and pride. "Male chauvinist pig" has become one of the more inelegant battle cries of our times. It is a chauvinistic slogan directed against others who are "different" in that *they* are chauvinistic. Confusing?

In cultural matters virtually everyone has chauvinistic tendencies and moments of chauvinistic behavior. In other words, it is very human to take one's own experiences and values as a starting place or norm for comparisons and evaluations of others. In some ways, this tendency is healthy: it indicates pride and appreciation for one's own heritage and situation. In some nations there is very little tendency toward chauvinism precisely *because* the people have low self-esteem.[5]

Rampant chauvinism is the basic stuff of intercultural ugliness. Dignity is sound; restrained pride is healthy. But puffed-up preoccupation with one's own superiority is ugly, contributing nothing good to intercultural relations. The expatriate should avoid petty debates about whose way of life is better. The mark of sophistication is cool avoidance of polarized arguments over the goodness or evil of any particular aspect of the host people, their society, political system, moral and ethical foundations, their religion, or any other aspect of their culture.

Appreciation is what culture learning is all about. One does not have to give up rock to appreciate Rachmaninoff or reject Warhol in order to grasp Rembrandt. There is nothing wrong with having preferences—even favorites. Indeed some things may always be rejected. You may never learn to enjoy *balut*, a Philippine chick embryo delicacy available at most rural bus stops—but you don't have to "shoot off your mouth" about it. Restraint pays. Keep your opinion to yourself when there is no good to be served by expressing it. Why remind your host-country friends and colleagues that you are having trouble coming to terms with their way of life?

Chauvinism, the bolstering of one's own ego against the insecurities which threaten on every side, is a temptation that wanes over time. If you discover that life can be more pleasant without it, you will be able to suppress it. But if you give in too often, it becomes a part of your new way of life; thus it becomes a fundamental handicap. Instead, let your confidence show by acknowledging the worth of others and their ways of doing things.

THE METRIC MENACE

Among the least admirable traits found among Americans is the habit of defending the status quo by appealing to extremist rhetoric. The debate over use of metric measures has brought the irrational streak into public view as have few other recent issues. In 1976, when the Federal Highway Administration announced that the measures on the interstate highway system would be changed from miles to kilometers, almost 5000 letters of protest put a stop to the plan. In 1975, Congress enacted legislation for a gradual changeover, but the timetable has been badly frustrated. The depth of cultural habits at stake has proved formidable.

Defense of traditions and the established view of the world can be formidable. In the United States it is not unusual for such defense to include even the allegation that change may be attributable to some sort of subversive plot. In 1977 Gallup found that Americans were two-to-one against conversion to the metric system, which American scientists have used as their standard since the nineteenth century. America has only four allies in this brave battle against the metric menace: Brunei, Burma, North Yemen, and South Yemen.[6] A sense of the absurd helps us detect the plot: Metric measures are a big totalitarian scheme to subvert the whole world. If any of our four powerful allies should fall to the insidious metric plot, it surely will be like a chain of dominoes and the Americans will then stand alone—defending the inch, pound, and mile, those great symbols of the glorious days of the British Empire! How the mighty have fallen: even Queen Elizabeth must measure her royal robes in centimeters today.

The metric argument will ultimately be resolved quietly because of the power of yet another deeply held American value: the trader's pragmatism. If it helps sell American products on the world market, never mind the rhetoric about communist plots and our dear friends in North Yemen; let's get on with it. Up with metrics! Down with ounces and inches! Just watch the Boeing Company; it is one of the big hold-outs.[7]

Meanwhile, as Americans, we tend to justify *our* way as the best way and to indulge in all sorts of chauvinistic speech and extremist actions to resist the very thought that someone else might have a better idea.

> Men, even good men, are commonly disposed to submit to the slavery of the actual; they literally cannot imagine themselves in any life situation other than the one in which they live.[8]
>
> *Daniel Berrigan*

THE MELTING POT

Americans have historically taken pride in their openness to people of other nations. "America is the great melting pot," our predecessors used to say. But today we know that the "melting pot" worked in only one direction. Everything put into it was expected to be transformed to become like what was already in the pot. So many of us are left with no sense of our origins and little linkage with the past. Thus Americans have become largely pragmatic creatures of the present. Who are we, really?

In fact, Americans have always been ambivalent about the melting pot idea. In this country, as in many other countries, certain ethnic stocks are seen as more desirable than others. Perhaps it was America's beginnings as a slaveholding society that started this process of discrimination. Africans were wanted—indeed *needed*—to produce economic wealth, but they were unwelcome in contexts other than the subservient and separated condition that slavery imposed. Elaborate social customs, fables, and pseudo-religious beliefs were created in the minds of the dominant classes to keep the blacks "in their place"—to enforce their separateness.

Among European Americans, by the second generation, Italians could marry Poles, English could marry Dutch, and Spanish could marry French. By the third generation even the ancient hostilities of Europe could be put behind and French could marry Germans, and English could marry Irish. From this tendency to let the common experiences of the New World outweigh the bitterness of the past grew the myth of the "melting pot." It wasn't a planned or decided policy. It was just a reflection of fact; in two or three generations white Europeans could "melt" into the American scene and be more American than Irish or German—if they wanted to.

But racial lines are harder to bridge, especially if skin color, hair texture, and facial features are significantly different. The "melting pot" never worked too well for native Americans (Indians), blacks, orientals, and the European-Indian mix that has pressed northward from Latin America (for example, the "Chicanos," the short-form name for Mexicanos, a Spanish and Indian mixed stock).

The pride some Americans take in the "melting pot" is a phony pride. Our ancestors in this rich chunk of wide-open geography were willing to move over and make room for European newcomers because of the need for population, not some altruistic concern for the hungry and oppressed. Yes, "we" made room for "them," but we *needed* them. Space was no problem, but the shortage of cheap labor *was* a problem, especially after the Civil War forced a change in the economy. Independence from the European colonial powers had shifted the market structures, and a need to be able to sell American-produced goods this side of the Atlantic was already in the wind: thus a larger base of consumers was needed. Immigrants were very much needed—but only the right kind.

The nonmelted immigrant Americans have two characteristics in common: (1) you can *see* that they are different, from a distance of thirty feet or more, and (2) their ancestors came to the United States at the request of Americans who were importing and exploiting low-cost labor. Like it or not, there is a not-so-pretty side of the American free enterprise system. Since its earliest days, some ethnic group is always the "low face on the totem pole."

First it was the African slaves who had been invited to help out in the New World by one of the most elaborate and well-organized systems of tourism ever dreamed up by a coalition of coastal Europeans, New Englanders, Southern planters, and Arabs. After white Americans finally were forced to acknowledge that blacks were also human—thanks to a persistent campaign of godly preaching, a horrible and fratricidal war, and one man of profound principles, Abraham Lincoln—there were no slaves to build the much-needed transcontinental railroads. Once again the creativity of New Englanders went to work and a new slave-substitute class was invited into the Republic. And so our second great group of unmelting ethnic groups came from Asia to replace the blacks at the bottom of the heap. They stayed on, first, to work in restaurants and laundries, and soon, to out-America the "Americans" in banking, real estate, and entrepreneurial business.[9]

Their situation as postslavery railroad workers and common laborers was sufficiently different from that of the Africans before them that the Asian immigrants were able rapidly to take charge of their own destinies. They had not been blighted by generations of demeaning slavery and so, even though they found themselves stranded as largely unwelcome aliens in the Western states and territories, they pooled their resources and began buying and selling (and laundering and cooking) their way into the mainstream of American commerce.

The third major group of "unmeltables" has a more mixed history and shares with the blacks a still uncertain future on the American ladder of "success." It might be argued that these people, the Latin Americans, were never invited in at all; they just sifted in. But considering their major immigration patterns, it is clear that they, too, filled the need for "cheap labor" for American enterprise. Texas, Arizona, New Mexico, and Southern California have always had these "Latinos" around. In fact, since this part of the country was Spanish long before it was American, one must raise the same questions as with the "American Indians": What do you mean *immigrant*? Who were here first?

But still today they come. The Rio Grande does not make an impressive national border. But even if it were the tumbling Niagara—which it surely isn't at El Paso, for example—it would take half of the U.S. Army on constant patrol to stop the immigrants. Further, we lack the motivation to do so. Just as surely as in the early American slave days, it is still in the best interests of the free enterprise system to keep such sources of cheap labor flowing, never mind the social tragedy that results. The hope for a better life is still a powerful magnet, and even in days of recession and job shortage, life in North America seems better than the life of a peasant south of the border. Canada holds the same magic charm; note the thousands of Haitians in Quebec and the thousands of Jamaicans and other British West Indies immigrants in Ontario.

Anyone can melt who is *invited* to melt. Melting implies being submissively assimilated more than adding a new flavor to the mixture. A more honest metaphor would be "washing pot." That's it. America is the great "washing pot." When you are invited in, it is for one of two processes: to provide the latest influx of cheap labor for the system or to be assimilated by washing. To be washed in the American washing pot is quite an experience: you abandon your mother tongue and adopt technological English; you trade in your old name with its complicated spelling—even if you hang onto Schneider, you name your son John, not Johann; your daughter becomes Alice even if her mother's name is Alicia; you buy a car and forget how to walk, you borrow lots of money, and obligate your future to the lenders just like a good American. Little by little others forget—and you forget—who you were.

Now and then an Alex Haley gets a longing for a linkage with the obscure past; he gropes to discover his "roots." Getting a sense of family identity and a sense of continuity with history from knowing where one has come from is a valid concern; but for many Americans historical identity was washed off in the washing pot—or as in Alex Haley's case, gouged out by oppression. So much for the good old American melting pot.

TELEPHONES, NOISE, AND FREEDOM OF THE PRESS

Many Americans feel a commitment to the United States of America that runs deep. So deep that they feel free, even obliged, to raise questions and challenges. Among our patriots and national heroes were flag-wavers and social critics. The latter have served the nation more substantially.

Having worked overseas under repressive governments, my own commitment to the exercise of social criticism has been intensified. What makes our nation great is its people's commitment to self-criticism and improvement. "We, the people" are obligated to an eternal vigilance, not merely of the defensive sort against attacks from outside, but more particularly to a defense of the internal concern for the engines of liberty themselves: the persistence of a quest for justice and an exalting of the common privilege of inquiry after truth. John Philpot Curran, Lord Mayor of Dublin in 1790, put it well:

> The condition upon which God hath given liberty to man is eternal vigilance: which condition if he break, servitude is at once the consequence of his crime and the punishment of his guilt.[10]

Whenever I return from overseas, I breathe a sigh of relief, not only to be home, though that is no small matter, but just to be back in *my* country. How often I find myself smiling—uncontrollably smiling because of happy thankfulness that I am an American. Perhaps I look suspiciously pleased as I approach the U.S. immigration officer; I wonder how many Americans share this feeling?

I'm home. Back again where our cities are relatively quieter—by world standards—because American laws require engine mufflers and social custom generally frowns on blaring sound systems. (In Japanese cities even posh and otherwise gentle neighborhoods are entertained weekly by the mobile "toilet-paper man"—giving free rolls in exchange for bundles of old newspapers—playing enticing toilet paper jingles at 100 decibels from a state-of-the-art sound system atop his truck.)

Back again where there is at least a beginning effort to deal with air and water pollution. Rio de Janeiro's sparkling beaches somehow lose their charm when you step in raw sewage; Taipei, as one example among dozens of smog-bound metroplexes, seems intolerably laden with poisonous gases.

Back where classrooms and public waiting rooms have architectural safeguards against the distorting and deafening "boom" that drives some of us berserk.

Back again where the telephones work. Yes, on the world standard our telephone system is incredible. In Paris, for example, the telephone directories are almost useless because the numbers are listed according to building owners, not occupants. In Jakarta, the streets are thronged with the cars, motorcycles, and bicycles of servants carrying written messages to and fro because the telephone system is so overburdened that a busy signal breaks in after the third or fourth digit is dialed. In many countries one must go to a telephone center and make a reservation for a booth in order to make a long distance call.

Back again where ice cream is safe, where water is safe, where products on the grocery shelf are generally fresh, where milk and cheese have been dated and refrigerated. Back where the stores are full of hundreds of thousands of items. Back where there are laws to protect workers from the maiming injuries so frightfully common in even such an advanced country as the Republic of China (Taiwan).

Ours is a materialistic society, and that isn't all to the good. But the fruits of entrepreneurial capitalism under reasonable government regulation and restraint have made possible a convenient life-support infrastructure. It isn't perfect and we continue to argue for improvements. But it is far better than most.

At the top of my list of things to appreciate is freedom of the press. Having had direct experience with the restrictions on freedom of speech and press in even certain so-called "free countries" overseas and seeing the deprivation induced by extremist governments, I am thankful to be back in a place where the biases in the press are more likely the publisher's than the government's! Here, if I don't like the interpretations I'm reading, I can always find another viewpoint. It can be depressing to live where every newspaper and magazine says exactly the same thing.

As Elmer Davis wrote, it is more than the freedom to speak, to write, to assemble, to dissent—it is all of this and more: "What makes Western civilization worth saving is the freedom of the mind."[11]

CONCLUDING THOUGHTS

People who work in intercultural situations need to have a clear idea about who they are and why they are living outside their own country. Lack of a clear self-image and a lack of awareness of how one's history relates to one's purpose can keep the expatriate from fulfilling his or her mission.

It isn't unusual to wake up in the middle of the night and ask "Where am I?" This happens to travelers quite commonly. But when it happens night after night and is accompanied by a crucial second question, "And why am I here?", you can be sure there's trouble.

Preparing for an overseas assignment is demanding, at best. All sorts of practical tasks and additional chores are piled on top of an already frantic schedule. It may seem to be a bad time to take on additional reading. For some people it's hard enough to find time for this one book. Nevertheless, you will need all the sense of American history and of your own roots that you can muster.

Learning to relate well in another culture depends to a great extent on your bringing to it a clear sense of who you are—as a person, as a worker, and as an American. Thus we must begin this preparation for overseas living with ourselves. Who am I? Why am I stretching?

FOCUS FOR SELF-EVALUATION

Throughout this book you will encounter practical suggestions. Some of these will be clearly stated; others you will "invent" for yourself as you interpret the meanings of ideas and experiences of others.

The intention is to invite the reader into a larger realm of thinking and valuing, to make the reading process as much as possible an *active* experience. Thus at the conclusion of each chapter a series of questions will be presented to encourage self-evaluation. The reader who is serious about the need for preparation will enter into this task with every bit as much gusto as into the reading itself. Underlining the suggestions as you find them or writing notes to yourself in the margin may be helpful, especially if you wish to take advantage of this chapter-end process of review and application.

Groups or families who use this book as a part of orientation training should discuss these reflections after each individual puts his or her responses in writing.

Reflection

1. For me, the most valuable new idea in the chapter is_____
_____

2. I had never thought much about_____
_____

3. When this chapter on overseas preparation started out by asking about me and my cultural background, my reaction was_____
_____

4. If I had written this chapter, I would have emphasized_____
_____

5. In what ways am I apt to be socially different from those with whom I expect to work overseas?_____
_____

Review

1. When I go overseas, with whom am I likely to live, work, and socialize?_____
_____

2. What are some of my strengths that will be useful overseas?_____
_____

3. What are some of my American characteristics which are likely to stand out? Which of these will be seen as desirable? undesirable?_____

_____

_____

Commitment

This chapter encourages me to be cautious about these matters as I prepare to go overseas:

1. My view of America:_____

_____

2. My own sense of pride:_____

_____

3. My political biases:_____

_____

3

Learning a Culture

RALPH LINTON, one of the great American anthropologists, defined culture simply as "the mass of behavior that human beings in any society learn from their elders and pass on to the younger generations."[1] This definition does not suggest that the people who are "passing" the behaviors do so altogether deliberately and consciously. How certain behaviors are passed along is fairly clear: some learning takes place at home, schools are responsible for other tasks, and the religious community makes specific contributions. In addition, and perhaps even more important, the simple fact of living in a certain place at a certain time among a certain mixture of people is the most important factor in determining which features of a culture are passed on to the younger generation.

Linton's emphasis on behavior is important. Culture is more than an abstraction; it is as concrete as what people *do*—how they behave, what they invest in, what they take time for, what they eat, what they don't eat, what they reward, what they punish. Culture is all this and much more; and as any trained anthropologist knows, it can be *observed*.

CULTURE

The essential core meaning of "culture" is elusive. We use the word because we need it, not because we agree on exactly what it means. As a word, "culture" is ambiguous in the same way as the word "moral." These words are tricky. "Culture" may refer to a general category of concerns or to one specific and usually desirable manifestation of those concerns. "The culture of the Navajo" suggests a general category—those things that are characteristic of the lifestyle and values of the Navajo people. A more particular use of the word, as in "to bring culture to the Navajos," might suggest specific images such as building a branch of the Metropolitan Opera at the edge of some southwestern desert.

Some of the misuse of the word "culture" comes from the confusion of those two common uses, the general and the specific. Using "culture" in reference to a quantity or amount is another misuse. It would not be correct to ask how *much* culture a person or society has. This misuse occurs in such phrases as "not very cultured," "lots of culture," and "adding to their culture."

Culture is. It may change, but it doesn't become less or more. It may become better or worse from the standpoint of some particular value or set of values, but culture, as such, just *is*.

Culture, especially in the minds of museum-goers and readers of the *National Geographic*, can be associated more with the things of a society than with the way of life and the values that the things represent. But to those who study culture the word means the people, their lifestyle, values, and the ways they relate to each other and to those outside their culture. The devices, machines, decorations, architecture, art, music, literature, and communicative-expressive modes (language, signs, and dance) are the *artifacts* of the culture.

"Artifacts" refers to the objects and tangible products that can be collected, photographed, or recorded by those who study and represent the culture. A knowledgeable student of culture never thinks of a collection of artifacts as being one and the same as the culture. Such things *represent* bits of a culture, but these bits are always incomplete. Without an intimate grasp of the meanings of these things within the lifestyle and values of the people who created them, they are just so many curiosities—nothing more.

A. L. Kroeber and Clyde Kluckhohn compiled a large review in 1952, attempting to put together all the ways culture had been defined in literature. After noting 164 extant definitions they offered the following conclusion:

> We do not propose to add a one hundred and sixty-fifth formal definition. . . . We think culture is a product; is historical; includes ideas, patterns, and values; is selective; is learned; is based upon symbols; and is an abstraction from behavior and the products of behavior.[2]

The most important thing to learn about the correct use of the word "culture" is that it is a *neutral* term. It should not be used to indicate something good, desirable, or perfected. To say that a person is "cultured" is usually an affectation; to say that a person is "enculturated" indicates that he or she has incorporated the norms of a given culture with such thoroughness that the person exemplifies that culture.

In reference to intercultural preparation, less emphasis should be placed on the *things* of the culture of others than on the enculturation process itself. The concern is to become an effectively adapted person in a culture other than one's own.

CULTURE AS CONSEQUENCES OF HISTORY

In the final analysis, culture is people—their habits, their language, their relationships, and their view of the world. To see culture as anything less is to miss the point. We *are* our culture. Our culture is the accumulated consequence of our history. In one sense this is as true of us as individuals as of societies. We share a history more like certain people's than others'.

I haven't experienced all the things my brother has experienced. I'm not into all the hobbies that my son enjoys. I'm unique. My brother and my son are unique. But we share many things. Our histories overlap.

In the same way, my personal history and the personal history of my Ethiopian colleague, Alemu, have come to overlap. Is he becoming part of my culture? Am I becoming part of his culture? Yes and no to both questions. In this rapidly shrinking world many of us are living in close relationship to more than one culture. We move back and forth, and we are changed in the process. Our personal histories are becoming more complex. Thus our cultural history blends and overlaps with those to whom we relate in life. The relationships that are warm and trusting make for increased similarity. Those that are hostile and antagonistic make for distance and dissimilarity.

Since world view and values are at the heart of the concept "culture," it might seem that sharing a common religion would be a strong factor in the direction of a shared "history," even for two people of very different nationalities. The rest of two such people's dissimilar cultural history would affect the meaning and form of the religious commitment, however. One should not expect to find an "easy" cultural identity simply because of a shared religion. A satisfying sense of common ground is likely to be found in this sharing, but coming to realize it in personal terms would require extensive experience together across time.

Certain of the basic human relationships can also provide a cross-cultural common ground of shared history. Motherhood, for example, is a powerful element of shared history. I have seen two mothers carrying babies of similar age encountering one another in an airline terminal, on the street, at church, or in another such place; what happens is almost predictable. Each mother focuses her attention on the child of the other. Since an infant hasn't yet sunk into the culture in which she or he is being reared, the infant presents less cultural dissonance to an observing mother from another culture than would, for example, a ten-year-old. Thus the apparent common ground of infant and motherhood makes a cultural bridge of considerable strength. Two women, acknowledging this shared history, can easily enter into a relationship which could, if desired, be nurtured into greater depths.

Sharing experiences with others is the primary mode of developing a shared history. Is it then any wonder that those who teach the skills of culture learning and those who provide intercultural orientation training are constantly urging people to do things together? Our history is the world we are making, as Rollo May once pointed out.[3]

SUBCULTURES

Despite the largeness and fuzziness of the idea of culture, when the prefix "sub" is added, the resulting term becomes easier to define and illustrate. "Subculture" denotes a particular set of values and a lifestyle which are characteristic of a specific group of people. The emphasis is usually on the distinctive features of a smaller group within a much larger cultural conglomerate (see Figure 3-1). The American Indians (now preferring to call themselves "native Americans" along with Hawaiians and the Alaskan tribes) are one example of subculture. In some ways they are part of the American culture, sharing an identity and certain values with other Americans, but in other important ways they are unique. Thus, within the general culture of New York City, for example, there is a distinct subculture of Mohawk Indians.

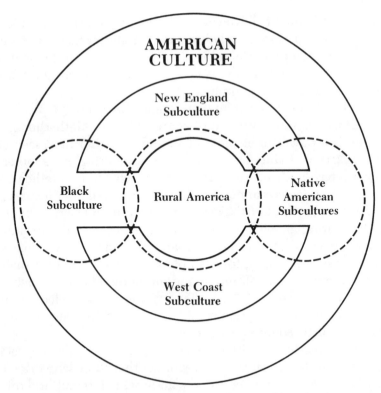

Figure 3-1. American culture and some of its subcultures

The specific focus on the values of a particular group within a larger society and its general culture is the correct use of the term. But subcultures also have their subcultures! So far, anthropologists have rejected the term "sub-subculture," but we do have a problem with the finer points. Just above, American Indians were described as a subculture of the American culture. Does this mean that the urban Mohawks and the Navajos of the Southwest are of the same subculture? No. All uses of "culture" and "subculture" are general and variable. The vocabulary of the field is confusing, though the actual phenomena may be less confusing. Only when we are generalizing do we get into these problems with language. When talking about the Mohawks, we use "Mohawks," "Mohawk tribe," or, better, "Mohawk nation"—*and* their culture. Then we can talk about the subcultural differences of the Mohawks who live in New York City, in contrast with their more rural cousins up the Hudson valley.

Culture learning is concerned with understanding cultural matters, whether focused on the mainline of a cultural group or on some subcultural variation. Understanding the culture learning task requires at least a familiarity with these terms and the general and specific uses in which they appear.

SOCIETY

Another of the ambiguities in reading and discussing culture is the word "society." This word has many widely differing common uses. "Society" can refer to a club or a professional association: The Michigan Historical Society, the Loyal Society of the Sons of Thunder, and thousands of others. "Society" also has a qualitative use, much the same as the use of "moral" to mean good or culture to mean the "higher" forms of music, art, and literature. Society, in this sense, carries a kind of snobbish connotation. One either is or isn't "in society," and if you aren't sure about yourself, you probably *aren't*, my deah.

To the social scientist, "society" has quite a different meaning: it refers to the ways people group and organize themselves. "Society" is the word used to emphasize the unity or the composite group-ness among a particular people. It is nevertheless a collective word. One can speak of American society, knowing full well that it consists of many levels. The middle-class society is one subdivision. The laboring-class society is another, not totally different from the former. Thus the freedom to use the word "society" to represent overlapping sets makes the layman very uncomfortable. It also suggests to many observers that social scientists are much too imprecise when they think and talk about concepts.

In defense of the field, it should be pointed out that all scientific terminology is arbitrary and that the people who invent taxonomies stand ready to teach newcomers how to use them. Ambiguous as such words may be, without the terms "culture" and "society"— with all of their subdivisions and levels of meaning—understanding human experience would be even more complicated. Figure 3–2 is a representation of how one can think about society. Overlapping circles represent all sorts of affiliations and institutional structures with which an individual or a family might be identified.

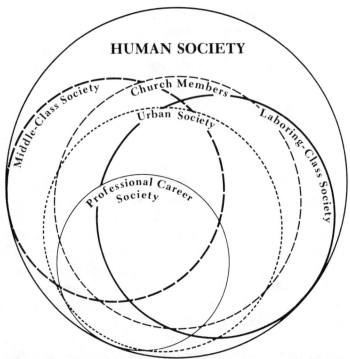

Figure 3-2.   The overlapping societies within society

CASINO'S MODEL OF CULTURE LEARNING

As a research specialist in the Culture Learning Institute of the East-West Center, Honolulu, Eric Casino has studied the process through which a person takes on the habits, outlook, and lifestyle characteristic of a given culture. Casino described two modes of culture learning: the sinking mode and the rising mode.[4] *Sinking* refers to the ways cultural patterns become our habits, so that we become unconscious of them. *Rising* refers to the elevating into conscious thought of the cultural elements in which we are participating. These two modes are the ways we learn a culture, our own or some other culture.

Sinking into Culture

In Casino's view there are four ways in which we learn a culture (see Figure 3-3); sinking accounts for one way of learning one's own culture and one way of learning another culture.

SINKING MODE   RISING MODE

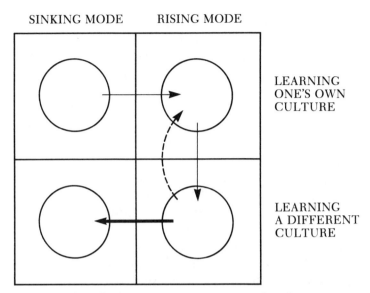

LEARNING
ONE'S OWN
CULTURE

LEARNING
A DIFFERENT
CULTURE

Figure 3-3. Culture learning: two modes, four forms

More often than not, when people are concerned about learning a culture or even learning *about* a culture, it is because they have become interested in some culture other than their own. In other words, Americans may want to learn about the Japanese culture, and the Japanese in turn may want to learn about the American culture.

But Casino asks the prior question: how did these people learn about their *own* culture? It is clear that neither Japanese nor Americans are born with knowledge of a culture. In fact, it is obvious that when humans enter this world as infants, they share what little they have of behavior styles with all other human babies. When they are thirsty, hungry, cold, hot, or hurting, they cry. Little by little they learn other ways to meet these needs. Little by little they learn about other needs and diverse ways to meet them. Little by little they become a part of the culture into which they entered at birth. They learn their culture.

Most babies the world over need only two to three years to become rather proficient in using the language that surrounds them. Everything about an infant's life seems oriented toward nourishment, security, and communication. Little by little the ways of his people become his ways. The foods of her people become her foods. The language of their people become their language, complete with the orientation to life itself and to the view of the universe represented by the language. In sum, they learn.

During these early years of life an American child becomes identifiably American. A Chinese child becomes identifiably Chinese. Even if the parents of both such children haven't the foggiest idea about the ways Americans differ from Chinese, the difference will be there. No one needs to identify or name these differences. The children have simply become awash in their respective cultural ways. They have "sunk" into their culture, it has sunk into them. They have learned their "first culture" in a *sinking mode*. This is what Casino means.

The learning of a culture in this "little by little" process adds up surprisingly fast, somewhat like the compound interest on any investment. But the process is quiet and subtle; no one even thinks about it. In the sinking mode, culture learning is never a spotlighted affair on center stage. It is as natural as breathing.

As one sinks into a culture, the first awareness of human variability develops in the form of consciousness of individual differences within and among one's own kind. Early in life one's values are very self-centered. "I am the standard; others who differ are differing from *me*," might be the way to put it in words. These little differences are both "the spice of life" and the source of personal anxiety and threat. If others are taller, it makes me uneasy. If others are shorter, it also makes me uneasy. If another is more competitive, more boisterous, more acquiescent, more anything, it is a source of potential uneasiness. The less secure one may be, the more likely one will be to see differences *within one's own culture* as a threat.

Herein lies one of the important sources of intercultural anxiety. If one is threatened by differences within one's *own* culture, how much greater is the likelihood that the differences across a cultural line will be seen as threatening.

Conversely, one of the important steps toward preparation for competent coping in a second culture might be a more thorough grasp and secure perspective within one's own first culture. In other words, before one risks the threats of encounter with those whose outlook is grossly different, one needs to make peace with those who are less significantly different.

Schools Are for Rising

People who have had the advantage of formal education usually know much more about their own history and culture. In contrast with the sinking mode and all its involvement with things that are learned without conscious effort, the intention of formal education is to make explicit, to name, to explain—to "think about."

Such experiences add to one's understanding of one's own culture. Casino calls this mode of culture learning the *rising* mode. *Rising* suggests the idea of coming up out of the amorphous background of the culture in which one is thoroughly immersed and, rubbing the eyes and clearing the head, becoming more explicit and "knowledgeable" about what is going on and why things are the way they are.

School provides the major rising mode learning of one's own culture. The formal history of one's people is studied. The prevailing assumptions underlying government, management, and interpersonal relations are presented and discussed. The geographical realities which affect life in the nation are identified and, to some extent, better understood. The arts and literature of the culture are examined.

Schooling does not use the rising mode exclusively to teach culture, nor is it the only way that this mode is implemented. Inevitably, every school has a "hidden curriculum." Values, intellectual perspective, and social bias as well as detailed customs are taught extensively, not because anyone consciously intends to do so, but simply because the participation of people in any social interaction or institutional experience contributes to further culture learning in the sinking mode. Conversely, many far less formal components of one's society serve to raise the implicit knowledge of culture into explicit awareness.

All sorts of little things add up. Most important are the experiences that lead one to reflective thought about those experiences.[5] Time spent talking with others contributes explicit knowledge of one's own culture. So do travel, reading, radio, and, last but not least, television. The sinking mode puts in place the habits and values of a person's lifestyle. The rising mode allows them to be identified and thus allows for critique and discussion.

Refinement of the values of a society depends extensively on the rising mode. In this respect, formal education plays an important part. Beyond the school's obvious "conserving" function in the society, it contributes explicitly to the human skills that allow a society to carry on dialogue toward the challenging and evaluation of its culture, especially on historical, ethical, or pragmatic grounds.[6]

Consciousness of Another Culture

What restricts a society—or a person—most severely is a lack of cultural perspective. If there were no possibilities for breaking out of one's own historical or pragmatic bases for valuing human good and bad, a society would be condemned to degenerating into itself.

Exactly at this point the urgency of cultural perspective and, especially, the importance of intercultural experience come into focus. Every society needs the perspective that comes from intercultural contact. It is enriching, but even more important it is essential to the survival of the society. Thus we see that learning one's own culture constitutes a prelude to becoming conscious of another culture.

Cultural differences can be seen either as the root of all human conflict and deserving to be diligently erased or they can be seen as the stimulating matrix of human creativity. There is something to be said for each of these presuppositions, but the second is more productive. If anything substantial is to come from intercultural experience, it is far more likely that the second will account for it. It is far more healthy to learn to live with differences, even to appreciate them, than to commit oneself to trying to change them.

For missionaries and for development assistance technicians this proposition creates a dilemma. On the one hand, their very reason for "being there" is concern about needed change. On the other hand, if difference is valuable, just what differences are to be seen as normal or desirable and which are undesirable? How can this dilemma be rationalized or resolved? The answer will come from the value system of the "outsider," but whatever answer is acted upon will be accepted or rejected on the basis of the "insider's" judgments. The alternative to this view of cultural difference is conflict.

What most people mean by culture learning begins with learning a second ("other") culture, beyond one's own, in the rising mode. Casino's analysis advances our understanding of culture learning in several ways, most particularly in respect to the following two points:

Effective learning of a second culture depends to a great extent on the explicit consciousness of one's own culture. In other words, people who understand themselves, "where they are coming from," and what lies behind the ways they think and act are far more able to learn a second culture.

Learning a second culture is inherently different from learning one's first culture, especially in the matter of where one begins. Despite the romantic exaggerations that occasionally show up in fictional literature, no adult ever learns a second culture, either in the sense of understanding it or fitting into it, apart from the *rising* mode. If a person has learned his or her own culture well in the *rising* mode, the understandings will serve as a platform for grappling with the "other" culture.

While it may be possible for a person who has never driven a car to learn to drive a truck filled with explosives on the job, I would prefer to stand well away from the road to watch. Many newcomers to the international scene lack even the foggiest notion of their own culture—what or who they are—in any sort of reflected-upon perspective. These people are in no shape to learn a second culture. Why would organizations hire such people for an overseas assignment?

We sometimes see such people in prefield orientation courses or workshops. They look like accidents on the way to happening. Such people need much help. The sorts of orientation they need before going overseas will be long and demanding. Those providing such training must give attention not only to the "other" culture, but to helping them develop a way of looking at themselves. These two modes of learning are interdependent, the one building on the other.

T. S. Eliot summed up this idea and the truth to which it leads:

> *We shall not cease from exploration,*
> *and the end of all our exploring*
> *Will be to arrive where we started*
> *And know the place for the first time.* *

How Wise Is the Second Sinking?

It does not follow that *sinking* into another culture is to be preferred over *rising* in consciousness of another culture. As a matter of fact, sinking into another culture is not always an option—few are ever invited to try it, and it can't be done without an invitation.

*From "Little Gidding V" in *Four Quartets*, copyright 1943 by T. S. Eliot; renewed 1971 by Esme Valerie Eliot. Reprinted by permission of Harcourt Brace Jovanovich, Inc., and Faber and Faber Publishers.

Of the four possible forms of culture learning, sinking into another culture is the most demanding and potentially the most illustrative of a commitment to the second culture. Isn't that what one's outlook should be? To accept the most exacting demands and to commit oneself thoroughly? It sounds good, but three major problems are encountered.

First, the last arrow in Figure 3–3 represents a movement from rational explanation of the culture into the realm of *less conscious acculturation*. To learn a second culture in the sinking mode implies the same sort of "getting awash in it" that is characteristic of sinking into one's first culture.

Even as this first sinking was less a matter of conscious decisions than of submitting to circumstances, so is sinking into another culture. Preparation for intercultural living, by its very essence, is a deliberate process. Sinking implies a totally effective "losing oneself" within or into the new culture. Yes, from time to time one sees the rare individual who has done this, but very seldom has this individual already been consciously aware of his or her own culture and of the new culture. Casino cautions that the final transition from rising into another culture to sinking into it is a theoretical representation, not often a practical move. Casino does not recommend it.

The second problem is the matter of *opportunity*. The outsider is an outsider; the foreigner is a foreigner. He or she may be accepted and valued as friend, sharer, and neighbor, but to attempt to cross over the invisible dividing line and become one with one's hosts is not an open option. If one is thus to be assimilated, one must be *invited* into the society. Yes, it can happen. But working toward such an invitation is likely not worth the effort. It implies a lifetime commitment and very difficult choice-making.

Abandoning one's first culture is a virtual necessity for sinking into another culture. This third problem is what makes it so very unlikely for most sojourners.

Acceptance as a foreigner is a thoroughly adequate basis for building virtually any sort of a human relationship (except, in some societies, marriage). Whether or not one should strive beyond this is still an open question. Starry-eyed young missionaries have been led down this primrose path by visions of themselves becoming indistinguishable from the nationals.

History shows very few highly effective missionaries, and surely no competent diplomats, who confused their friends in the host culture by attempting to "sink in." Did Albert Schweitzer abandon his piano and pipe organ to "sink" into the musical culture of West Africa? No. He was consciously Alsatian to the end. And Mother Theresa? Has her effectiveness arisen essentially from her adopting of Indian dress and lifestyle? Has she withdrawn from her European and American connections? Is she not still respected as an effective foreigner?

Partly because missionaries and development workers identify themselves with a supranational cause, they sometimes try too hard to escape from their own first culture. Such efforts can turn a person into an ambiguous blob. Everyone needs an identity and a consciousness of that identity.

Some good things can be said about sinking into a new culture. The well-accepted expatriate will be invited to little excursions into the sinking mode. Sometimes it is even possible to fantasize that one is becoming one with the nationals. Warm feelings are sure to accompany those moments when one's foreignness seems to have been forgotten. They can enliven one's experiences; but make no mistake about it, the competent intercultural worker continues to learn the culture in a conscious and deliberate manner, and in turn, reaps the benefits of an enriched rising mode comprehension of his or her own culture.

GOING NATIVE

Now and then an American who has "gone native" bobs to the surface. A sort of mystique has grown up about the American who is so thoroughly adapted to another culture that he or she has become indistinguishable from a local person. Is this good?

Historically missionaries have been drawn into a close relationship with their converts. When newcomers observe this, they sometimes attempt to take shortcuts to acceptance. Eagerness to identify with people of the host country and to show solidarity with them causes strange and sometimes unbecoming behavior. Such an expatriate usually starts by wearing the local style hat or head scarf. Such items of clothing are usually highly functional, which encourages more copying. Soon it is the local muu-muu or sarong, the sandals, and, when thick skin has developed, the bare feet that seem to symbolize a total "acculturation."

This pattern is seen far more often in rural situations, of course, and it often reflects a sincere interest in adapting oneself to the local situation and lifestyle. The danger lies in giving offense to people as a by-product of a misguided effort to become accepted.

In many situations, perhaps most, the outsider will be accepted most easily if she or he *remains* an outsider. People feel more comfortable relating to a foreigner who looks and acts like a foreigner. A foreigner who adopts too many of the ways of the local folk arouses suspicion and uneasiness. The American is trying too hard; why does he or she want to be like us? Some will even be saying, "This American is stupid; I would give *anything* to have an American passport, and he doesn't seem to value his."

Reverse the situation and think about the ways that Americans relate to respected foreigners. European orchestral conductors and virtuoso musicians are *supposed* to talk with thick accents. Their old-world hand-kissing, bowing, and dreamily squinted eyes are part of their charm. No major symphony orchestra association would suggest that a European conductor should look more American. Foreignness does have its own mystique.

"Uncle Murph"

But missionaries, for example, tend to be ambivalent on this matter. On one hand, they want to be honest and faithful to what they really are and to what they stand for. On the other hand, they don't want to see themselves merely as "culture carriers."

The first case of a missionary's "going native" I encountered was many years ago in Brazil. An elderly man walked into the house where I was staying, dusty sandals and all. He was incredibly dirty and his clothes were in need of repair. He resembled so many of the farmers of the region, but there was something about him that immediately whispered "American." To this day I can't put a finger on it, but when I spoke a word of greeting, I chose English, not Portuguese. He replied in perfect English, and I began an acquaintance with one of life's unforgettable characters. He is gone now, but his work among the people of that impoverished region lives on. He lived frugally, accepted little assistance of any sort from the outside, and attempted in every feasible way to become one with the people. His efforts were effective. One must wonder if indeed his dress had anything at all to do with his success, but no one doubted that he was deeply loved and respected—by the Brazilians.

To the other missionaries he was both a mystery and a threat. Many saw him as an unattainable ideal; they tried to rationalize why they couldn't be like "Uncle Murph": Bachelors like Murph could "go native," but since most of the rest were married, and since they planned to return to the United States eventually, there was no way that they would do as he had done.

Others saw him as a crackpot. No one needs to go that far, no matter how sincere! These people picked at every idiosyncracy and every flaw. Nothing that Uncle Murph did was worthy of better than scorn.

I was appalled. The major effect of Murph's choice of lifestyle was alienation from the rest of the missionary community. That much was quite clear. Whether there were any unusual benefits for Murph or for his relationships with the Brazilians wasn't nearly so clear. Indeed he had taken every step to become one with them, and they seemed to value that, but in certain matters they related to him as to any other American. There was some little element or some small set of clues that made him special and distinct—not really quite a Brazilian. I wonder now if it wasn't exactly that point of being special and distinct that accounted for his real influence. Maybe the "going native" was only a by-product of the great heart of compassion that motivated Murph's every step. In any case, it would be unwise to try to follow artificially or superficially in Murph's footsteps hoping to achieve the effects he achieved. The soul Uncle Murph revealed can't be explained in terms of dirty, ragged clothes.

An American in China

The American who "gives it all up" is still a captivating theme, I'll admit. About fifteen years after the massive exodus of non-Communist Chinese to the island of Taiwan, I was doing an errand on the back streets of Taipei. As I passed each of the little criblike stalls of vendors and craftspeople, I peered in. Most had half-doors which doubled as service counters and as barriers to keep the smaller children in. Here an herb shop, there a tinsmith, next a seller of flashlights and umbrellas, then a tailor. A glance into a shoe shop: cross-legged on the little platform that marked half his space above the dirt floor of the stall sat a man with an old-fashioned awl and very coarse waxed thread. My eye took in the tools of the trade and the curiously "backward" technology in a city then struggling to come into its own as a rival of Hong Kong. Not until I got beyond the fleeting view did it hit me: He had red hair. A red-haired Chinese? Hardly. So I turned around and walked back past the stall. Yes, as he raised his head to observe this curious foreigner, I could see, even in the light of his single, dangling, bare bulb, that his eyes were blue. I stopped, and for a second that seemed more like an hour, I stared. Then I spoke: "Hi, there, I'll bet you're an American." With a snort that suggested that he understood English, he shot an angry glance at me and turned back to his work.

It was an electric moment. In many ways he was Chinese— dress, occupation, posture. But still, something said *American*. How much had it cost him to sink into this second culture? What had motivated him? Did the Chinese really accept him as Chinese? Now an American-Chinese shoe cobbler, he had simply traded in one cultural narrowness for a different one. Tragic. This is not the proper end for the otherwise liberating art of intercultural adaptation.

FOCUS FOR SELF-EVALUATION

The likelihood that you will learn something that will make a practical difference in your overseas competency will be increased by the time and effort you invest in thinking specifically about the following matters.

Reflection

1. On what matters do I tend to have self-centered values?_____

   _____

   _____

2. What has motivated me to go into overseas service? In what ways does my motivation represent my cultural values?_____

   _____

   _____

3. What do I most hope to find in the people with whom I will be working?_____

   _____

Review

1. What is the difference between the "sinking" and "rising" modes of learning a culture?_____

_____

2. What are the major forces and events in my "personal history" that have shaped my values?_____

_____

Commitment

What expanding of my "personal history" do I want?_____

_____

_____

4

Accounting for Differences

CULTURE LEARNING is concerned with unusual people and the movement of those unusual people into other parts of the world where they encounter still other unusual people. The human family worldwide has much in common, but there are wide variations in all sorts of obvious and subtle characteristics. The differences hit you long before the common ground becomes clear. So it is best to start out with the assumption that the first task is to become able to cope with the unusual.

THE WE/THEY HABIT

The tendency to oversimplify and thus to dichotomize is not new, nor is it unique to Americans. In matters of right and wrong, the Pharisees of Jesus' time were dichotomizers of the most stubborn sort; things were either lawful or not, and the Pharisees maintained the rule book. At the same time, close by in Samaria a more distinctly cultural form of we/they dichotomy was maintained. All religious issues were boiled down to a formula: "We Samaritans worship at Mount Gerizim; you Jews worship in Jerusalem."[1] There it is: *We* are this way; *they* are that way.

Since the dawn of human society, the emphasizing of difference and the tendency to dichotomize into *we* and *they* is at the root of many intercultural conflicts. It doesn't follow that solving intercultural conflict is as easy as abolishing the distinction between "our kind" and "their kind"—indeed not. Distinctions are real. The contrasts of lifestyle and values between any two cultures are substantial and often quite stubborn. But if a person wishes to move freely back and forth across cultural lines, it is well to avoid the habit of thinking in we/they terms. <u>Instead, it is preferable to see oneself in two different "we" forms. *We*, when I'm here, and *we*, when I'm there.</u>

The idea of two or more forms of social identity is not far-fetched. Every person already maintains several such relationships. A healthy family relationship is a "we;" so too is a constructive work relationship: "we at the office," "we who are missionaries," "we in our family." Simply extend this sense of we-ness to a sense of identity with people who are culturally different and you are on your way to a constructive relationship.

An American cannot think in terms of "we Brazilians," but there is nothing to prevent a person identifying as one who shares a place of residence, "we who live in Brazil," or shares an outlook, "we who stand together."

If you never think "we" but always "they," you will never enjoy the warmth of those you serve embracing you in *their* understanding of "we." Instead they will always see you as "one more of those Americans who prefer to remain aloof from us."

How much better to get beyond Kipling's self-perception as an outsider:

> *Father, Mother and Me,*
> *Sister and Auntie say*
> *All the People like us are We,*
> *And everyone else is They.*
> *And They live over the sea,*
> *While We live over the way,*
> *But—would you believe it? They*
> *   look upon We*
> *As only a sort of They!* *

---

*Excerpt from "We and They" by Rudyard Kipling from *The Definitive Edition of Rudyard Kipling's Verse* reprinted with permission of The National Trust for Places of Historic Interest or Natural Beauty and Macmillan London, Ltd., and Doubleday & Company.

THE COMPARATIVE AND THE COMMON

People are alike in more ways than they are different. Regardless of culture, there are more common factors than different factors, especially if one gets underneath the *apparent* differences to find the common roots. "Cross-cultural" refers to what is common across two or more cultures, for example, family structures. The particular features of family roles and behaviors will vary, but beneath the variations is a cross-cultural concern: family.

"Intercultural" refers to the contacts or exchanges between cultures. When the concern is primarily practical, as it is in the matter of relationships and the skills needed to work and live effectively in a culture not one's own, the task is *intercultural* but the knowledge base is *cross-cultural*. Thus the leading specialized publisher of practical texts and learning materials for people preparing to move overseas is named the Intercultural Press, but when a leading social scientist of the field compiles and reviews the research, he entitles his book *Cross-Cultural Encounters*.[2]

The concepts and terminology of intercultural preparation are drawn mostly from the field of cultural anthropology. The relative newness of the literature and research traditions in cultural anthropology leave much room for doubting even the things that we *think* we know. The sensationalized debate about Margaret Mead's earliest major field study, *Coming of Age in Samoa*,[3] serves as a warning that not all is settled.[4]

The field of anthropology, in general, has gone through several historical phases as it has emerged among the modern social sciences. A tug-of-war between emphasis on the common and emphasis on the peculiar has characterized the field throughout its history. Even today, some anthropologists seem transported into ecstasy over what can be found in one culture and nowhere else in the world. For example, in a small tribe in Papua, New Guinea, people count to five on their left hand then point to designated left-arm positions from the wrist to the neck to finish out the count to ten. Other anthropologists seem much more entranced by the common denominators that underlie the apparent cross-cultural differences. For example, regardless of whether people count on their fingers or on their arms, all people everywhere have some method of counting and a traditional way to visualize the counting process.

It need not be an either-or matter. Appreciating difference is important. Underneath a given difference is some sort of human theme

with which a perceptive outsider can identify. The difference is neither more nor less important than the underlying common theme.
The newcomer must cope with difference as the reality of the intercultural encounter. As a matter of intellectual process, difference
can be grasped more effectively if it is seen as an equivalent of something more familiar. The Inuit's igloo or the Hausa's mud hut are
similar to my house in Michigan because they are (1) built essentially to match the neighbors' houses; (2) decreed by custom and
laws to be substantially similar to the domiciles of the neighbors and
the regional cultural norm (in most of the United States the rules are
called "zoning codes"); (3) built from materials that can be made
readily available at the building site; (4) designed to provide insulation from the discomforts of prevailing weather, privacy for the
family, and protection from interferences by other creatures. In
Michigan, the bears, wolves, and jackals are not as likely to be a
major nuisance as are two-legged outsiders, but the motive is cross-
cultural. Being intellectually alert to all of these common denominators can help me comprehend, but it won't help me cope with the
smoke if I am in an igloo or mud hut. My upbringing did not include that adjustment. I can learn to cope with the smoke and
odors; but I'm not comfortable.

UP FROM THE SAVAGES

An old theory of cultural development still shows up among otherwise well-informed Americans. From the viewpoint of our highly
technological era, it is tempting to assume that many other national
groups are following in *our* footsteps. This idea is even more credi-
ble because many in the Third World are obviously grasping after
the things of science and technology—television, refrigerators, air
conditioners, airplanes, nuclear power plants, and the like. Given
time and resources, they will catch up, so the theory says. Ethnocentric chauvinism suggests that by the time the have-not nations
"catch up," America will still be out front in many ways not even
imagined today. Maybe.
　The major fallacy in this sort of thinking is its presumption that
all societies are moving on the same path—a single path with only
minor variations. Thus differences between one nation and another
are a matter of how far along this trail they may be.
　Today's more enlightened views of culture and the development

of societies rejects this old theory. The major criticism is that it over-
simplifies the vast array of human variations. It especially overlooks
the differences among people's values. A society progresses or develops in terms of its own values and aspirations. For sure, values
and aspirations are sometimes adopted from other societies; in some
respects the technological cravings of the "modernized" nations
have been adopted by the less wealthy nations. Television may even
bring a sort of worldwide realignment of values: materialism and
individualism seem to be just around the corner in many formerly
familial societies. But this hardly justifies the old theory. If there is
any sort of following along a single path, it is on a downhill path,
hardly worthy of the concept "cultural development."

Expatriates of technological nations should be careful not to fall
into the error of one of our "Founding Fathers." Brilliant and insightful though he was, Thomas Jefferson held the old "up from the
savages" theory. He saw the American Indians at one extreme and
people like himself at the other. In his last years, at age 81, Jefferson
put together this remarkable commentary on cultural development:

> Let a philosophic observer commence a journey from the savages of the
> Rocky Mountains, eastwardly towards our sea-coast. These he would
> observe in the earliest stages of association living under no law but that
> of nature, subsisting and covering themselves with the flesh and skins
> of wild beasts. He would next find those on our frontiers in the pastoral
> stage, raising domestic animals to supply the defects of hunting. Then
> succeed our own semi-barbarous citizens, the pioneers of the advance
> of civilization, and so in his progress he would meet the gradual shades
> of improving man until he would reach his, as yet, most improved
> state in our seaport towns. This, in fact, is equivalent to a survey . . .
> of the progress of man from the infancy of creation to the present day.[5]

DOWN THE SAME TRAIL?

Since social evolution has strongly influenced Western thought, it is
only a short leap from the belief that all societies are becoming more
and more advanced to the notion that all societies are at one point or
another on the same trail. This latter view makes the contrast between America and Ghana, for example, simply a matter of time
and resources; given enough time and the necessary things to work
with, Ghana will someday "catch up" with where the United States
is today.

Whether the comparison is with France, Spain, and Japan, or India, China, and Mali, the question, "How far down the trail have they come?" is simply the wrong question. There are many trails and there is no trail. The development pattern of each human society is different, and only in the most technological and materialistic sense is any nation "following" any other.

Every nation must be understood in its own terms. It is a serious mistake to presume that because of its material wealth, military power, large-scale commitments to the arts—or even because of its beneficence and motivation for humanitarian assistance and religious missions—the United States is either the front-runner in a single-minded race or the great example being eagerly copied by many others.

LITIGATION—THE BREAKDOWN OF HONOR

One useful way to look at differences is to compare emphases. Some things are seen to be more important and thus are more emphasized in one culture than in another. Sometimes the difference is a matter of substituting one value for another.

Going to court, or at least threatening to take someone to court, has become an American pastime. It is good for the lawyers, of course, but not so good for the quality of life. If people accept the idea that someone else will have to decide, it reduces the contest to a stand-off. It subverts the human process of negotiation and peacemaking.

If someone offends us, we threaten to sue. If someone plants a tree or builds a fence a few inches across our property line, we threaten to sue. The matters people take to lawyers and onward to courts are often trivial and peevish. The result of all this is a national disgrace in America and in a few other nations, most notably India: clogged and delayed court schedules, overworked judges, rich lawyers, and perpetually angry people. It is no idle joke to suggest that the high incidence of heart disease and hypertension among Americans may relate in part to the tendency to fight about things rather than seeking compromise and harmony.

By way of contrast, a Japanese friend has been building a large private school in a secondary city in Honshu. While on a visit there, I was invited to visit his half-completed pride and joy, the new school. The cluster of buildings is located in a small area, with a mountainside behind, a tight cluster of middle-class homes on one side, and a busy highway curving around to complete the boundaries. The buildings had already begun to show their elegance. Their solid but flexible engineering reminded me that this was earthquake country, and a four-level adult-education center had to be built to stand and yet sway.

Admiring the rectangular lines and its uniquely Japanese character, I noted an oddity: a television antenna was attached to the corner of the roof-frame nearest the cluster of houses. From the antenna ran a veritable spray of antenna leads, one to each of the twenty or so houses. So, I thought, these technology-loving Japanese have figured out a way to improve their reception by using my friend's new building as an antenna mast.

My Japanese host noticed that I was observing the way all the houses were linked to his new building. "It's just temporary," he said. "What do you mean?" I inquired, using one of the handiest of all intercultural questions.

"It's a long story," said he, starting out once again toward the inspection tour of the construction itself. For some reason, he preferred not to explain, so I decided not to push him.

As we completed our tour and turned back toward his car, I glanced up at the antenna one last time, hoping he would say more. If there were something embarrassing about it, it would be very rude for me to push the matter. Japanese share with many other Orientals that intriguing exaggeration called "saving face."[6]

I decided to try just one gentle nudge in addition to my fairly obvious glance at the wires. Were he an American colleague or friend I might have said, "You aren't going to leave that mess of wires like that after the building is done, are you?" But such an implied criticism and the bold imputing of ugliness would have been totally wrong with a Japanese friend. So I tried a positive approach, complete with an implied compliment—a safe technique in any culture: "Your neighbors are likely very happy to have such a nice high place to put their TV antenna."

He smiled a huge Japanese smile, the kind saved for very special occasions, and he began to tell the whole story. Because now he was telling it on his own terms and in a context of acceptance rather than criticism, I needed to ask no questions at all, just to listen and learn.

It turned out that while the first major structural steel was being erected for the frame of the building, the households of the nearby cluster began having trouble with their TV reception. The higher the steel, the worse it got. At this point neither the construction crew nor my friend, the owner, were aware of the problem. It would be rare for any individual to come to complain about such a thing. Such boldness is bad manners among proper Japanese. Instead, these householders talked to each other and came to a very Japanese conclusion about what should be done. One of the oldest men in the neighborhood was selected as a messenger to approach the owner on behalf of all householders. An old person is presumed to be wise and deserving of great respect; any message such a person carries must be given attention as a matter of honor. He was not sent empty-handed. The people of the neighborhood had each contributed money so that an expensive gift could be purchased to serve as one of the key elements in this age-old ritual of the aggrieved.

After all was in readiness, the old man visited my friend in his home, presented the gift, and assured him of the best wishes of all of the householders. And, oh yes, by the way, was he aware that there was this one little problem? Of course, it was surely not more than a simple coincidence, and the people were certain that he had had nothing to do with it, but the television signal from the city was now almost gone. Did he have any idea what these poor householders might do so that they could have television again?

My friend promised that he would have an expert come to study the problem.

And he did. The expert said that, sure enough, the new building was blocking what had formerly been a straight-line signal from the city. The only solution would be to raise everyone's antennas higher than the new building—at staggering cost, or to set up some sort of community antenna system distributing the signal from one very tall antenna.

At this point my friend needed no one to urge him or to tell him what he ought to do. His project had created the problem; it would be necessary for him to provide the solution and bear its cost.

Thus a large antenna was fastened to the roof frame. This was only temporary—a self-standing antenna was on order and would be installed in the community soon. At that time all the festooned leads would be replaced by inconspicuous cables running along with the telephone lines.

Only in Japan, I thought! Not only did he order the costly community antenna, but he put up this temporary arrangement so that he would not create a problem for others even for one more day. What made him do it? Honor.

A heartwarming story? Yes, but altogether true. The Japanese system of justice is built on honor just as surely as the American system of justice is built on the litigation of adversarial relationships. But the Japanese also have a pragmatic streak. In this matter they are very much like Americans. It showed itself just after my friend finished his story of the antenna problem. I responded to the story in an American way: "That surely will cost you a lot of money!" I exclaimed.

"Ah, yes, but not nearly as much as the cost of an American lawyer and a long series of court battles!"

This Japanese gentleman, wise in the ways of the East *and* the West, prefers the ways of the Orient. And saves money too!

WALKING IN THE STREETS

While in Arlington, Texas, for a conference recently, I was reminded of my first visit to Brasilia. Brazil's modern, sprawling metropolis, splashed across the desolate prairie of interior Brazil, was designed with very little concern for pedestrians. For me, walking serves three purposes: it is a highly functional way to get from one place to another, it gets one closer to a practical level for observing life, and it is great exercise. But in so many places nowadays walking is almost impossible unless one risks life and limb at the edge of an overcrowded highway. I discovered that Arlington's new sprawl is virtually devoid of sidewalks—just like Brasilia. Perhaps it is assumed that people will walk in the road in any case, and sidewalks are thus unnecessary. Perhaps there is no money for sidewalks, or perhaps people are to be discouraged from walking. In Brasilia and Arlington the first and second reasons seem unlikely, so we are left with the third.

Those who enjoy walking and especially those who *must* walk have reason to resent the lack of concern for pedestrians. As in the developing third world nations, one observes now that in America—especially the new suburban America with its extensive reliance on shopping centers—there are fewer and fewer sidewalks. The world is not made up of neat divisions between nations that do and nations that don't have provisions for the people who must walk.

In Taiwan, England, Japan, Greece, Italy—you name it—you will find yourself wishing there were sidewalks. Even where there are sidewalks, they seem often not to be where you want them or so fully parked with motor bikes that they can't be used. You stumble along the rough and ragged roadside or, in harmony with the local folks, you venture onto the streets and roads right along with the trucks, motorcycles, and cars. Under your breath you may mumble about the careless disregard for life and limb. So backward, you say. So underdeveloped. Remember Arlington, Texas, and the thousands of other new American neighborhoods and business areas where it is blithely assumed that everyone will be driving or riding. The "underdeveloped" shoe sometimes fits American feet.

WHEN BACKWARD IS FORWARD

Dealing with a West African airline can compromise your will to live. Anyone who overlooks the inconvenience, discomfort, delays, and anxieties of travel and bureaucratic red tape in Ghana, Nigeria, Liberia, Sierra Leone, and their neighbors should be cited for extraordinary patience. One must take a very long view of the recovery process to believe that postcolonialism can even survive the serious breakdown of technology and relationships with westerners who still expect the old colonial levels of service.

Each postcolonial nation is now doggedly putting together its own expertise. A new era is dawning, but development takes time. When the colonial masters pulled out, they not only took with them the vital keys to the institutional structures they had put in place over several generations, but they left relatively few trained technicians, professionals, and competent managers among the national persons.

Inherent in the evil of colonialism is the necessity to suppress creativity and resourcefulness. Once they were on their own, postcolonial peoples' creativity and resourcefulness emerged promptly, but often in undisciplined and greedy forms.

To assume that the problem is "African ignorance" or "African selfishness" would be vicious. In the first place, the problem is certainly not uniquely African—a week in Indonesia or Jamaica will correct that misconception; and further, the problem was created by colonial powers in the first place. It is grotesque to blame victims for being victims, no matter what the form of rape.

Southeast Asia and Africa are still in the first generation of postcolonialism. The fact that Latin America still suffers from the heel prints of Spain, Portugal, the Netherlands, and Britain a century

and a half after Simon Bolivar's death should warn us that recovery
in Africa may be slow.

Just thirty years ago John Gunther's landmark book, *Inside Africa*, was published, journalistically documenting the African nations of that day when *Uhuru* seemed just around the corner.
Uhuru—the Swahili idealization of freedom—has turned out to be
costly and elusive. Gunther's optimistic picture of the prospects for
an economic and political vitality is put into the harsh reality of recent history by David Lamb's *The Africans*, a report of four years'
travels in 48 African countries. "The colonialists designed the scenario for disaster and the Africans seem to be trying their best to fulfill it," he concludes.

Behind the scene, every African nation affects every other. But
these relationships and effects are largely ignored by the American
press and, curiously, by the local press in African cities. It takes a
careful reading of a survey such as Lamb has provided to grasp the
whole of it—however tenuous that grasp may be. Perhaps Lamb
dwells too much on the horror stories, but such treatment is required by honest realism.

> In Somalia the average government ministry has eight hundred servants. On any given day, a senior government official told me, only
> sixty of them show up for work. In Zaire a $1.8 million international
> grant to repair Kinshasa's broken-down city buses is swindled down to
> $200,000 by the time it reaches the transportation ministry, and ends
> up accomplishing nothing at all. In Nairobi a man calling the police
> station to report that his house is under attack by a band of bandits
> with machetes is told he will have to drive to the station to pick up
> some officers; the department has no cars on duty that night. In Zambia hundreds of government cars sit rusting in a huge parking lot outside Lusaka. Many need nothing more than a new carburetor or fuel
> pump. But with no mechanics around, and not much initiative to
> spare even if there were, it is easier to junk them and buy new ones
> with an international grant.[7]

In addition to providing abundant documentation of human
greed and craving for power, Lamb reminds that the unresolved racial tension that infects Africa is a smoldering fire fueled by the
stubborn hammerlock on much of Africa's mineral wealth, expertise, and industry that is master-minded from Johannesburg. If only
South Africa were a part of Africa's whole, in the sense of humane
sharing and economic cooperation, two things could begin to happen: continent-wide balancing of resources, markets, and, especially, food supplies would make African nations more interdepen-

dent and less dependent on outside donations. Second, the level of
agitation and anger could be reduced, ushering in a period of Pan-
African political cooperation.

No American should take up an assignment in Africa without an
awareness of the symbolic meaning and the practical effects of
South Africa's apartheid policies. It is, to Africans, what it would be
to North America if the states of Illinois, Michigan, and Indiana
were controlled by a minority of blacks (proportionately fewer than
are in these states now) who allowed whites to work in mines, in
lower-level jobs in agriculture, and in the city businesses so long as
they remained willing to walk or take jammed buses back to their
packed villages at night. Frustration and anger would fill the whole
continent. So it does in Africa.

When you use West African public transportation on the last leg
of your travel to take up residence there, you begin to learn patience—and it is important to be a quick learner. The travel experience with its almost useless timetables, its chaotic terminals, its ca-
caphony of meaningless noise and mindless responses to even the
simplest questions tells you that you are in the midst of some of the
worst consequences of colonialism to be found anywhere. Almost
the worst. . . .

What may be worse, because it speaks of a recovery not even yet
begun, is the veneer of servile deference and the "comfortable" resi-
due of the "Yes, bwana" spirit that still hovers over many another
place in Africa. For the visitor and for the expatriate, this willingness to go with the white folks wherever they wish, this "whatever
you say must be right, ma'am and mister," is a reminder that the
broken human spirit sometimes recovers slowly.

East Africa, in general, *seems* more advanced than West Africa.
The East Africans were the plantation hands for the Europeans, the
West Africans drew back into their dark interior and left the coastal
cities to the Europeans. To this day one can see the differential effects. Now that these "less cooperative" West Africans have come
out of their forests and marshes, they run airlines rather badly. But
backward as the airlines may be, the Africans are running them.
That's progress.

BORDERS DON'T MAKE NATIONS—PEOPLE DO

To the European explorer, rivers were the means of discovering the
interior. To people whose motives were travel, trade, and commu-

nication, waterways provided access—the means to move people, ideas, and things.

To some extent the coming of the "iron horse" and its twin ribbons of steel changed all that. The waterways became barriers; expensive and somewhat unreliable bridges became necessary. Rivers, in simpler times, were the means of holding people together and of extending one's sense of interdependent community. But to the technology-dependent "modern" societies, rivers became less necessary, less valued, and, ultimately, were perceived more as barriers—fences, borders, defensive lines rather than unifiers.

Such was the great clash of cultural values and perceptions at the time of the borders created in many colonial regions of the world, especially in Africa. As in ancient times when the great kingdoms had been created around waterways—the Babylonians of the valley of the Tigris and Euphrates, the Egyptians of the Valley of the Nile and the Red Sea, the Romans and later the Moors of the Mediterranean, and the Vikings of the North Sea—the nations and coherent tribes of Africa were largely organized around rivers.

To the Europeans, whose nations were themselves in the process of being reshaped according to the new values of the Industrial Revolution, rivers had come to be understood as "natural boundaries." Thus today's map of Africa shows nations largely carved out and bounded by waterways. In fact, however, the tribal "zones" or regions of tribal kinship do not often coincide with these Europe-imposed colonial boundaries. No nation in today's Africa has been able to do much about this problem, but it remains one of the sorest points in African political life.

Especially when the boundaries of a nation have been drawn by outsiders, and are, in fact, splitting ancient tribal zones right down the middle, it is hard to drum up much patriotism or even loyalty to a central government.

In other cases, Nigeria for example, the idea of "one nation indivisible" is continually threatened by the reality that the nation consists not of one but of many tribes. Of these, three (the Ibo, the Yoruba, and the Hausa) are the dominant tribes and have long been at each other's throats. Thus almost every disagreement or governmental issue bursts into flames along tribal lines.

The solution does not lie in hundreds or thousands of single-tribe nations. Some sort of combination is absolutely necessary, but especially where tribes are split by the river-based colonial boundary lines, some redrawing of maps might help. Of course that solution

isn't feasible either, because relinquishing land is something that nations rarely do voluntarily!

The Gambia, one intriguing example of pragmatic map-mak-
ing, is a river basin within a largely French, Portuguese and Dutch-
dominated tropical forest area of West Africa (see Figure 4–1). During the peak of the slave trade, the mighty British navy and
mercantile establishment were able to hold this water highway
against all threats. Today it is a nation—20 miles wide and 200
miles long. With English as its trade language, its tribes sprawl
across the regions of Senegal and Mali where French is the trade
language. Logical? Maybe not; but it is a creature of European history. The same can be said for most of Africa.

For the expatriate, the difference between a unified nation and a
tribal mixture may take some "getting used to." In general, family,
extended family, and tribal identity are matters of greater intensity
than loyalty to the central government. But it isn't wise to take anything for granted. Watch and listen in order to discover the patterns
of patriotism and loyalty.

PICK YOUR FIGHTS CAREFULLY

Getting tuned in on the local folks' lists of "good guys and bad guys"
is important. Especially in postcolonial nations, Americans often
discover that the "friendly nations" we take for granted are deeply

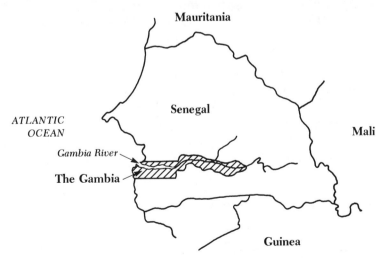

Figure 4–1.

resented. During the Falkland Islands fiasco, Americans in Latin America had to be careful not to play up our "English heritage"; those British were the bad guys. Among our Indonesian friends it is better not to mention the Dutch. And nowhere in Black Africa is it wise to speak fondly of the Republic of South Africa. In every nation the cast of characters shifts. Deeply held sentiments emerge, flourish, and fade. You have to keep up with current events.

It is far better to pick your fights than to be forever falling into them. Other people have their reasons for their attitudes, too. In another country you will discover that there are grievances against this or that nation, against one or another ethnic group based on events, circumstances, and traditions that you have never heard about. Did you think you knew everything? Did you know that the United States has "hit the beach" to intervene in one after another Caribbean, Central American, and South American nation 95 times in the history of our Republic? Sooner or later you will be reminded of this statistic by a Latin American acquaintance.

Take for example the decision of Pope Alexander VI which led to the division between Portuguese and Spanish settlements in South America: the hard feelings live today, nourished by antagonisms and bitterness dished out by both sides whenever Brazilian and Spanish-language nationals get together. Latin America, we have been taught to think, includes Brazil. Maybe it does on the map, but don't use the term to include Brazilians if any are present. They are likely to insist that you say "Latin America and Brazil." Brazilians simply don't like to be wrapped into any collective description that puts them into a peer identity with *Spanish*-speaking people. The Portuguese (and their Brazilian offspring) are intensely proud, nationalistic, and, for the most part, anti-Spanish.

Even the Portuguese language itself, though derived from Spanish—and thus clearly a "Romance" or Latin-based language—was deliberately constructed so that it would be hard for Spanish-users to understand. To this day it is more common for Portuguese-speaking Brazilians to understand Spanish than it is for Peruvians, Chileans, or Argentinians, for example, to understand Portuguese.

HANDBAGS AND HANDHOLDING

Many Americans are hypersensitive on matters pertaining to gender roles. In several places in Europe and here and there in Latin America, men carry purses. Not just *little* purses—more like handbags. Many have wrist straps, a useful deterrent to purse snatchers, and now and then they even have shoulder straps. Many Americans do a double-take the first time they see a man carrying a purse. The sight can be seen in some American cities, but many Americans haven't yet noticed.

As with many a "strange custom," there is a functional reason behind the purses. When super-tight trousers became stylish about ten or more years ago, the pocket purse or billfold became an uncomfortable and "unsightly" bulge. Pocketless tee shirts came in at the same time, so especially in the warmer countries, there was no place within the clothing to carry one's money, documents and cigarettes. The purses also solve the problem of carrying things that nowadays cannot safely be left in locked cars.

Perhaps it was the documents that forced the issue, but since Americans don't share this need, we tend not to be familiar with the reason for purses. Americans are among the very few people in the world who are not required to carry identity papers. In some countries, one even has to carry an employment record and/or travel authorizations. A fellow just can't slip these bulky documents into a slim pocket with a bit of silver, a one and five and still show his manly slim rear. A purse is the best answer. Americans may stare. But the purse-stares are tame compared to the stares for male hand-holding.

In many Arab nations, here and there in Europe, and in many cities of South America, it is common to see male friends walking down the street hand-in-hand, much as pub-hopping Irish and Japanese men stroll down the street with arms around each other in high spirited camaraderie. "Back home" you just don't *do* that. If you want to see some wide eyes, watch an American tour group as they notice the custom for the first time—and elbow each other discreetly.

STARING

Have you noticed how little children can stare at you? Children usually display whatever curiosity they may have with a total lack of concern for whether or not you enjoy being stared at.

In some societies, but not all, children are taught not to stare at people. Learning not to stare is part of the socialization process. In

Western societies, a person who stares is likely to be interpreted as infantile, feeble-minded, overly tired, or very ill-mannered.

In certain highly stylized societies of the Orient—Japan for example—staring is even less acceptable. No matter how curious or how much one may want to establish a contact, keeping one's eyes on another person for more than a fleeting second at a time can be offensive. Among Chinese, in certain tribes of Africa, and among New World Indians, a direct, eye-to-eye contact is impolite. Respect for authority or for an elder is shown by looking downward while talking. For Americans, this presents a difficult problem. Accustomed as we are to using eye contact—perhaps accompanied by a smile, a nod, or a wave of the hand—as a communication or appreciation and as a basis for further contact, this nonverbal communication is often misunderstood. What to us is a simple display of respect and human warmth can be interpreted as an insult.

Conversely, the people who are on the receiving end of our prolonged eye contact often feel uneasiness and fear. Our putting a smile with the eye contact doesn't help much. There are even places where smiles are reserved for intimate situations.

Then there is the other side of the story. In some parts of the world children are not discouraged from staring—especially if there is something curious at which to stare. The same American who must be cautious about not extending a polite glance more than a second or so in certain situations finds an almost infuriating "invasion of privacy" as people sit and stare—sometimes by the hour. In my experience, it occurs most predictably among rural people or isolated societies—as in Micronesia or the Caribbean. Standing at a porch railing with a shaving mirror propped so that the early morning sun assists in my shaving, I have been startled to discover squatting figures—indeed, swelling crowds—giving their undivided attention to the mysterious ways of this foreigner. Do I shoo them away? Smile and nod? Ignore them?

The first several times one encounters this situation, it is a "problem" to be solved. Deciding what to do seems important. But after awhile it becomes merely an experience, not really a problem. One merely does what seems most humane. I usually try to ignore them until the "performance" is over—shaving, loading the car, writing in my log book, or whatever. Then, when I am finished, a smiling glance and a nod or an appropriate word of greeting, in their language or mine, is met by murmurs of returned greeting and, often, the smiles which mean so much to me.

This very basic human process, watching another human being, represents both the simplicity and the complexity of the intercultural accommodation. Consider these reflections:

- Curiosity is normal, shared by all, and should not be denied nor inhibited. It is one of the most powerful motivators of learning.
- One's culture establishes the ways and the extent to which curiosity is to be regulated lest it become offensive to others.
- What is offensive in one culture may not be offensive in another. Each culture's standards and styles are, to some extent, a violation of another culture's standards.
- The prepared expatriate accepts the responsibility of accommodating insofar as possible to the standards of the host society and its culture.
- Competency of the prepared expatriate always includes two aspects: acceptance of the local behavior and adjustment of one's behavior to the norms and acceptable styles of the host culture.

WHEN IN ROME . . .

Rigidity leads to breakage. The green branch is hard to break because it bends so easily; the dried branch snaps.

So it is with adaptation to culture. For some people, even the thought of "giving in" to ways that are different threatens their sense of worth and well being. Stubbornness can be tragic, whether it springs from deliberate chauvinism, pride, or just plain habitual rigidity. A closed mind or hostile attitude leads to rejection of that which is different. There is nothing but trouble ahead for a person who resists adaptation.

Within limits, the old advice is still valid: When in Rome, do as the Romans do. As a basic way of coping with cultural difference, it provides a good starting place. It suggests conforming and adapting as the requisites of "getting along." It suggests a mindset and willingness to forfeit some or all of one's distinctiveness in order to achieve a presumed greater value: "fitting in."

Herein lies a rub: deeply held values cannot be violated or compromised without pain and loss. "When in Rome . . . ," if taken as an excuse for violating one's moral and ethical values or religious beliefs, can become the source of grief and heartbreak. The overseas experience provides every sojourner the occasion for looking carefully at the values and beliefs held most dear.

Staying in one's own society, especially living out one's life among those who share the same subcultural values, is likely to cause those values to become more a matter of habit than of reasoned thought. Only in moments of lapse or violation does the value become clearly focused in mind. The result is a kind of "doing what comes naturally"; within this sort of habit-oriented life, one may exhibit many good and desirable attributes, but they are apt not to be very thoroughly thought through. Why do you value what you value and believe what you believe? Your life is more responsible, and likely more moral, if you know what you believe and why.

For the person who goes overseas, *consciousness* of values becomes more characteristic. Thus it can be said that a period of intercultural experience will cause one's values to "come clear." Only that which is real—to which there is real commitment—will survive. When "doing as the Romans do" jolts one's value system, two choices are clear: to accept the new value or to return to the old with greater dedication. The latter, especially, has a character-building quality.

In simpler matters of taste, personal preference, and aesthetics, where moral issues are not at stake, "do as the Romans do" can be the best advice. Whatever you do or fail to do has the effect of causing you to stand out like the proverbial "sore thumb." Distinctiveness of personality and personal style need not be sacrificed, but all sorts of simple things can be adjusted in order to fit in better. Consider the following:

Symbols of American Affluence

The camera around the neck screams "tourist" in many languages. Get a smaller one or leave it in a purse or knapsack, according to local custom. Conspicuously costly items, especially those that are different from the local norm, will draw attention. Fancy-printed umbrellas, elegant thermos bottles, and the many other things carried into public view should be "tuned" to the local equivalents. In every society some things are *supposed* to be ostentatious while other things are not. Hold off on some of your choices and purchases until you can see what will be the style and pattern of those with whom you will be working and engaging in social activity.

Clothing

Americans are aware of the importance of dressing appropriately for the occasion. One would not want to be the only person in shorts at a given occasion in the United States. This commitment to conforming, in matters of dress, should be as firmly maintained in a foreign society. There will be plenty of mistakes made, since it is much harder to ask and get a straight answer when one is in another culture, but the effort will be worthwhile in the long run. In any case, one should be a good enough observer to avoid making the same mistake twice.

Displays of Stubborn Individualism

For many Americans, some little quirk of clothing or mannerism is dearly preserved as a reassurance of one's individualism. At the risk of becoming psychoanalytic, it might be suggested that such displays are ways of seeking attention, calculated to compensate for basic insecurity. So the silly plaid hat, the Donald Duck tee shirt or the Texas-style boots are adopted as an affectation. Americans are accustomed to these little "trademarks" of particular individuals and little is said or thought about them. But the cost of such an idiosyncracy in some cultures can be high. People can become irritated—whether or not they say anything about it—with a person who insists on being unique through the use of such artificial devices. Surely in the Orient, where the mass of humanity tends to suppress individual identity, Americans can feel a deep craving for standing out in a crowd; but it should be clear that the American *does* stand out because of the *real* distinction of being a certain sort of foreigner—there is no need to add a dangling six-foot gold scarf to increase one's visibility.

GO WITH THE FLOW

In matters of planning, especially the dates and timing for events, the sojourner must be able to "go with the flow." In the negative form, the following advice might be given: Don't push. But what do you do? Unpredictability and the changeability of schedules can be wasteful and disorienting and progress suffers.

In every culture there is a sense of pace and space. If you get too far outside the pace expectations, you will find your influence and even your newfound friendships slipping away.

As an American, accustomed to organizing and planning to gain predictability, control, and efficiency, I had to learn two vital lessons in Asia. First, the necessity to mesh my commitments to an international development assistance fund with the realities of Indonesian government bureaucracy convinced me that Western concepts of scheduling can be a source of continual friction. Only when I assigned the task of scheduling for our project to an Indonesian did things begin to happen. Not that they happened as quickly as my sponsoring agency might have liked, but at least they happened. What had been going on before might best be called nonaction. Because so much Indonesian effort was put into proving that my schedule wouldn't work, there was little energy left for anything else. Once I conceded the issue to their better judgment, Indonesian concepts of time and effort came into play.

I learned the second important lesson about scheduling on another assignment in an Asian country even more prone to mysticism and the inscrutability that Kipling called to the attention of his compatriots. The fact that I had to make this discovery through mistakes in the field rather than through reading and scholarly preparation illustrates the importance of being able to learn from experience.

"Would next Wednesday be a good day for the five of us to visit the provincial headquarters?" The hemming and hawing over such seemingly routine matters became annoying. It seemed that we could never come to a decision. Or when we did, as often as not the schedule would come unglued before we could put it into action. I trusted these people and respected them, but there were times when I wanted to pull out my hair and scream.

My "bridge person" in the project tried to help me, but I wasn't paying enough attention to him. "Sometimes we pick the wrong day," he said; this didn't ring bells until long afterward when it finally dawned on me that I was taking into account only the logical and rational concerns when establishing schedules and calendars. My Asian colleagues wanted ever so much to follow through on my suggestions, but their hands were tied until they could check out the days and dates with an outside consultant. Determining the "auspicious" date for a certain kind of event is taken very seriously. Before we could really commit to a schedule, a numerologist (some would say, "spiritist" or "witch-doctor") had to be consulted. I began to wonder if the project might not move faster if we put the consultant on our payroll and asked her to sit in on the planning sessions!

As a matter of fact, I knew full well that there are many people in the world who take numerology very seriously. The mystical meanings of certain numbers, and, especially, the astrological significance of dates is a very important concern of widely distributed religions and cults across the globe. The concern is so deep and the variables involved are so complex that in many matters a specialist must be consulted.

Even among many people who are in the "modern" sector, Christian converts included, this concern with numbers and the zodiac continues. When one considers that even in America today, many office buildings and hotels are numbered so as to omit a thirteenth floor, this problem seems less exotic.

For these two reasons, different concepts of appropriate pacing and the issue of numerology, it is wise for the sojourner to go with the flow. Don't fight it.

Then there are holidays. But that would take a separate book. Here it may be sufficient to say that the wise sojourner makes a list of each and every national and religious holiday in the country. Recurrent shut-downs are a nuisance to Americans who have become accustomed to certain stores and services being available 365 days per year. Beware! In many countries holidays are a very serious matter. By American standards, they are very, very frequent.

Don't be surprised if your household staff expects to be off duty when you most need them. Your maid will probably spend Ramadan in her village with her family. Find out what that's all about before you are asked.

THE SPIRIT WORLD

Those who see the human being as more than flesh and blood should not be surprised to discover that in some parts of the world people are more aware of spiritual matters than in others. Modern western sophistication, under the mistaken impression that science reduces the credibility of matters of faith, tends to disbelieve or disregard anything that cannot be observed empirically or rationally explained.

The sojourner who gets off the tourist's path and into the inner workings of an oriental, African, or aboriginal society in Latin America, Australia, the Pacific Islands, or elsewhere sooner or later will encounter the spirit world in undeniable ways. It would be wrong to assume that this is exclusively a matter of the witchcraft of

"primitive" societies. Some of us have run into witchcraft and Sa-
tan-worship in such cities as Paris and London. The persistence of
spirit forces in modern Hong Kong, Taipei, Tokyo, and Singapore is
also quite evident.

Arnold Mayer, an expatriate American audiovisual specialist
and media producer in Nairobi, writes:

> This has been a difficult letter for me to write because for many years I
> thought of demons and spirits as something out of another time. How-
> ever, as I have gotten very close to my Kenyan friends and have under-
> stood better the influences that control their lives, I have become con-
> vinced that the spirit world exists as a real everyday experience for
> many people. . . . The results of this influence extend to those who live
> and work around the possessed person. I have had to readjust my
> thinking to allow for such a world to exist at the scale that I am discov-
> ering is really here.[8]

In an accompanying narrative, Mayer describes a spirit-possessed
person he calls "Naomi."

> Naomi had developed a withered leg early in her life, probably as a
> result of polio.
>
> A crippled person in Kenya is known as *kiwete*. In Swahili there are
> six different classes of nouns. By the prefix of a word you can tell what
> class of noun that word falls into. Some of the classes include trees and
> growing plants, others include material things like chairs, shoes,
> knives, and tables. Another noun class deals with animals and people.
> A person is known as *Mtu*; people are known as *Watu*. So we say that
> the people class is the m-wa class. When a person has a major physical
> handicap he is reclassified into the *things* class. So *kiwete* (a crippled
> person) or a *kipofu* (blind person) is classified in the ki-vi class which
> includes things that are used around the farm or house. They are no
> longer considered part of the *people* class. I mention this because you
> need to know a little of how Naomi may have felt as a crippled person.
>
> When Naomi was twelve, several spirits came to her one night and
> asked if they could dwell within her. Some of these were spirits that
> had been dwelling in her mother. Evidently in this family there was a
> long history of spirit possession. These spirits said they wanted to live
> within her and give her great powers so that she would again be re-
> spected in the village.
>
> You can see the dilemma that Naomi faced. She was looked upon as
> something less than human because of her crippled leg; by inviting
> these spirits to come in she might gain powers that could help her re-
> store her dignity in the village. However, when such spirits possess a
> person they may make demands. Going against the spirits' wishes can

cause sickness and injury to the possessed person. As Naomi worked together with these spirits, she developed the ability to cast out lesser demons from other people, to tell fortunes, and even to heal some diseases that were prevalent in that area.[9]

Encounters such as this have been told and retold by Western sojourners, especially those whose backgrounds in rationalized and verbally preoccupied religion give them little basis for anticipating such experiences.

BUT WE DON'T LIKE DURIAN

When you are thoroughly committed to accommodating yourself to the differences in a new cultural experience, you may occasionally try too hard. You may find yourself doing things that some of the local folks avoid. In such a situation it is quite acceptable for a newcomer to politely demur.

"Have you ever tried durian?" It wasn't the first such question that day. In fact we had stopped for fruit of various sorts and stopped for so many photographs of scenic vistas that I began to wonder if we would ever get to Jogjakarta. But what can you say?

"No, that's another new one for me."

"Would you like to try it?"

"Sure, why not," I said with all the enthusiasm I could muster. The car swerved to a stop, throwing Indonesian gravel in all directions. After a few minutes of polite conversation and negotiating, we were on our way again, leaving the roadside fruit vendor a few rupiahs less impoverished. Reflecting back on the experience I recall a sort of knowing glance among my three Indonesian partners, but it meant nothing at the time. The sack of fruit went into the trunk with no insistence that we peel it and eat it as we drove on. For that I was thankful, because my hands were already far too sticky to be comfortable and far too dirty (by American standards) to wrestle any more exotic fruit into my mouth.

Later, after we had checked in at the government guest house, the durian became the subject of our conversation. All the other fruits that day had been peeled and divided by one or another of my colleagues, usually with skill and a certain amount of ceremony. This time, for the durian, nothing would do but that we should have the fruit properly cut, peeled, and arranged on a plate. A houseboy was called and a rapid-fire discussion ensued in what I think was Sundanese. Twice in the exchange everyone chuckled (except me—language ignorance is the worst kind) and I began to wonder if the Indonesians had invented their own version of the good old American "snipe hunt."

Sure enough, when the plate of durian appeared, at the end of the houseboy's fully extended arm, I smelled a trap. Or was it the durian I smelled? Surely both.

It turns out that durian has a basically disagreeable odor—more than likely nature's way of saving it for some poor creature in the ecology with no sense of smell at all. Indeed, I had seen some Indonesians eating it at the roadside, and these durians were prime specimens. But as the plate arrived, my colleagues stood and filed out, smiling weakly. I was left with an enormous pile of durian.

"What is this?" I called after them. "I can't eat all this by myself. I need help!"

"But we don't like durian. You're the one who wanted to try it; not us."

In that moment I learned quite a lesson! It doesn't follow that all Indonesians like durian, even if it is a "typical" fruit. It doesn't follow that all Americans like hot dogs, Chevrolets . . . or even apple pie.

As a newcomer I was free to try things for myself and just as free to like or *not* to like. I could be as honest as they were being.

Meanwhile, what to do about the durian? It was in the nature of my childhood to turn down any food that smelled even slightly disagreeable. My adult nature had put a level of rationality in place to blunt this instinct. Thus I had learned to eat—and enjoy—okra, papaya, turnips, and various other of my childhood turn-offs. So the durian was a challenge. I started in. It tasted somewhat better than it smelled; but not enough. At first I thought I might try to clean up the whole plateful and "amaze" my hosts. But two bites persuaded me that I should try a different tactic. There was no place to dump it or flush it down, so I decided to be honest. (That rarely seems to occur to me as the first strategy, I must confess.) I had managed about the fourth sizable chunk when one of my Indonesian colleagues stuck his head in the door to see who was winning, me or the durian.

"Like it?"

"Not really, but I can eat it. It's maybe something you have to live with for a long time," I replied.

"No, I don't think that helps." His shake of the head was conclusive.

Just then the other two joined us and after a few words of congratulation for my brave try, they took the remaining durian to the courtyard and deposited it under an innocent bush. I was sure then and I am sure today that eating all of that durian would have been a big mistake.

There is nothing wrong with having tastes and preferences. Wherever you go you will find that others have them, too. Trying to adopt tastes and values to match those of a "standard" Indonesian is as unnecessary as walking on your knees to match the height of the "average" Indonesian. Variations *within* a society render such words as "average," "standard," and "typical" almost useless.

Be yourself. Try not to be preoccupied, overtly curious, or self-conscious about the differences. Learn to take everything new in stride. Adjust yourself when possible, but don't expect to "give in" on everything.

SKATING ON COCONUTS

Being half-prepared for surprises can be fun. By "half-prepared" I refer to expecting that some things won't make sense at first, but enjoying the surprise or humor of it when such an encounter occurs, and then going on to try to figure things out.

The first time I saw coconut-skating I was so sure it was a joke that I laughed out loud. The scowl that came back was enough to tell me that I had completely misunderstood the situation. In the Philippines a maid tends to be all business, especially when working for Americans.

But there she was, barefooted as usual, with half of a coconut shell under each broad foot, systematically skating around the room. So help me, *skating*.

If this performance wasn't for my amusement or hers (and her face said it wasn't), then she had gone out of her head. It wasn't the first time, nor the last, that my working hypothesis was that a certain local person was at least a part-time lunatic.

I backed out and strolled down the hall, trying to look cool and calm.

"Ismelda . . . Ismelda is skating in the living room," I said to Mary, who didn't even look up from the desk where she was typing.

"Yes, this is Thursday, isn't it." Startled to find a second luna-tic—and this one an American missionary, I held my cool and calm style only with great difficulty.

"She skates only on Thursdays? That's nice," I said as I beat an awkward retreat from Mary's little study room.

"Oh, you mean *why* is she skating—right?" Mary called af-ter me.

"Yes, I guess that's the major question," I replied.

Mary, who had done part of her prefield orientation training in one of my workshops, decided to give me a dose of my own medi-cine: "Go out there and watch her skate; then come back and tell me what you see." And so I did.

Her typewriter clicked on, scarcely missing a beat, until I ex-claimed from the living room hallway, "I've got it!"

"Well, good for you; you're never too old to learn." Mary's voice had just enough sarcasm in it to call me up short on how I must of-ten sound to others. And while the typing went on I stood there ad-miring nature's own polish for hardwood floors, coconut oil, being applied by a very effective Southeast Asian method.

FOCUS FOR SELF-EVALUATION

When first confronted with cultural difference, one is likely to be resistant or even negative. The competent sojourner learns to get beyond the irratio-nal reactions and *think* about things. Reasoning out differences is a good habit, even if it doesn't always work—some things have no apparent rea-sons, they just are the way they are. The Chinese, for example, ask why Americans put ice in tea. No reason. They just do—sometimes.

The following pattern of reasoning can be used to think through the differences one encounters in another culture.

First, make a list of those things you have noticed or heard to be differ-ent in the culture to which you are preparing to go. Be as specific as pos-sible.

For each item on your list, answer the following questions:

1. What did I expect or what would be less noticeable to me as a new-

   comer?_____

   _____

2. Why would an American have done it differently?_____

   _____

3. Why do these people do it the way they do?_____

   _____

4. Is there any chance I might enjoy or appreciate doing it as they do? Why? Why not?_____

   _____

5

The Skills of Coping

THE COMPETENT SOJOURNER copes with culture. Culture is to be encountered, related to, dealt with, and grasped. The necessary skills are active processes rather than passive reflections. Culture is active and alive. The sojourner-in-preparation should mark this well; to move into another culture with confidence will require alertness and capacity to make sense out of what can be observed and experienced. It's all there. It all stems from more or less understandable roots. Those who seek will find.

COPING: AN ACTIVE PROCESS

The way to get on top of things is to develop a reliable strategy for coping. Intercultural encounter is full of surprising events—like life at home, only more so. It is simply not possible to be specifically experienced or specifically prepared for anything and everything. One attempts to grasp what lies behind something—whether it is the meaning of a strange encounter or the probing of one's own vague and mysterious feelings. Adequate coping with culture depends more on general understanding and willingness to take each event on its own terms.

In cultural matters one develops a familiarity with patterns without expecting the exact fulfillment of a given pattern each time. One develops a feeling for the tactics and procedures of interpersonal encounter without expecting the tactics and procedures to work exactly the same way each time. One learns a style of approach—a way to *be*—in order to put oneself into the action, not as a reacting robot, but as a full participant in the shaping of the outcomes of the experience.

Coping is a matter of handling something effectively that might otherwise become a problem. The emphasis is more on the fact that you actually do handle it than on the judgment that you were highly successful. To cope is more a matter of surviving against odds than it is a matter of conquering. For most Americans a sirloin steak is not something to be coped with; eel with leeks is.

Coping has become an important theme in many programs of intercultural preparation. The emphasis on coping is an acknowledgment that not every experience in a new cultural setting will be easy to handle. To give any other impression, and especially to puff up a person's enthusiasm unrealistically, would be reprehensible. No matter where a trainee is headed, the responsible prediction would be that some matters will prove to be difficult—some few, at least, will be very trying.

Even people who never leave their own culture discover themselves anew day by day—encountering new experiences and handling them, whether expected or unexpected. So what is different overseas? Only frequency and intensity. People who try to cope are in many ways the same everywhere. Each person develops ways to deal with various types of new and potentially threatening experiences. Some of these ways may be defensive, others may be based on aggressive "counterattacks" directed against the perceived threat, and some may be an outgrowth of curiosity, a craving to turn a negative to a positive, or a sort of game-playing motive that sees winning or losing as "less important than how you play the game."

The earlier methods of orientation training, with their emphasis on knowing and understanding, often set up trainees for a fall. Modern intercultural orientation programs are based, in part, on the proposition that people need to know how to cope. Since a person cannot know in detail what is going to be needed in an intercultural assignment, the most appropriate preparation will encourage the trainee to develop ways to apply a specific set of coping strategies.

BECOMING SHOCK RESISTANT

The expression "culture shock" may not deserve to be weeded out and purged from the literature of the field of culture learning, but its overuse has led to unfortunate negative connotations. Surely there is such a thing as intercultural *conflict*. Surely there is such a condition as *inadequate competency*. Surely there is such a state as *intercultural incomprehension*. Any combination of these can result from improper or inadequate preparation. But to call this syndrome "culture shock" diverts attention from more important matters. It can lead ultimately to educational approaches that are less a matter of preparation than of remediation—patching up and gluing back together rather than adequately preparing in the first place.

What would happen if the idea of "marriage shock" became popular? Surely there are profound adjustments to be made when two persons bring their separate identities and contrasting life histories and value systems into a commitment to unity. Or parenthood—is there anything in life that so predictably turns out to be much more demanding than was anticipated? But do we talk about "parenthood shock?" The term "culture shock" has been with us for over a quarter of a century, and it is not likely to go away. Those who teach and write in this field do talk about it, whether or not we believe that it is a good idea to do so. It is a popular way to look at the matter, so we play along.

Fear is a strong motivator. Fear of the unknown is especially easy to exploit. Even among people who ought to know better, there is a tendency to play on the anxieties of people who need help. What is needed far more than the rude act of shaking sleepers into startled fear is helping them cope with what they will find when they awaken!

THREE SHOCK ABSORBERS

What can be done to make culture shock less severe? In workshops for people going overseas, we try to develop three skills—empathy, observation and exploration.

Empathy

How a person relates to others is the foundation for cross-cultural effectiveness. Can you trust others? Do you accept help from others?
Do you try to *feel* life from the point of view of the other person?
Many Americans place great importance on being independent and
having their own way. That may work out fairly well in our own
country, but there are very few places outside North America and
Europe where independence is socially accepted. In most of the
world, especially the third world nations, people are expected to
need each other, especially within the extended family to which
they happen to belong. This sort of mutually dependent relationship
is built on a sensitivity to the needs and feelings of others.

One of the more useful ways to assess your level of empathy is to
isolate some behavior or attitude you see in someone else and try
hard to think of a possible reason why the other person does this or
feels this way. You'll know that empathy is emerging when you begin to be really generous and nonjudgmental. You'll begin to make
up alibis and excuses in your mind for other people, and you'll be
more willing to see their side of the story.

Observation

Observation games and drills can dramatically increase perceptual
skills in a number of ways, often within a short period of time. Test
yourself with the following exercise: Close your eyes and reconstruct
the setting in which you are now located. With your eyes still
closed, try to spot something in your recall of the general scene that
you haven't already thought about. Why is that window down from
the top? How did that paint get scraped? Who might have left that
small green object over there in the corner? Why? And so on. Then
take a very quick peek out the window or off to the left and start the
game again.

If you repeat this exercise several times a day over a period of
weeks, you will find that your skill is increasing. As a bonus, you
will develop a lot more self-confidence about your ability to observe. You will enjoy awareness of the interesting little questions
that can be raised about things otherwise taken for granted. Perhaps
the greatest values lies in learning the usefulness of asking yourself
"Why?" Even as a child asks "Why?" because he or she wants to

learn, you will find yourself carrying on a continuous internal inquiry about your own environment.

Transactional Exploration

Are you learning to deal with new and unknown experiences by relating to them experimentally? Rather than becoming rigid and frightened because you lack information, or becoming "lost" for lack of a model to copy, do you get actively involved and try out your hunches?

This "trying out" is what we call transaction: do something and see what happens. As a child you learned more this way than any other. You never lose this capability, though as you grow older you tend to depend more on previous experience and the knowledge it has built within you. When you encounter something really new, something that your past experience doesn't cover, you can always resort to transactional exploration. Make an effort to rediscover this tactic.

Scientifically, transactional exploration is called "inquiry learning" or "discovery learning." In common-sense terms, it involves finding out through trial and error. Though in cross-cultural matters you don't want to do too many things that are going to make matters worse, it is usually better to do than not to do—to act rather than to freeze up. When you freeze you stop learning!

Robert Kohls, an expert in the field of intercultural training and the Director of Training and Development for the International Communication Agency, draws a useful distinction between frustration ("uncomfortable, but short-lived") and "culture shock." *Frustration* arises from the following:

- Ambiguity of a situation in which you find yourself
- Mismatch between your expectations and the reality of a situation
- Unrealistic goals which you now realize are out of reach
- Inability to see results
  - —Because the need is simply too huge
  - —Because the work to be done is beyond your skills and understandings
  - —Because the work to be done is in reality different from the view held by those who are defining your mission

—Because the amount of time available to you is inadequate (or your period of service too short) to see the slow-paced efforts

- Growing awareness that the wrong methods are being used to achieve the intended objectives[2]

Culture shock, by comparison, is a longer and larger problem with the following characteristics:

- Culture shock does not result from a specific event or series of events. It comes instead from encountering ways of doing, organizing, perceiving, or valuing things which are different from yours and which threaten your basic, unconscious belief that your enculturated customs, assumptions, values, and behaviors are "right." It comes from being cut off from the cultural cues and known patterns with which you are familiar—especially the subtle, indirect ways you normally express feelings.
- Culture shock does not strike suddenly or have a single principal cause. Instead it is cumulative, building up slowly from a series of small events that are difficult to identify.[3] It comes from these realities:
  —Living and/or working over an extended period of time in a situation that is ambiguous
  —Having your own values (which you had heretofore considered as absolutes) brought into question—which yanks your moral rug out from under you
  —Being continually put into positions in which you are expected to function with maximum skill and speed but where the rules have not been adequately explained.[4]

As use of the term became more popular, research on "culture shock" increased. Especially in reference to the Peace Corps, studies of "culture shock" were conducted for about fifteen years. As funding of the Peace Corps diminished, this research emphasis faded rapidly.[5] No clear consensus was reached; "culture shock" remained at the level of a "folk generalization."

Kohls sees it as a sort of homesickness. Brislin proposes this definition:

Culture shock refers to the accumulated stresses and strains which stem from being forced to meet one's everyday needs (e.g., food, cleanliness, companionship) in unfamiliar ways.

Culture shock . . . summarizes sojourners' reactions after they lose the security of familarity.[6]

WHEN THINGS DON'T MAKE SENSE

While granting that deprivation of the familiar is surely a triggering problem in any intercultural encounter, the thing that concerns me most is learning to make sense out of the unfamiliar. This concern comes out of the 1959 use the term by Edward T. Hall: "Cultural shock is simply a removal or distortion of many of the familiar cues one encounters at home and the substitution for them of other cues which are strange."[7]

Self-assessment should focus more on things you can do something about rather than those things that are probably beyond your control. Overseas experience inevitably involve the loss of familiar cues; in fact, that's part of the charm of it! But what about those "cues which are strange"? Must they *remain* strange? Indeed, no.

What happens to the inadequately prepared person is far more than the removal of the familiar. What determines whether or not shock results is a matter of what one does with the unfamiliar and the "strange." If unfamiliar experiences are processed actively using specific tactics for coping, they need not be overwhelming. Are you learning to handle new experiences this way?

One of the best explanations of this skill is based on a communication concept: When you think of the human mind as an information processing system, "culture shock" can be seen as an overloading that blows the fuses.

Your senses, especially your eyes and ears, are constantly feeding signals into your brain. Some you ignore, but others you "process." You make sense out of the signals by connecting them with experiences from your past. "What's that blinding flash?" Oh, sure, just another photographer with a strobe. What sense could you make of portable lightning if you'd never seen a flash camera before?

Blah, what a taste! No problem, it just needs some salt. Making sense of data in the environment lets you decide what to do. But if an experience doesn't ring any bells, you may not know what to do. And when you don't know, you may become afraid to do *anything*.

The tremendous cultural chessboard we live on at home is too easy to take for granted. Up, down, sideways, diagonally, everything has a familiarity to us—we're used to it. Take a look at the decorations and trimmings on your clothes right now. They all fit together to make an "okay" appearance. Of the thousands of ways to put things together, it's your culture or subculture that says what's okay. Why do you eat with your fork in your strong hand? Why use a fork at all? When is it acceptable to eat with the fingers? Why? With whom should you sit? With whom should you *not* sit? When do you smile? Why?

What does it mean when someone belches? When someone laughs at you? When you aren't asked to sit down? When someone shakes a stick at you? When the agreed time to meet arrives and there's no one there but you? These questions have cultural meanings, and when you don't know the "code," you feel left out and, very likely, more than a little frightened. Are you becoming more aware of your own codes? Are you prepared to adjust to codes that are different?

IT'S REAL

Each of us will encounter "shocking" problems in various experiences. The results of "culture shock" boil down to four conditions. Are you becoming more capable of dealing with them?

Emotional anxiety: Being in strange surroundings

Disorientation: Being unable to predict what other people are going to do

Discomfort: Not knowing what to do to handle a situation

Overwhelming sense of incompetency: Experiencing too many sensory stimuli that don't have clear meanings, and locking into a feeling of impotence

Most of us can handle short periods of any of the first three conditions without going into shock. But when the first condition leads to the second, the second leads to the third, and then the fourth takes hold, you're in trouble. All the signals coming in are getting blocked. Nothing makes sense. What's that funny noise? Why is he doing that? Where did she go? What's that for? Why are they looking at me like that? Why? Why? When? What? Who? Where? . . . Help! Overload.

COPING WITH "CULTURE SHOCK"

Brislin writes about "culture shock" in terms of the need to cope: "The stresses which accompany a cross-cultural experience often stem from attempts to cope with situations which *seem* familiar but which are puzzling because of cultural differences such as the importance of time constraints or the number of people who have roles in a situation."[8]

"Coping" implies a practical and action-oriented way to respond to new and unfamiliar problems. Some writers in the field refer to "coping" but never bring their advice down to practical suggestions. Kohls is one clear exception; he suggests a five-part coping strategy to prevent or cure culture shock:

1. *Gather information.* Keep looking for things you overlooked before. There is always more to see and to learn. Some of it will make sense.
2. *Look for logical reasons behind the strange and the unfamiliar.* What is most important is the consciousness that things aren't inherently irrational simply because you haven't yet made sense of them. Keep trying—with a positive and open outlook.
3. *Fight off the temptation to take out your frustration on the people of the host country.* "Stupid natives!" is hardly a useful thing to say, even inside your own head. Avoid expatriates who talk and think this way; they will drag you down deeper into culture shock.
4. *Discover and affiliate with a person of the host country who can help you interpret experience.* Just as surely as language differences can be bridged by a good translator, a culture-translator or "bridge person" can help you understand the mysteries. Don't depend exclusively on fellow Americans to provide this sort of help. Many misunderstandings can be passed from one American to another. Learn to trust people of the host country.
5. *Have faith in yourself and in the underlying good will of those in the host country.* The most trying experience can turn out to be a valuable milestone if you don't give up—on yourself, or on others.[9]

MAKING A GAME OUT OF UNCERTAINTY

Even awkward moments can be turned around into learning experiences, often with good outcomes. The satisfaction that can come from a delighted host or hostess can make it all worthwhile. So when in doubt, make a game—a sort of detective game—out of your uncertainties and look for solutions.

"I notice that you do that just like we do!" Whether it is eating your soup last, taking off your shoes when you enter a home, bowing when you shake hands, or whatever, it can be fun to observe carefully and to copy the behavior of host-country people.

They will tell you that you should feel free to do things whatever way you want. People of every culture seem willing to let outsiders do things their own way, but what really delights them is to find you quietly copying their ways.

In some parts of the world meals are consumed one course at a time—soup, then salad, then the main dish, then vegetables, and then dessert. In other places it is the custom to sample this, then that, then the other—round and round, never quite "licking the platter clean." How do you know which and what? You could ask; and it's better to ask than to ignore, but on these little things, why not make a game of it? Observe, copy, and await your reward! The secret of the game is to be unobtrusive. You don't win if you are forever asking, "What is it I'm supposed to do next?"

Calling attention to the idea that their ways are not your ways is the right of your host. You are the outsider. Your calling attention to differences, even in little things, can create awkwardness, sometimes tension or embarrassment. But if *they* call attention to differences, it will usually be in the form of a compliment—especially if your host should come across with the *big* one: "Most Americans don't do it the way we do—you're different." It can be fun to hear this, especially in reference to something no one ever told you— something you noticed and figured out for yourself.

My first experience with the *mandi* of Indonesia was of this sort. As it turned out, there was no one to observe, but there were plenty of clues all around. My host had handed me a towel and invited me to "cool off . . . take as long as you want." He pointed outside to a little shed attached to the house. I nodded and headed for the shed. Inside I found a waist-high cubic concrete tub filled with water, a pair of hooks high on one wall, and a floor covered with wooden slats and slightly tilted toward a low spot where a sizable drain hole was covered with a small square of metal screening. Now what?

Was I supposed to get in that tub? In spite of the extremely hot and sultry weather, I didn't relish the idea of climbing in to such a large tub of unheated water. Furthermore, whoever had installed the pipe (yes, there was only one) had positioned the faucet almost directly over the center of the tub. How could you get in and out with that thing in the middle? I was confused and not at all comfortable, so I did what uncomfortable, confused people do—I found a scapegoat: stupid Indonesian plumbers. And, as usual, that helped in no way whatsoever—except to remind me that "stupid locals" is an outsider's cover-up for his or her own ignorance.

So I looked around some more. This time two more things came into view: There was a plastic sauce pan with a long handle. Could it be an oversize dipper? And a small plastic box was perched on a crosspiece of the wall frame some distance from the tub. What was in it? Aha! soap; but why so far from the tub?

While all this observing and thinking was going on I got out of my clothes. Although I wasn't sure what to do next, I didn't imagine that Indonesians could keep as clean and neat as they do by daily face-washing. And with my pants in hand, I looked for a place to put them. The hooks high on the wall! Indonesians come in fairly short sizes, so I wondered at the height of the hooks. But, unlike my long-legged problem in many an American bathroom, the cuffs weren't going to get wet here, I thought. And then it began to fall into place.

Standing right there on the slatted floor was where my "shower" was to take place. The dipper was my shower, the tub was my ample reservoir, and the faucet was to refill the reservoir when I was through. At least all those ideas fit together.

It seemed to be a reasonable set of hypotheses. If I could just confirm any one part of it, I'd give it a try. The reservoir idea—why not just work directly from the faucet? I turned it. A trickle. More turns. Still a trickle. Never could you shower with that little flow. But over time, it would accumulate in the reservoir and you could have plenty to shower with. Further, as the cold tap water stood in the tub it would be warmed to a more pleasant temperature.

Fingers in the water. Right. Exactly the temperature to refresh without inducing a heart attack on this steamy day.

Here we go. The dipper. A half-cup down the left arm. A bit of soap. The water ran to the floor-slats and headed across to the drain. Aha! The open-air plumbing does work, after all. A little more water this time, and again.

Suddenly a childhood reading experience flashed into mind. Was it Kipling in India? Stevenson on his visits to Polynesia? I had read them all. (Childhood reading and my Great Aunt Mabel had got me into all of this in the first place.) I recalled the writer singing at the top of his voice as he splashed (yes, that was the word), splashed, and "threw water everywhere" (yes!). So I tried it. First the singing, then the splashing. And a bit more of each until the whole household could hear that I had found one of the profound pleasures of Indonesia, the *mandi*.

In the process I discovered why the clothes hooks are high on the wall. When the celebration of elemental values of life came to an end, I rebuttoned the not-too-wet essentials and emerged. My host was grinning from ear to ear.

"You've used a *mandi* before, I gather," he said with a slight bow.

"No, but it doesn't take me long to learn."

"I should have explained it to you, but I didn't know if you needed me to."

Here's an important point: I could have asked. Perhaps I should have asked. Indeed, I would have asked if it had remained a mystery after I had taken a good look. But I didn't need to, and even if I had done something fundamentally wrong—even had I climbed bodily into the tub and displaced two hundred pounds of water, my host would have accepted it. I was an outsider. My ways were not his ways. But he wouldn't have been quite so delighted that I could enjoy *his* ways even without being told.

And then came the reward: "Did you turn on the faucet when you finished?" he asked.

"Yes," I replied. "It likely will take thirty minutes or so to replace what I used from the tub."

"Yes, about that. I'll turn it off after a while. Do you know you are the first American ever to visit us who knew to leave the water running?" And his smile became even warmer.

A little thing. But these little things add up. They tell your host that you care.

THE CLOSED MIND

No one knows how minds become closed. Children demonstrate curiosity and openness to inquiry. But they also seem to become, day by day, more fixed in their ways and opinions. Distaste for certain foods, stubbornness, resistance, and discomfort with the unfamiliar emerge early in life.

What keeps a mind closed is the refusal to try a new idea. Just as surely as learning to like spinach requires some effort and willingness, so it is with opinions.

Arguing, especially that childish sort of my-way-is-better-than-your-way bickering, badly serves a person by keeping the door clamped shut.

"No, it doesn't."

"Yes, it does."

"No, it doesn't."

"Yes, it does."

New ideas haven't a chance. Worse, the rigidity of old ideas hardens. The potentiality for deeper understanding diminishes.

Dealing with this issue from the perspective of traditions and values, Fred Graham of Michigan State University's Department of Religion shared an observation on National Public Radio:

> I think we can have firm convictions without being closed-minded, mean-spirited and always assuming the opposition doesn't know what it is talking about. Consider the Biblical admonition to "speak the truth in love." Speaking the truth means having convictions about what is true. Speaking the truth *in love* means that I assume the other person also has convictions, that those convictions were arrived at honestly, and that our mutual concern for truth forces me to listen to the convictions of the other person as attentively as I want mine listened to. When I do that I can be surprised, better—*we* can be surprised, by truth that neither of us had expected.
>
> Christians have argued among themselves bitterly for centuries about how Christ is present in Holy Communion. Jews were never brought into that argument, of course. Catholics said Jesus' words, "This is my body," means this bread *turns into* my body. Lutherans said no, to them it means. "This bread *contains* my body." Baptists said, no, it means, "This bread *commemorates* or *reminds* of my body." Calvinists said no, it means, "This bread *conveys* you to my body," and so on. One day some Christians, tired of arguing with each other, decided to talk to some rabbis. There they found out that the words of Jesus suggested, as does the language of the Passover Seder, that what happened long ago is made present in the meal and that people who share the meal and the words are transported back in time to the original Passover and the Flight from Egypt. In the course of the new, non-dogmatic dialogue with Jewish scholars, Christians are gaining insights different from any of their arguments, transcending old language, opening new perspectives and refocusing the issues.
>
> So truth breaks in when people take others seriously: when they *speak the truth in love.*[10]

COPING WITH OLD-TIMERS

It's probably true of "old-timers" anywhere, but since becoming an old-timer occurs earlier among expatriates, reminiscence about "the old days" is very popular. After someone has been *anywhere* about five years, a preoccupation with the past emerges. Who knows why? Perhaps it represents some deep craving to be seen as part of something one has never quite felt to be one's own. Or maybe it is just that this form of bragging about one's capability to survive is gratifying as a display of superiority. No matter why, it does happen, and the newcomer hasn't got a chance to contribute a fair share to a conversation that turns toward "the old days." The best advice is don't try. There is no more sure way to sound silly than to try to use a one-year-ago story to compete in the big league of five-and-ten-year-ago people. Instead, listen closely, be entertained, and remember a few of the better stories. After a respectable time, you can retell these same stories in a slightly altered form: "When I first came here I knew an old-timer who told about when they put up the first traffic light—it wasn't all that long ago either. My, how things have changed."

Among those who know where to get outstanding food in various capital cities, there are frequent games of can-you-top-this. My favorite candidate was an absolutely marvelous filet mignon in Bogota. On several occasions I had returned to this simple little side-street steak house and, by myself or with friends I wanted to impress, ordered this great steak dinner for well under the equivalent of a U.S. dollar. The place may not even be there anymore; it has been some time. I don't know what their price would be today, but it was great while it lasted.

Once I was telling my old-timer's story about the 93¢ steak in Bogota, and one of the other fellows leaned forward and said,

"I know that place, on Calle Zipaquira, right? Just around from the Hotel Ponce?"

"Yep. Exactly."

"Greatest steak in Colombia. Only it was more like forty-five cents when I first found the place."

You can't win 'em all.

COPING WITH INSULTS

"Sticks and stones may break my bones, but words will never hurt me." Good advice is implied in this childhood verse. It isn't wise to react overtly every time you are called a bad name. For many adults, especially those who have worked in humane environments and lived in genteel families, being called a "bastard" or some such derogatory epithet brings a flush to the cheeks and unpleasant memories of childhood (or the army) to the front of the mind. "Fighting words," we used to say. And, of course, that's exactly what the antagonist wanted—to get you to "blow your cool" and react. The whole idea of the game is to get you to swing and miss. Then you are laughed at, from all sides. As a youngster you probably learned the fine art of selective deafness: Hear what you want to hear, ignore the rest.

The old skill needs to be dusted off. Not only are you apt to be challenged on the street, at some point, but you will also discover a whole new use of the skill of selective deafness. Sooner or later, in polite company, at a party, as an aside in a pleasant introduction to some new business or neighborhood acquaintance, it will happen—usually when you are off guard because you least expect it. Someone will take a deep verbal dig at your race, your nationality, your religion, or your organization. And it can sting. The temptation can be almost overpowering to swing back—at least verbally. *Don't.*

"Sticks and stones may break my bones, but words will never hurt me." Well, hurt, maybe, but words will never *kill* you. And a scuffle just might. No, not kill you physically, but it could wreck or seriously damage your mission. Wounding your pride is a worldwide trick to get you to overreact and take a suicidal plunge while defending a relatively unimportant point of prejudice that can't be resolved by argument anyway. Don't take the bait. Especially in a linguistically mixed situation, your selective deafness will be interpreted as a lapse of your language skills or those of the attacker. Try to let it pass unnoticed. After a few tries, your message will be received as an honorable and acceptable one: You are not willing to fight over biases and prejudices. Fortunately, this message is appropriate in most polite groups throughout the world.

COPING WITH PHYSICAL THREAT

If you want to get stoned, travel in Israel and include the back streets and off-highway roads in your itinerary. Israel is surely not the only place where this happens, but in the "Holy Land," stoning has a long, long history and the current inhabitants haven't broken with the past. Stoning automobiles has largely replaced the stoning of persons, thank goodness. Today stoning doesn't mean execution.

When you are in the wrong place—such as driving through an Arab village with Jewish friends, or when you are in the right place at the wrong time—such as driving into an Hasidic orthodox district on the Sabbath, your car may get pelted.

Occasionally there are some windows broken, and especially if someone gets out to confront the molesters, there can be an ugly incident. But more often than not the stoners aim for the car's painted surfaces, and their aim is generally quite good. You should just assume after the first stone hits that more will follow and a trip to the dent-and-paint shop is inevitable. Don't fight it, just keep moving— but *don't hit anyone.*

What is such behavior all about? Hostility is the name of the human game in many a troubled part of the world. Today's sojourner needs to be ready to respond to hostility. For Americans, bristling in the face of even such a little matter as name-calling is second nature. It isn't easy to find a calm and less emotional way to behave at a moment when all of one's instincts are screaming, "Don't let them get away with that!"

The best advice is that an inflamed crowd is more likely to become violent if one engages in argument or fighting back. Whether it is a policeman challenging your right to walk near a military post or a crowd blocking the street down which you wish to drive, a bullish insistence on your "rights" can be costly. It is far wiser to give in and adopt a behavior that gives less provocation.

As events in Colombia, Italy, El Salvador, and Nicaragua have shown, this won't keep you from getting killed. But it does increase your chances of walking away, or driving away, from an otherwise very ugly situation.

- Stay calm (that's the hardest part).
- Stay in the car (play for time).
- Follow orders (unless it is painfully obvious that to do so will make matters worse).

HE WHO LAUGHS LAST, LAUGHS BEST

Not all stories of assault and battery have humorous endings, but here's one. For a number of years it was common for gangs of three to six young toughs to roam the main streets of Bogota, literally bowling over almost anyone they felt like "hitting." It was so common that you actually planned for this possibility. The attacks were generally quick, but could be seen coming for several frantic seconds just before you found yourself on the sidewalk. The favorite technique of the assailants was a frontal attack that involved a rapidly approaching elbow-to-elbow group of similarly sized older teenagers who looked you straight in the eye as they plowed right into you. Even if you were with three or four friends who tried come to your defense, it was usually futile.

Since these dramatic events took place on crowded streets in the modern part of the city in broad daylight, there rarely were any weapons involved and little if any more physical attack than the rather rudimentary act of being knocked to the ground. The motive was first intimidation and then pickpocketing. The tales of lost wallets and purses were commonplace. "Sooner or later it happens to everyone," the expatriates shrugged.

So you coped by carrying an expendable wallet—not a bad idea anywhere—with just enough in it to satisfy the assailant that he (or she) indeed had gotten away with something but had unfortunately misjudged the wealth of the victim.

On the particular day in question three friends and I were on our way to inspect a project in the rural *campo* several hours north of Bogota. It involved a long trip on a bus that was always crowded, so we had our pockets jammed with provisions for the day. In this one a sandwich, in that one a couple of boiled eggs. We looked "loaded," I'm sure. But no briefcases or shoulder bags—just a rolled up newspaper and a tired-looking note pad in hand.

After sharing a planning session over breakfast at a little center-city coffee shop, we headed for the bus station, two by two down the relatively narrow sidewalk.

"Look out! Here it comes." That's about all the time there was before Greg and I were down flat. Four fleeting figures melted into the crowd behind us and the episode was all over. Our two Colombian colleagues helped us to our feet, we brushed ourselves off, checked quickly for bruises or scrapes and counted our blessings as we moved off once again toward our destination.

Greg started chuckling and I discovered a pocket full of mashed boiled eggs.

"What's so funny?" I asked.

"Did you bring any toilet paper?" Greg asked.

"Of course, why?"

"So did I, but I may need to borrow some of yours. Mine's gone."

"Did they get it?"

"Must have. That pocket must have looked like it held my bill-fold." And the four of us laughed all the way to the bus station.

LEARNING TO TAKE POSITIVE ACTION

"Don't get into trouble" is useless advice. Coping requires positive action. How an experienced driver copes with oncoming high beams at night provides a useful example.

Night driving for a beginner presents a persistent terror: what if the oncoming car's headlights blind me? A very good question; finding the answer *promptly* can be a matter of life and death. The fact that so many people survive for years though they drive at night suggests that there is an adequate way to cope with the problem of oncoming headlights.

My grandfather taught me to drive. The first time we tried it at night, he said, "The idea is to avoid looking at the other guy's headlights. If you look, they will blind you for a few seconds." Like any other advice to youngsters, the warning and the intrigue of danger were just too much—I had to try it! As a front seat passenger, I had often looked directly at oncoming headlights, and I had experienced the slight pain and the aftermath of black spots wherever I looked. As a passenger, it was an amusing diversion. As a driver, I had to find out. . . .

My grandfather's firm hand on the wheel let me know that he knew I'd been blinded. He was shrewd yet patient. No lectures, no scolding, just a quiet question: "Want to know how to handle it?"

After just this one embarrassment, I was ready to listen. "Keep your eyes locked on the right edge of the road just as far ahead as your headlights reach. You'll be surprised how easily you can see the oncoming car and anything else you'll need to see. Just keep your eyes locked on the edge of the road—way out ahead—until the oncoming car goes past." As usual, he was right. It worked. There may be other strategies one can use to cope with this problem, but I still use the one my grandfather taught me when I was fourteen.

Consider the elements in this story: a problem to be warned against, an encounter to affix its reality, a strategy to use to cope with it, a successful application of the coping strategy, and finally, after much practice, a habit.

Coping with culture is much the same. There are real problems. Each newcomer brushes against them to determine their reality—warnings and "don't" advice serve not to deter or prevent but to sensitize and increase one's awareness so that the problem can be more clearly identified. At this point what one needs most of all is a coping strategy—something to do that will head off, reduce, or side-step the problem.

BASIC COPING STRATEGIES

A coping strategy is somewhat like a stock answer for a given question: it will work much of the time, but not all the time. A well-oriented sojourner is constantly evaluating and revising coping strategies. Learning from experience and proposing refined approaches and responses can work together to refresh one's repertoire of coping strategies.

In general, a coping strategy is a particular answer to a "what do you do when. . .?" sort of question. The master coping strategy is *copying*. What do you do when you don't know what to do? When in doubt, do what everyone else is doing. Following this advice in Japan, for example, you will find yourself bowing a lot. Never mind; it will help to give the impression that you have been around a while; thus others are less likely to take advantage of you.

This section lists a number of the circumstances in which a sojourner will experience uncertainty, uneasiness, and unpleasantness. For each of these one or two simple suggestions are offered. Think of these suggestions not as rules but as a starting place for your own process of discovery. Not every suggestion will work in every situation. Moreover, everyone is different, and what works for one person may not work for someone else.

How to Handle Being Stared At

Look away and say to yourself, "I'm different and it shows. So what?" Then forget it. Or stare right back. It can be fun to violate your own cultural norms on such matters and note how it feels.

How to Handle Rudeness

Look away and say to yourself, "Maybe I misunderstood or maybe they don't think that's rude." Remember it. It helps to be prepared in case the same thing happens again.

How to Handle Politeness

Express appreciation exactly as you would in the United States. A smile and a "thank you" in English will suffice. Better yet, see to it that your very first learning in the local language includes the right words and tone for spoken appreciation.

How to Handle Deference

You need to decide why someone is deferring to you rather than making the decision or taking the initiative. If it is because you are a newcomer, tell the person what you would prefer, but say that you would be very happy with the decision he or she might make. If it is because you are a friend, treat it the same way you would with a friend in the United States. If it is because the person habitually defers to whites or to Americans, negotiate a deal. "I'll decide this time if you will next time. Agreed?"

How to Handle Aloofness

When people stand back or even become quiet when you enter the room, it suggests their anxiety about displeasing you. Try to reassure them. Instead of showing your anxiety or displeasure, overlook the aloofness and close in the distance—physically and emotionally—with your own initiatives. Try conversation, close identification with several of the local colleagues, or, better yet, find some excuse to share some snack foods or a meal. There is nothing more universally useful for breaking down social distance and aloofness than eating together.

How to Handle Being Left Out

The discovery that you are being left out is likely to be an indication of language problems, style of dress, or perceived lack of interest in the local ways.

Try to use the local language in as many contexts as possible, particularly in social contacts with the families of one's colleagues. Dress responsively to the levels of formality of the local people. It isn't necessary nor always desirable to adopt local costume, but at least give it a thought. More important, use the American equivalent of the local *gradation* of formality. If you wear a suit at work, don't assume you should wear one when joining your colleague's family for a drive to the hill country. Observe or ask what he or she wears on such occasions, and select your clothes to parallel the local level of formality for given occasions.

Take the initiative in learning about the local culture. People are reassured when they hear you say you want to see their country, their artifacts, and their shrines. Until they discover your interests, they may leave you out simply because of unwillingness to "impose" on you.

While on my first visit to Bangkok, a Thai friend from graduate school days set aside a full day from his busy schedule to escort me around the area. His position in the government was evident for all to see: there we were, seated in his spotless white Mercedes, a uniformed driver waiting patiently for orders. With Oriental deference, my friend Sai asked, "Where you wish to see?" "Whatever you think; I'm ready for anything, Sai." "No, you must decide." "I really want to see some of the *wats*; should we start there?" "Ah, you wish to see *wat*? I show you *wat*!" With enthusiasm, he gave the order and sat back as we sped down the narrow streets toward his favorite *wat*, one of the several thousand ornate temples so characteristic of Thai Buddhism.

"I thought you might want see floating market; all tourists see floating market, but it not really good Thailand. *Wat*. That good Thailand. We see many *wat*." And we did. His delight was that I had wanted to see *his* Thailand and that I had known just enough to give him the opportunity to show me Thailand his way.

As we parted many *wats* later, he urged me to get up early the next morning to board a tourist boat for a tour of the floating market. It was legitimate for an American to want to see it, but preferably not with him!

So often sojourners are left out because their interests are assumed to be those of a tourist. The more you act like a tourist, the more likely you are to be left out.

How to Handle Conversing about Unknowns

Some negative advice here is imperative: Don't fake it! If you don't know what's being talked about, there are three and only three responsible things to do: (1) *Keep quiet*, listen, and learn. It is a very gratifying experience to let others discover your willingness to listen to them, not to be the center of attention. (2) *Ask questions*, but not too many nor too often. Sometimes the questions of an out-of-it newcomer will be off-center. Especially if there is a language problem, you can drag down the pace and depth of the conversation with just two or three inept questions. If you ever catch yourself saying "But I still don't see . . . ," you've gone too far. (3) Cautiously try to join the flow. As your understanding grows, join gently into the murmurs, chuckles, and nonverbal approbations. Just don't be too obvious about it or you might be seen as faking more understanding than is reasonable to expect.

Show interest in landmark monuments and date-named streets: "Avenue of July Twenty-Three, what happened on that date?" Ask questions about concrete rather than abstract topics until you are in tune with the people around you.

Assume that some conversations are going to go over your head. Don't force other people to relate everything to your level of understanding.

How to Handle Language Hang-ups

Differentiate two types of situations: (1) language hang-ups in which you need to get an idea across to others and (2) language hang-ups in which someone else needs to get an idea across to you.

In the first case, you need to take all feasible initiatives, generally in this sequence: First, use the local language, with several repetitions because your tonality and "accent" may require that your listener get accustomed to how you sound. Next, try English. Someone within hearing may be able to help you translate. Then add to your English some improvised sign language. As a rule, sign language doesn't work well all by itself. In fact, it is very demeaning and quickly resented in many cultures except as an adjunct to oral language. Just keep talking, but don't shout. Turning up the volume doesn't make English any easier to understand.

In the second case, when someone else is trying to get an idea across to you, the best way to cope is to let the other person take the initiative. The more you try to *guess* aloud and to act out what you think you may be hearing, the more apt the other person will be to hold you responsible for the hang-up. Better to appear to be dull and dumb than to appear to be insolent and disagreeable. Even an altercation with an officer of the law may come to a shrugging conclusion and dismissal if the outsider appears to be hopelessly dull.

How to Handle a Different Sense of Time

Americans tend to take time very seriously. In some places in Western Europe and in some metropolitan centers elsewhere in the world, time-consciousness is part of the lifestyle. But the jokes about "Asia time" and "Africa time" are based on a very real fact: many people in the world have no particular concern about time. When it is light, they get up; when it is dark, they sleep; when they are hungry, they eat—if there is food.

Always plan an alternative or auxiliary activity while waiting. You will do a lot of waiting, so take paper and pen. Adjusting to "mañana time" is a great opportunity for letter writing or reading a book.

Slow down the pace of your efforts, or you will constantly be at odds with your local colleagues.

Try to minimize the references to time. You won't accomplish much by subtle reminders that "we were supposed to get started at half past three." You won't change the culture at large, although you might be able to train your own local staff to behave like Americans. But then, how much is it worth?

How to Handle Delays

One of the most frequently reported frustrations of overseas Americans is the constant and recurring sense of delay. The more dependent one is on outside supply and communication lines, the greater is this problem. Despite our complaints about slow mail service, inefficiencies in the stores, and the tendency of parts suppliers to send the wrong-size gasket, Americans are really sitting atop the heap. On the world standard, no one could possibly have more support and supply systems going for them than we do in our home country. When the sojourner encounters delays, it can turn readily into frustration. Just try to get *anything* done without delays! No way. Add time to your plans to allow for the delays.

Duty and customs regulations make importing from home costly and slow; higher probability of losses in the mails means that we can't count on systems that we once took for granted. If the projector bulb burns out, that could be the end of it for three months or so. When the windshield wiper motor gives out it may be quicker to take it to the little back-street shop in Cochabamba and have the motor rewound (a practice abandoned forty years ago in the United States) than to await a new one from the importer.

For these and other ailments, friends and co-workers among the internationalists and other expatriates can be of help by serving as "mules." In the luggage of a returnee from furlough one can find anything from a mixer beater to a new carburetor.

I recall a large and heavy toothed gear that fell from a damaged suitcase in the Managua airport. My travel companion simply muttered, "Jeep parts are hard to find here" as he picked it up.

Coping with delays can work toward the building of patience and virtue if you can "roll with the punches." Here are some practical suggestions:

- Learn to rely more on things that *are* available; reduce dependency on the trappings of industrialized society.
- Use local transportation and gear yourself to its schedules. My Indonesian friends taught me that one main event per day is all anyone should plan; and getting somewhere always counts as one day, even if it's only fifty miles.
- Anticipate long turn-around times on *everything*. Make no lock-step plans. Thus occasionally you will be delighted by something that happens before you expect it.
- Take the side of *explaining* delays rather than *complaining*: "Well, you see, they probably had to send to Miami for the part, and you know that takes time. . . ."

How to Handle Ambiguity

Americans like to get things clear. "Now let me see if I understand what you're saying. . . ." And the reply is nothing but a shrug or tel-

ephonic "Si," spoken in a sing-song tone indicative of no conviction
whatsoever. Grrr! . . .

Though Americans tend to despise ambiguity, they will accept
lies spoken with conviction. We make allowances for error as readily as people in other societies, but our rules of the game are different. We would rather be told the wrong diagnosis with conviction
than the right diagnosis tentatively. Perhaps this is because the technological mind can think in terms of experimentally testing a hypothesis so long as it is related precisely. But ambiguity is alien.
Coping with ambiguity is a skill to learn for overseas.

Accept the halfway answers and generalized messages. They are
often the best you can get; there is no use in pushing.

Attempt to discover the worth of living by faith rather than by
confirmation.

If necessary, construct a question or two that will politely test
the level of knowledge of your informant—this approach should be
used in place of the more American form, "Are you sure?" Instead,
comment "I wonder when that was decided," or "If we wait until
then, the additional problem will be such-and-such." The idea here
is to engage your informant in conversation criticizing or challenging the earlier information without directly disagreeing.

Do all within your power to be as explicit as possible about the
situation from your side and perspective. Often if others are clear
about what you want, need, and understand, they will meet you
more than halfway. Give them a chance.

If all else fails and you feel yourself falling into despair, take a
break. Nothing will reduce the tensions produced by ambiguity
quicker than diversion into your favorite hobby or recreation. It
may be stress resulting from ambiguities more than the more commonly cited "time on their hands" that makes swimming, tennis,
horseback riding, and collecting (antiques, art, butterflies, and
stamps) so popular among expatriates. Hang loose. Stay open. Enjoy the moment. Confucius (or somebody) said, "The bough that is
not flexible will break."

How to Handle Roundabout Ways

Closely akin to other matters that produce delays and anxiety are
the cultural rituals which get in the way of straight-line planning.

Roundabout ways of doing business are a bore and a bother if
one lacks an awareness of the good to be served. In a more tradition-

bound culture, the meanings of certain procedures may have evolved so long ago that no one is able to explain them. Thus it falls to the outsider who craves an explanation to create one for himself.

Start with the assumption that rituals, though they seem to slow down business transactions, are probably rooted in some ancient respect for the feelings of people.

Accept the probability that a routine or ritual will ensure against hasty errors. Even in America this possibility is respected: "Haste makes waste."

How to Handle Bribes

Yes, this matter of bribes—called by various polite and quaint euphemisms wherever you go, "dash," *baksheesh*, "goodwill," commission—is sure to come up. To the American whose sense of morality may be offended by the very thought of paying a bribe, the reality can force a very weighty decision. The extent to which bribes are a part of American business industry and government is obscure. In our society bribery is, at the very least, not a topic of polite conversation. In some countries it is much more open; here and there it is regarded as honorable in its own way.

This notion of honorable bribery becomes slightly easier to grasp if one considers the role of tips in American restaurants. If it were not for the tacit agreement between employer and patron that the employee will get hardly any salary at all unless the patron helps out directly, the American restaurant system would fall apart and fast food would take over once and for all. This is not bribery, of course, but neither is it a responsible wage system under ordinary American standards.

In certain Islamic societies it is expected that the responsibility for one's family—aunts, uncles, and cousins by the dozens—entitles a person with many mouths to feed to skim off a bit of whatever goods or funds pass through his hands. The rules that regulate this "right" are vague and its practice is mysterious to any person unfamiliar with the culture. Its justifications are venerable and ancient, some traceable to (or at least not in conflict with) the biblical teaching about the right of the ox to partake of the harvest while it is threshing out the grain.[11]

Nevertheless, one never quite gets comfortable with the discovery that one's passport is being held for ransom at the immigration desk (always some sort of "mistake in the visa—an extra fee of $5 will take care of it") or the interminable "not ready yet" that is pre-dictable in all sorts of government offices, signalling that the only way to speed up the process is to "grease the skids" with extra money. Extortion? Yes and no. Tips? Yes and no.

Americans don't like to be told they *must* tip. When 15 percent for "service" is added to the restaurant or hotel bill, the reaction is more apt to be indignation than appreciation—never mind that the injustice of a noncontracted commission scheme for the waiter has replaced the pot-luck system of tips. All of this is understandable, and yet when the post office clerk suggests that he needs an extra dollar so he can find the misplaced registered letter, the American tends to get hysterical.

Instead of fretting about bribery, your mental health might be improved if you think of it as a tip. Your protest alone isn't going to change the system or solve your problem. The local folks may be embarrassed by your protest, but they won't be much affected— they know how to live with it.

Try a calm ignorance approach if you feel that your baggage, goods, documents, or whatever are being held for ransom. If there is any place where ignorance of the language (real or pretended) works to your *advantage*, it is at airports, where customs officers and the like may consider you just too dumb for them to bother with. If you intend to play it this way, never open your purse or reach for your wallet. It will be taken as an affirmative bargaining signal. Try a hands-folded-on-the-counter stance. And keep calm. The moment you communicate anger, the stakes go up.

If you have the time, try a calm sit-down strike. If there is any-thing that public officials in such countries cannot comprehend, it is a patient American, especially one who is willing to sit on a chair or even on the floor in a corner to await the mythical bossman-who-has-to-sign-the-papers-and-he-won't-be-in-today. Expressing a willingness to wait will put the whole game into your command. From here on your presence is a silent rebuke and, where "face" is important, the longer they make you wait (for nothing) the more sure their ultimate loss of face will be.

"But don't you understand? He won't be in today. If I sign it for him, I will be taking a serious risk. You should come back tomor-row." He won't be there tomorrow either, but the "risk" will then have a clear-cut price tag.

"Yes, yes. I have nothing else to do. I will wait." It must be said with a smile. This procedure will not work at all if you threaten or argue about anything. If he says you cannot wait in the room, then wait in the hall—in full view. If they want to shut down for lunch, wait in the doorway, always in full view. Bring a book to read or some letters to write. Prepare for a long day and start in mid-morning. Only twice have I ever had to eat my bag lunch on the premises; for some reason, about two hours of the mysterious American who doesn't shout, threaten, and claim to have friends in the government is about all these people can handle. It's always gratifying when a completely distraught civil servant comes up as you are sitting on the dirty floor or leaning against a stained wall reading your book, shoves the signed documents into your hand, and says, "You go now, please."

Even if it doesn't work every time, the satisfaction of an occasional win makes it a marvelous game to play. Hint: If you tire of the game, quietly disappear and start over in another day or two. It beats paying a ransom.

How to Handle Beggars

One fact of life in much of the world is that certain outcasts, children without families, handicapped persons, and rural people who have been forced off their land and have come into the city with no marketable skills are forced to beg in order to survive. The human services setups in very few countries are able to be of any help whatsoever. Further, the grim contrast between rich and poor makes begging more socially permanent; thus it is taken for granted. Newcomers are often shocked; because of this rather than because of the social reality, one's local hosts are often embarrassed by beggars— whether on the street or at the front gate.

A second fact of life is similarly predictable: Wherever begging is a necessity, professional begging also exists. With nothing more to gain than a small fraction of the paltry amounts that may be given by passing pedestrians, there are people enmeshed in "underworld" schemes of professional begging. Working in much the same ways as organized prostitution, the exploitation of misshapen and hopeless people in the great cities of the world is one of the most pervasive evidences of inhumanity.

What advice to give? How to cope? Whatever one can afford to share can be shared first with those who are trying to earn and merit their pay: Get your shoes shined often. Let a child help you carry your packages to your car. Be generous with the car-park "supervisors." If you find an old man and woman with a tolerably clean bucket and rag, pay them to wash your car.

When you give money on the street, follow local traditions. Note what your colleagues do. If they avoid the practice altogether, ask them about their views of begging. Learn from them of any humane options that may exist.

How to Handle the Unfamiliar

You don't have to know everything in order to get started in a new culture. Far from it; in fact, learning how *to learn* is the most important culture learning skill. Coping with the unfamiliar requires observational skills, sensitivity of feelings, interest in people, and a capacity to test out the meanings of what things appear to be.

Be willing to try things—foods, activities, and ideas. Fight off the natural tendency to avoid the unfamiliar and to abhor the taboo. Yes, Americans have their taboos, especially in terms of food. Turtles, snakes, lizards, monkeys, dogs, cats. The good Lord couldn't possibly have intended us to eat these poor creatures. Or sheep's eyes and testicles. Now we've gone and done it. No more! Help! I won't do it! Okay, so don't, if that's the way you feel about it. Everyone draws a line somewhere. Just don't draw your line until you need to. Fretting about it ahead of time is the very worst thing to do.

How to Handle Coping Fatigue

To paraphrase Abraham Lincoln, you can cope with all of the problems some of the time, you can even cope with some of the problems all of the time, but you surely won't cope well with all of the problems all of the time. In the first place, just when you think you've got things under control, a new problem shows up—usually like nothing you've handled before, and so you must once again become an inventor.

The ultimate all-purpose ever-ready hang-up–removing coping

strategy requires two people—usually two expatriates, though one could be a close local friend. In some ways it is more a ritual than a true coping strategy, but it is important. "You can't win 'em all" is still wise counsel for anyone who deals with human beings, especially in the area of human relations and services. The coping strategy recommended here is a quick eyeball-to-eyeball lock-on—just an instant will do, but it must be purposeful and mutual, accompanied by an informally agreed-upon code word or phrase, preferably spoken in unison by both persons.

A number of people in various overseas assignments will look purposefully at each other and mutter, "Cope!" This is one of the best ritual code words because it is right on target. Other words and phrases that I have heard during such moments of here-we-go-again include the following: "Lovely," "Punt," "Ah, so," "Home, sweet home," "And away we go," "Play it again, Sam," "Your shot," "China—one, visitors—zero," "They told me there would be days," "Awa,"[12] and "Why me, Lord?"

Such a ceremonial means of coping with frustration, disappointment, or rejection has a long and revered history. One well-documented case concerns 35 pairs of trainees whom Jesus sent out to heal the sick and announce the coming of the Kingdom of God. Jesus anticipated that the trainees would encounter rejection in certain communities, and so he told them, "Go into the street and say, 'Even the dust from your town that sticks to our feet, we wipe off against you.' "[13]

Surely the most thoroughly prepared and well-oriented person will encounter situations which will be unproductive and unpleasant. Does not this happen "back home"? Why shouldn't the sojourner expect some "down" times and some disappointments?

A positive outlook and self-confidence to weather the storm will see you through. Meanwhile, as we learned to say in the high school band, "When in doubt, trill on B-flat!"

SUMMARY: THREE KEYS FOR COMPETENT COPING

Coping successfully depends in large part on a positive outlook, a willing spirit, and an active style. You can't turn every difficulty into a rainbow, but it helps to assume that you can learn something useful from every adversity. The basic idea of coping can be summarized in three recommendations:

Get Information and Keep on Getting It

Any coping strategy should build on and add to one's knowledge background, ideally including language skill. The first step to take in preparation for any overseas assignment is to get background information. Reading is valuable; so is talking with others who have been there. After you are on the field continue the habit. There is always more to learn.

Copy a Reliable Model

The skills of observation and effective copying can be developed. Make it a habit to wait for someone else who is more "at home" to set the example before you go blazing ahead with your own notion of how something should be done. Be alert to all sorts of social cues.

Using Your Best Insights, Act!

The third and most open-ended coping strategy is to act creatively upon your best insights, watching the effects and quickly making appropriate adjustments. Think of it as a game: you observe and draw inferences, act on the inferences, observe the feedback and consequences, and revise your inferences and act accordingly.

FOCUS FOR SELF-EVALUATION

The possibility of "learning on the go" through the development of appropriate coping strategies is the major message of this chapter.

Reflection

Of all the items in the section on basic coping strategies, the following three will be most useful for me to add to my skills:

1. _____

2. _____

3. _____

Review

1. To what extent are the following pieces of advice sound? Under what circumstances might I follow this advice?

   a. Try to behave as much like the people of your host country as possible._____

   _____

   _____

   b. He who laughs last laughs best._____

   _____

   _____

2. Describe the steps that might be taken in dealing in an experiential way with a completely new or highly ambiguous situation._____

   _____

   _____

Commitment

I intend to take the following steps to find and develop friendship with a "bridge person":_____

_____

_____

_____

6

Interpersonal Relationships Are the Key

THE MOST IMPORTANT FACTOR in your effectiveness and happiness overseas is the way you relate to other people. All of your concern for culture, your knowledge of the country and its people, and your skills in coping are less important than your manner of dealing with fellow workers and people of the host country. Indeed, some overseas Americans are doing reasonably competent work despite interpersonal skills that are close to zero; one way to cope with the foreign, the strange, and the irritating is to be pompous, self-important, and graceless. But there are better ways.

Many sojourners are more task-oriented than people-oriented. The compulsive concern for getting the job done promptly and well causes relationships to suffer. According to Kipling, "pushing" and "hustling"—the tendency to shove people around—was seen by the British as necessary to fulfilling their mission:

> Now it is not good for the Christian's health to
>   hustle the Aryan brown,
> For the Christian riles, and the Aryan smiles,
>   and it weareth the Christian down;
> and the end of the fight is a tombstone white
>   with the name of the late deceased,

> *and the epitaph drear: 'A Fool lies here*
> *who tried to hustle the East.'**

Kipling was right, of course, and his observation still holds true today. His images of India are familiar to the expatriate—anywhere in the Orient, the Pacific Islands, or in much of Africa. The matter of riling and smiling—oh, how often one sees this!

Two words will become very familiar to the well-oriented expatriate—"imperious" and "arrogant." The words are very useful to describe much of what one sees as expatriates deal with host nationals. It is so easy for the expatriate to be too blunt, too pushy, downright bossy and rude—all in the interest of getting one's job done or in assuring that one's helpers are "doing things right." Asking oneself over and over if "arrogant" or "imperious" have begun to describe one's behavior and relationships can help to turn back this hazard before it gets out of hand.

The smile that comes back when the expatriate gets really angry is perhaps, itself, the greatest stimulus to anger. Americans like people to smile at them *except*—and how important is this exception—when those people are being scolded or reprimanded. But in many parts of the world it is natural to smile to cover one's embarrassment. So instead of doing as Americans do and glancing about sheepishly or putting a hand to one's forehead, the berated person may look right at you and smile. And as Kipling says, the infuriated "Christian" takes another step toward his own tombstone.

PUSH, PUSH, PUSH

On a restful Sunday afternoon I heard a truck pull into the compound. The familiar sounds of a caravan being loaded reminded me that tonight the medical team would set off for a two-week assignment, providing replacements for the fatigued team in the field. Two doctors, three nurses, several Kenyan drivers and assistants would be in the cabs of the several vehicles. I went to the window of my little cottage to see how many vehicles were going this time. The largest lorry we had (truck—in the British-influenced parts of the world it's called a *lorry*) would be at the center of the procession be-

*Rudyard Kipling, prologue poem in *The Naulahka*, vol. 9 of *The Works of Rudyard Kipling* (New York: Scribner's, 1925), p. 63.

cause its load of needed supplies was almost as important as the re-placement personnel. The view from my window was reminiscent of the colonial era. Two white women and one white man were standing well behind the Mercedes-Benz lorry and the man was ap-parently giving the orders as four Africans hoisted the huge bundles and containers into place. I went back to my reading.

After a time I became aware that the pitch and intensity of the white man's voice had risen considerably. Now I was sure who it was—the British executive who was in charge of the whole opera-tion. My first reaction after recognizing his voice was a sort of warm approval. Here it is, Sunday afternoon, and the chief himself is helping get the caravan ready. How nice! Ah, these former Empire folk have really learned what democracy is all about. Back to my reading.

Again after a time my attention was drawn back to the caravan-loading project. This time there were no voices. But those thuds— what was that all about? Thud. . .thump. . .clank. I returned to the window to observe the last of the crates being shoved off the lorry. The shovers were the white executive and one African. The rest were standing at the side watching. The women had left. What was going on?

This time I didn't go back to my reading. For nearly an hour I watched, unbelieving at first, as the Britisher—with only one helper on the truck—wrestled each crate, bundle, and box into place and personally lashed each one with rope. By now it was obvious what had happened: either because the Kenyans hadn't fitted it all to-gether to his satisfaction, or because he thought he could get more on if he did it his own way, the white *bwana* began to push. Before he finished he had banished even his one remaining assistant to the ground. He became both the supervisor and the one-man crew. The four Africans just watched as he tied every last knot.

I was too far from them to be sure, but as I watched this marvel-ous spectacle of a very riled Christian, I wondered, with Kipling, were the watchers smiling?

RELATING TO OTHERS

The essence of effectiveness in interpersonal relationships is accept-ance. Basic honesty, openness, and trustworthiness are impossible to fake. The person who "puts on a good act" for others is soon found out; this fact has no cultural limitations—insincerity looks very similar and has similar consequences in most human societies.

The qualities of personhood and personality that constitute a sound basis for human relationship are so basic and so deeply ingrained in what already is *characteristic of a person* that it almost seems futile to review them. Nevertheless, they are so important that a responsible review of intercultural competencies cannot omit them. Perhaps if one is aware of their importance, the transition to an overseas assignment will provide a significant opportunity for renewal or recommitment to these virtues.

Effective interpersonal relationships depend on the following:

Kindness. It seems to "come naturally" for some; it requires continuous self-reminding for others—no matter, it pays large dividends in one's own sense of worth and in a healthy respect for others. "Be kind to one another" is still sound advice.

Patience. The "get-ahead" person is especially apt to be impatient. Being able to accept the time it takes others to think and act is basic. Learning to be more patient with oneself helps too.

Valuing people. Sometimes *things* are allowed to become more important than *people*. Even getting one's job done "well" and promptly tends to get in the way of a proper focus on people. People, not things, are what life is about.

Politeness. The proper mixture of respect for customs, respect for other people, and willingness to be a person among persons goes a long way toward offsetting the dissonances that naturally arise from the differences between oneself and others. Irritability, harshness, and the need to be noticed can work against good relationships.

Thinking the best of others. Showing respect demands investing trust in others. Suspicion, aloofness, coldness, and "distance" come between people. Holding a grudge or keeping a list of one's hurts, real or imagined, is a sure way to turn a relationship sour. Even when it seems that someone has let you down, try to find some way to look at the situation that gives the other person the benefit of the doubt.

Persistence. Some might call it faith—faith in another person, or faith in others, in general. Fidelity and stubborn commitment to make things work will pay off. Building and main-

taining good interpersonal relationships require a commitment that is strong enough to persist in the face of all sorts of
setbacks.

Getting along well with others is never easy; it requires effort.
The effort must be based on well-established values in one's personal
commitments to life and the pursuit of happiness. Especially in intercultural situations, it takes all of the skills one has developed over
a lifetime at home.

FELLOW USERS OF ENGLISH

One surprise that awaits the American overseas is the difficulty of
establishing satisfying relationships with others who speak English—for example, the British. Those who speak the same language
and presumably share a cultural heritage can turn out to be unexpected problems. Perhaps because we expect greater understanding
and similarity of values and outlook from them than from "real"
foreigners, others who speak English can sometimes be too much
taken for granted.

As it turns out, even the language itself can become a source of
tension in relations with these people. Just as surely as English is *our*
language, it is possessively held by everyone in Australia and New
Zealand, and by the formally educated people in Singapore, Malaysia, Hong Kong, India, Kenya, Tanzania, Uganda, Nigeria, and so
forth. But English is surely different in many ways in each of these
countries. Whose English is "right"? Who can claim the right to be
the world's arbiters of English vocabulary and forms? Surely not the
Americans!

Resisting the temptation to "correct" other people's English
grammar or pronunciation will go a long way toward improved relationships. Learn to listen and accept other accents and forms.

WHEN FORWARD IS REGRESSIVE

Every time you blurt out that terrific idea that has just now occurred to you, you reinforce a stereotype of Americans held by
many in the world. Forwardness—being pushy and verbally
blunt—is inappropriate behavior in most of the world, especially

for a newcomer, and Americans are widely considered among the world's worse offenders.[1] As a newcomer, you will have much to learn. You will need to "pay your dues" by living with the situation a while before you earn the right to propose change. The length of the apprenticeship varies widely according to region and culture, but it is usually longer than Americans are accustomed to at home.

The "hotshot" newcomer is usually deeply resented, even one who is fifty or sixty years old with a Ph.D. or M.D. Unless a wise old-timer is willing to adopt you and give you some firm advice, the only thing that will protect you from falling on your face is your self-discipline and your sensitivity to the feelings of others. Pay attention. Practice *asking* rather than telling. Defer to others. Assume that you may not be able to see the whole situation. Humility, even for a professional, is a wise and worthy virtue.

FINDING FRIENDS

In unfamiliar surroundings, and especially among people you barely know, finding a friend can be hard. Loneliness is a more serious problem than fear, but among a whole new set of contact persons, how do you get beyond the first level of acquaintance? Being able to share your interests and concerns with close friends is very important. The sojourners must get to work early on the friendship-building task.

On the other hand, instant friendship is suspicious stuff. In any society the too-warm-too-soon sort of person is apt not to become a lasting friend because of the very forwardness itself. One American trait that turns away potential friendships in other cultures is this tendency to rush things.

A better approach is to do what people of Oriental background often do: (1) show interest without asking too many questions, (2) let your "openness" unfold gradually and with one or two friends at a time, (3) find things to do in company with your new friends, and (4) look for opportunities to trade favors—deeds of helping and kindness. Be careful not to let things develop in a one-way flow of attention and giving. Americans can learn to appreciate a somewhat lower level of overt warmth and, especially, overt enthusiasm. Personal relationships should develop gradually and should arise out of genuine liking rather than out of your resolve to prove your ability to win friends.

Even if it proves to be difficult, try to build several close friendships. Your earliest friendships will probably be with people who can speak your language and with whom you can more readily identify because of their capability to handle the intercultural encounter that you represent. Therefore you will find their friendship not only personally fulfilling but also useful in practical ways. You need such friends to help provide the "bridges" you need to broaden your involvement in the culture.

BRIDGE PEOPLE

A well-oriented newcomer will be open to all sorts of new friendships. Three special friends should be sought out: an experienced and bilingual old-timer among the American expatriates, an age-mate person among the recent newcomers to the field or area, and a bilingual host-country person.

The old-timer can help you "learn the ropes" and warn you away from persistent local pitfalls and minefields. The fellow newcomer can provide the very important sounding-board and co-learner functions—a person to learn with, for whom the development of perceptions of new experiences is also a current preoccupation. The host-country person can provide the finest sort of bridge into the culture, helping you make your way across the initial barriers of language and customs. Of these three, my own experience suggests this third friendship is most important. And for the sense of stimulation and encouragement, the age-mate fellow newcomer is a close second.

TOO CLOSE FOR COMFORT

Now and then you will encounter an entrenched expatriate who persists in antagonisms and petty meanness to cover for his or her own intercultural incompetency. Whether missionary, educator, business person, or diplomat, there are still those folks (and they are not always the old-timers) whose major purpose in life seems to be to belittle, "coach," criticize, and backbite the newcomers who show genuine interest in the people of the host country.

What can you do about it? First, preserve your ideals. Second, save your skin. If the first and the second are incompatible, try number three: go underground. A colleague who is defensive, traditional, and resistant is rarely changed by frontal assault. It is too hard for such a person to lose face; he or she will make your life miserable rather than concede that the old ways of relating to host-country persons should be changed.

You may believe that developing a warm working relationship with your host-country counterparts is an important reason for going there, and you may think that mutual trust is an ideal to be sought after. Well, watch out.

Old-timers may try to help you on this sensitive matter, but there may still be a generation gap. You will be warned about getting too close to the host-country persons. Believe it or not, getting "too friendly," especially if you take nationals into your confidence, can result in criticism and the "cold shoulder" from some of your colleagues. Some of your least pleasant relationships may be with fellow expatriates whose embarrassment about their own poor relationships is beginning to turn to anger.

You will run into these and other unfortunate aftereffects of the old ways. In the matter of loaning money to nationals, however, the old-timer's advice is probably still apt: don't. If you do, you very well may lose some money on "bad loans." Instead, take steps to build trust over time; it may be worth it. Swallow your frustrations and disappointment and work toward humane relationships—even if you have to work "underground"—quietly, unobtrusively, and gently.

TRUST

Trust is hard to define, harder yet to prescribe. It is necessary to attempt both because nothing else so persistently shows up among the lists of attributes needed for effective intercultural living.

Trust, at one level of meaning, is a commonplace—everyone knows what it means and everyone means the same thing by the word. At a more technical level of meaning, however, trust refers to choices—usually choices made on the basis of previous experience, by the intuitions and "feelings" that whisper their irrational guidance on the back side of our eardrums. Thus we have "trust" in the roller coaster at the park, but not in a footpath at dusk. And the same friend whose driving is trusted in the car pool may not be offered the weekend use of our car while his is in the shop. Such are the little matters of trust.

Trust is a precious commodity. At the interpersonal level, trust is the foundation of human relationship. Virtually every act with or toward another person reflects a basic commitment of trust—or lack thereof. The quality of relationships and the strength of one's ties into the several communities of life depends on how trust is invested.

TRUST AND SURVIVAL

It pays not to be too free with one's trust. Unscrupulous sellers of phony investments, defaulting insurance schemes, "effortless" paint remover, and "problem-free" used cars linger as constant reminders that you never can be too sure!

Gullibility is not considered to be an asset, though it is a sometimes companion of a trusting nature. "Keeping your guard up" is the way to avoid a surprise. All sorts of experiences in modern life teach a person that it is better to be prepared for the jolts than to let them catch one off guard. Not all of this advice and socialization relates to interpersonal relations, of course, but much of it does, and a sort of "cool" distance and reserved attitude toward others has become almost stylish.

Intergenerational stress hasn't helped the situation much either. "Never trust anyone over thirty" has become a motto for many young people, and the tensions of degenerating families, splitting churches, and unhappy school experiences all flow together to produce in many an expatriate a deadly backlog of trust-destroying toxins. Not all orientation programs help much with this problem, and these toxins can ultimately destroy the expatriate's chances to establish effective relationships.

To some extent, trust is a matter of faith. Since "you can't win 'em all" and there will certainly be times when misplaced trust will backfire—perhaps even threaten your life—what do you do? Freeze up? Trust nothing? Trust no one? If you choose this extreme, you forfeit the game.

It is far better to take a leap of faith and run the risks. Vulnerability has always been the price of true friendship. One cannot always be the self-reliant, self-made expert. Trust placed outside oneself may threaten the ego of a person who wants to be self-sufficient, but for the person who draws strength from relationships, trust is the foundation of success.

WORDS OF WISDOM

The gaps that are most likely to frustrate communication among expatriates are less likely to be culture gaps than generation gaps or subculture and interpersonal problems. Gloria Tiede, a TEAM missionary in Japan, recently summarized her observations and experiences in an article entitled "With Sympathy."

> When you arrive on the field it will be a while before you feel a part of the new country and culture, so you look to the mission to fill the gap. You've heard about the "mission family." I'll tell you a secret. The mission is pretty good, but it's not a family—certainly not a family like the one back home. You have joined an organization. Relationships don't come ready-made as they did when you were born into a family; you have to build them.[2]

She hit the nail right on the head. It is up to every newcomer to build the friendships and develop the trust relationships that will facilitate entry into the community. The imagery of "family," "colleagues," "fellow servants," and the like are just so many hollow labels until one puts them into action.

The newcomer who fits in and yet makes a self-satisfying contribution to the whole of an overseas effort will soon begin to think like an old-timer. Since turnover among expatriates is fairly frequent, the newcomer who succeeds can become an old-timer relatively quickly. To be accepted, the newcomer needs to be cautious about new ideas and quick fixes for old problems. Nothing is so likely to annoy old-timers as naive ideas from people who haven't yet learned the territory. The first task of newcomers, then, is discovery, not dissemination.

Tiede reminds us that what counts most among the skills of the sojourner is the capacity to recognize and the will to accept a different point of view.

> . . .When you're hurt it's always good to check the other fellow's frame of reference. After you're an expert in recognizing the frame of reference, then you can begin to learn to accept the validity of each different frame of reference. That's even tougher.[3]

HUMOR—A POWERFUL TOOL

Every society has one or more minority groups, neighbor nations, or ancestral forebears designated as the bad guys, the dumb guys, or the fall guys. The French can hardly stand their ancient enemies, the Germans. The British put down the French—"Frogs," they call them. The Irish detest the British and call them "Brits," said with a kind of spitting sound. The mainland Canadians bounce their version of "Polack" stories off the people of Newfoundland. Stereotypically, other Canadians tend to think of Newfies as being a bit slow.

Some nations take on their very parentage itself as the brunt of their spite, as do the Brazilians toward the "backward folks" back home in Portugal. In Taiwan it's the "mainlanders" versus the Taiwanese and vice versa.

The "moron" stories that once circulated in the United States have now resurfaced as "ethnic" jokes with any number of targets: blacks, Italians, Polish people, and so on. All Americans, but especially those who are going overseas, should be reminded that other people have their sensitive issues, too. A newcomer can never be sure what he or she is getting into with racial and ethnic stories. The safe rule is to stay away from them altogether.

Motives of Humor

The motives of humor are complex. The healthy values of jollity and good fun are widely appreciated. When people can laugh together, the levels of trust go up and the basis for warmth and friendship is broadened. Humor can release tension and clear the air. In its best uses, humor facilitates communication.

But sometimes humor is used to demonstrate superiority, or at least to bolster the ego of one person or group at the expense of another. Hostility is the basic motivation for many of the stories and jokes that pass as humor. When one person needs to laugh at another or when one group has developed a cultural habit of laughing at another, there is something very unhealthy about that the relationship.

Humor can even be used to draw others into a community of shared guilt. The social demand is to laugh when others laugh; but to laugh at something that violates your values will compromise you. Others can thus ensnare you in their sense of inferiority or guilt.

Humor and Identity

Humor serves as a kind of reassuring ritual. Like religious repetitions of a formal pledge ceremony, laughing together becomes a ceremony—an induction. Newcomers are often inducted into a group by participating in the group's humor. When a group of people laugh together they show their solidarity. Telling racial or ethnic stories is a favorite device of people who have a need to demonstrate their own superiority and power. By using a common repertoire of humorous situations or directing humor at a common target, people take "humor-shots" at outsiders. It can be subtle; sometimes it takes the practiced ear of a linguist or the trained eye of an observer of culture to see the social purposes of humor.

To paraphrase a famous biblical profession of loyalty: "Your jokes shall be my jokes and the people you laugh at I will laugh at."[4] Accepting, or pretending to accept, the humor of a dominant group is a cheap way to adopt an identity, and it can backfire.

During one of my longer assignments in Brazil I developed a real taste for Brazilian humor. Many Brazilians have a very good sense of humor. They love to tell funny stories, most of which characteristically have several punch lines, one after another, so the laughter is shared in incremental waves as the story unfolds. The favorite butts of Brazilian jokes tend to be the Portuguese, and joining in the laughter and the telling of this particular variety of the "Polack" story seemed to be a quick way to become Brazilian. I was getting pretty good at it. I felt more like a Brazilian insider every time I told one, until one day a Brazilian friend whom I particularly admired didn't laugh at my put-down of the Portuguese. He turned on me and snapped, "What do you have against the Portuguese?" It was one thing for him to laugh at the Portuguese—after all, they were his ancestors; but they weren't my ancestors and I had no business doing it. At one level this may seem irrational or inconsistent: why should he care, especially since I was simply copying what he did? But at another level, it was much like what happens in our culture. I can complain about something that's *mine*—my car ("It *never* starts when I'm in a hurry") or my son ("He seems dedicated to making baggy shirts into an art form"). Whether in jest or seriously, it's one thing for *me* to say it about my son or my car—but it is quite different when I catch someone else talking about them like that!

Laughter as Assault

Laughter can be vicious. Most everyone has experienced the knotted stomach that wrenches one's very soul when it becomes clear that others are laughing at you. To walk up to a group of friends and discover that you are being talked about and laughed at behind your back is completely demoralizing.

No one likes to be laughed at unless he or she has deliberately invited laughter—by making a face, wearing a funny costume, or acting the clown. Humor is dangerous stuff when it has even the slightest tendency to hurt others.

What people talk about in derisive ways tells you something about their values. What makes people feel anxious, embarrassed, or threatened often is revealed in their humor. Mother-in-law stories can be told by people who really do respect and love their in-laws. But they are more commonly an assaultive way of getting revenge for strained relationships. Humor can be a socially accepted way to act out aggressiveness and hostility. Uneasiness about one's own dignity and worth can lead to worse forms of racism, and humor can be an early symptom. If people who are in humanitarian service careers, especially, could take stock of themselves and consider that degrading others can degrade oneself, there might be far less of this sort of the "parlor-game" assault that passes as humor.

The intercultural sojourner is well advised to leave back home that dangerous tendency to tell "funny" stories that are put-downs. They are morally reprehensible and pragmatically dangerous. Don't take the chance.

TRUE PATRIOTISM

Those who pull others down in order to make themselves look better have not yet been delivered from the limitations of childhood. Awareness of one's own worth is never enhanced by defensiveness and bigoted ethnocentric pride. A mature sense of self-worth accepts others.

So it is with patriotism. The true patriot's feelings for country, people, and history depend far more on self-respect than on a sense of superiority and a critical attitude toward others. True, patriotism reaches its fever pitch in times of war when there is a keen consciousness of a common enemy. Putting down that enemy raises the patriotic flags even higher. But this form of patriotism is far from healthy.

What really counts is dignity and a sense of the worth of a people. And dignity never depends on superiority. Would that all American expatriates were people whose respect for their own country allowed for and encouraged others to hold their heads high. Said Queen Elizabeth II, "True patriotism doesn't exclude an understanding of the patriotism of others."[5]

FOCUS FOR SELF-EVALUATION

Matters of trust and interpersonal relationships are hard to evaluate without feedback from others. Nevertheless, some self-assessment here may be helpful.

Reflection

1. What signals do I receive from others about their interest in being around me? Their acceptance of me? The way they see my acceptance of them?

   _____

   _____

2. What is my attitude toward politeness? Do I try to be polite? Am I aware of politeness when others relate to me?

   _____

   _____

3. In the matter of trust, where do I see myself?

   SUSPICIOUS   ALOOF   TRUSTING   GULLIBLE

Review

In what ways can sincerity and a conscientious attitude toward my work

get me into interpersonal difficulty?_____

_____

_____

Commitment

I intend to take these steps now, during preparation, to make my affiliation with co-workers and family warmer and more trusting:_____

_____

7

Language Can Be Barrier or Bridge

AN IMPORTANT choice lies just ahead: You can learn a new language and open up your world; or you can put it off, making excuses about insufficient time.

Resistance to language learning can be a big problem. Too few Americans are exposed to a second language early in life. Unfortunately, language learning does get harder as you grow older. Thus the fear and resistance that is so common among Americans has its roots in reason.

For adults, language learning is a lot like losing weight. You don't do it unless you want to—*really* want to. Like losing weight, language learning is good for you; and you get tired of hearing about how important it is. Unless you are strongly motivated, you persist in hoping that your destination overseas will be an exotic location where you can get by with just good ol' English.

Because there are many such places—too many, perhaps—overseas Americans quite often lose their resolve or start a lifelong procrastination, putting off biting the language bullet.

ENGLISH, ENGLISH, EVERYWHERE ENGLISH

English is spoken wherever Americans go. At the very least, the Americans all speak it with each other, and since there are Americans in almost every urban location, the usefulness of English is impressive. The problem lies deeper. The language you speak limits you to the society of others who speak that language. If you speak only English, you can relate in expressive, thought-sharing ways only to four groups of people: (1) other Americans; (2) educated internationalists—expatriates from European nations, especially, whose educational background can embarrass you because of its richness and variety compared to your own; (3) persons in the host country who have learned to speak English just well enough to sell you things or otherwise serve your needs; and (4) educated upper-class nationals who are not typical of the host country as a whole. Tourism is built on the first three groups. Thus it is common for American tourists to hold the dangerous opinion that "you really don't need anything but English—everywhere you go people speak English well enough so that Americans can get by."

Being limited to English can turn a difficult situation into a sour one, though. It is amazing how few police, military people, hospital staff, automobile repairmen, post office employees, and others with whom you really have important reasons to communicate are able to speak English—especially at night! (In some countries it seems that they pull in all the bilingual people at sundown!)

Imagine yourself on a large intercity bus in Africa. As elsewhere in the Third World, the typical way to get from one metropolitan center to another is by bus; buses range in quality from the sublime to the ridiculous. Even in some relatively blighted countries there are buses with a level of comfort and service well above the best in the United States, and other buses (lots more of them) that allow chickens inside on passengers' laps and pigs on top if they are firmly "hog-tied." So here you are, on a bus that is about halfway between these two extremes, and the night is very dark.

The capital and its complex of outlying villages is many hours behind you. Have you noticed that English has also been left behind? This is rural territory, and clearly it is tribal territory. As people have gotten on and off in the last hour or so there have been no reassuring phrases of English—only the babble of an unfamiliar dialect. Whatever it is, it surely isn't based on Latin!

Not surprisingly, you are unable to sleep, since the remoteness has made you somewhat anxious. Nothing very interesting has happened, and that is just as well. The stories they tell about bus breakdowns and the old tales about highway pirates are probably exaggerations anyway. Furthermore it can't be more than three or four more hours until dawn, and then the trip will become more interesting.

The bus is slowing down again. Perhaps another shadowy figure at the roadside with a bundle of produce for the market in the city. (The rural folks seem to travel all night to get their vegetables and fruit to the city; when do they rest? What a life.) No, not a stop for passengers, there's a fire ahead. A big fire. Out here? There's no town. Lots of people. Several reflectors—taillights of trucks and buses at the roadside. Arms waving dead ahead. We stop.

First a hush among the passengers. Then a burst of excited conversation. People everywhere in the world communicate emotions in remarkably similar ways, with their faces, tone of voice, and body language. You can read this much: there's something going on that has your fellow-travelers *very* agitated. What is it? If only you could understand what they are saying. But you can't. You try English: "What's happening?" No one answers. Even if any of them can understand you, they are too excited and upset to go to the extra trouble of speaking English. After all, you aren't buying anything *this* time.

A rag-tag uniform of some sort—or is it? Anyway the fellow wearing it is talking to the bus driver. They are not happy with each other. The stranger in the uniform has a gun. No question about which of them will win the argument. *What is going on?* Please someone explain. No way.

"Everyone off!" At least it's clear enough what that phrase means though it is linguistically as foreign as all the rest. Everyone is pushing toward the front door. Here we go . . . out into the night, a million miles from anywhere. Please, someone explain. No way.

The fire is not far ahead; it isn't a burning vehicle. It looks like a bonfire. What? right in the middle of the road? To block our way! Some sort of an ambush? The only comfort is that there are so many other vehicles here—and perhaps a hundred people are standing in the roadway. Are they friendly? They seem to be angry. All of them. Who are they looking for? Then it hits home: curiosity and all of your unfulfilled anxiety suddenly turn to panic. Yours is the only white face to be seen anywhere in the mob. You thought you knew what it meant to be a minority. Surely you have recognized yourself to be a member of a minority race—it only takes a few hours in Africa or Asia to become aware of this. But in the pit of your stomach, and with a wrenching tightness across your upper back, you suddenly *feel* like a minority—and a targeted minority person, at that.

Though I would not wish such pain for any fellow human being, there is an educational value in such a feeling. In this flash you know—*really* know at the gut level—what fear does to people. It shrinks you, it weakens you, it degrades you; you feel like a trapped animal. Your reaction isn't anger—anger takes more time and effort than you can muster just now. No, it is helplessness—utter vulnerability—and once you have felt it, you don't need to *know* it.

Self-recrimination comes first. It's my own fault. How did I get myself into this situation? Why didn't I take the plane? Yes, it costs five times as much, but it surely would have been worth it! Better yet, why didn't I take the daylight bus? Can't even remember. What got into me. A night bus? In this part of Africa? Stupid. Stupid. Stupid.

As this is going on in one corner of your mind, something else is happening in another: You remember a book you read before you came to East Africa. It described a similar situation. The book said that there was a fine line between annoyance and panic. What was it? Yes! It said, "If you know what's going on it's only annoyance. If you don't know what's happening, it's panic." Remember it clearly. It is the key to such situations. How important it is to know what is happening, to be able to ask, to understand the answer. Oh, to know the language!

As you step off the bus you make two discoveries, both of them very wet. Your shoe disappears into the mud, and your eye catches rippling reflections of the bonfire all around. There is water everywhere—lots of water. A flood. Just beyond the bus is the bonfire; just beyond the bonfire the road has disappeared under a rapidly flowing river. Here in this darkness, it's hard to make any estimation of the extent of the washout, but it seems extensive. That's the situation: the road is impassable. End of the line. Now what? And your panic settles back into annoyance.

In the next hour several more annoyance-to-panic-to-annoyance cycles occur as you deal with one after another of the by-products of the flood. Where can you safely sleep? What variety of mosquitoes are these? There must be millions of them. Floods always drive out snakes and lizards; has anyone thought about that? Why are they backing up your bus? Now they're turning it around. But your fellow passengers don't want to get on. Why not? It's better than spending the next week out here at the edge of the world waiting for the water to recede. So you get on. All alone. Not even the driver seems pleased about this. He sets the brake and goes into a long and agitated speech. The free translation seems to be "Stupid American, you are making a big mistake." But that's only a guess, because he's apparently speaking Swahili—the standard intertribal language in this region—and your Swahili lessons took too much time away from your work. You stopped attending after the third session and even had the nerve to try in vain to get a tuition refund. Not so smart. You need Swahili now; that's for sure.

There's nothing to do except get off. You watch as the bus pulls to the side of the road and stops again, this time headed back down the long six hours toward the capital. Now what? Please, someone explain. No way.

The sounds of laughter are reassuring. These Africans seem more readily able to adjust to annoyance than Americans would be. They have each other to laugh with—and most important, they have language. Language is very important in the fulfilling of what we are as human beings. Without it we slide into a frightening pit of mire and mystery. With language, we have each other.

You can't sleep. The mosquitoes are everywhere, and you ache and itch from toe to head. Especially your head. It's a miserable night. You wander from one little cluster of Africans to another. They sit in circles around fires. It isn't cold—not even chilly—but these folks have built their own smaller bonfires; some have walked back to high ground to bring back scrub fuel for the fires. The smoke hangs low, and where there is smoke the mosquitoes have dispersed. How reassuring it would be if someone were to invite you to join the circle around one of the fires. Maybe they have. Several times someone has shouted at you from a fire-circle. In your panic it sounded as if they might have been saying, "You filthy white dog, we will kill you before dawn." But now that the mosquitoes have become your major enemy, it occurs to you that these people could have been saying, "Join us, friend, we have no mosquitoes here in the smoke." But how would you know?

Across the flood ahead a pinpoint of light brightens into a pair of headlights and for the first time you can see clearly the extent of the flood across the road—maybe two hundred yards. The Africans seem excited, pleased, in fact. As you stare intently, the distant light flickers. Look more carefully: Sure enough, there are people in front of those headlights—people walking toward us through the water. In due time they emerge on our side of the flood. Baggage and sacks on their heads, wet to the waist, and laughing. Soaked shoes or no shoes, laughing. Calling back and forth to one another and to our groups. All laughing.

A perfectly respectable African solution has been reached: they take our bus, we take theirs. A bit wet and tired, yes, but in a short time we are once again rumbling across the miles of East African vastness—in the right direction. And now you can sleep.

It only takes one or two emergency situations for an American's motivation to learn the language to increase dramatically. Should you await these motivating events? Why not just *imagine* such difficulties and the jams in which you might find yourself and get to work on the solution. There is never a good mañana in the matter of language learning. The time for language learning is always *now*.

WHY LEARN THE LANGUAGE?

Americans are so accustomed to having "foreigners" meet them more than halfway in matters of language that they fall into a sort of linguistic lethargy. Shake yourself loose and get on with it. It may be hard for the intercultural newcomer to imagine, but the positive side of language learning is there, waiting to reward you. Besides making you more secure and less apt to panic, there is much more to language skill. Consider six main reasons why you should apply yourself to language learning.

Exchanging Ideas

Knowing the language of the people with whom you are working allows for a much more free exchange of ideas. There is no substitute for eye-to-eye conversation in the local language. To converse in English in the middle of Osaka is to remain foreign. Sights and sounds are Japanese; the signs are Japanese; the ideas they communicate are Japanese; the lifestyle is Japanese. Thus the conversation is either in Japanese or it is foreign. Being concerned about this sort of foreignness is important. Even if your Japanese friend speaks excellent English and is quite willing to converse in English, you should be sensitive to the fact that when you require him to use English, it puts both of you in a relational context that is foreign to Osaka. Free exchange of ideas and thoughts will suffer, no matter how strongly he may be motivated to be "free" with you.

Being Accepted

When the expatriate is able to use the local language, he or she will enjoy a higher degree of acceptance. People of any country take it as a compliment when outsiders learn to use their language. In most countries, even a few words and a brave willingness to try to use them will help you win admiration and acceptance.[1] Such people are so accustomed to having to make all the efforts to bridge the language gaps with Americans that they are warmly responsive when an American tries to meet them halfway. Not speaking the language of the country can suggest an insult: in effect, you are saying, "Your language is not important enough to merit my time and effort." Although there are some remarkable exceptions, it is common knowledge that American diplomats and foreign service officers who are unable or unwilling to use the local language can create irritating intercultural problems through their very communicative style that can undermine their positions. Ironically, their very presence in the host nation is for the purpose of promoting the best interests of the United States. Like the Russians, Americans are seen as technologically skilled, but too preoccupied with our own affairs to be interested in others except in terms of our own well-being. Thus even our efforts in relief, aid, and technical assistance are assumed to have ulterior motives. People everywhere in the world find it easier to trust those who speak their language; those who are unable to do so are likely to arouse suspicion.

Freedom of Movement

Among the most common anxieties of Americans facing first-time overseas assignments is the fear that they won't be able to move about as freely as they do in the United States. This concern usually focuses on not having a car, not being able to read the road signs, the quality or lack of highways, and the differences in driving regulations. As it usually turns out, these factors are not so important as the lack of ability to use the local language. It is *language* that keeps Americans in their houses or apartments in the evenings or on the weekends, not the quality of the highways!

Whether in your own car, in a chartered vehicle, or on public transportation, you won't feel very confident if you don't speak the language. If you get on the wrong road or miss a bus, how do you find out what to do next? Greater freedom of movement and more enthusiasm about travel and exploration await those who develop language skills. Since mobility is a major source of security and well-being for Americans, this should be motivation enough for language learning even if there were no other benefits.

Labeling and Classifying

Effective communication in another country, even among those who can meet you on your terms, using English, depends to some extent in knowing how others organize their thoughts. Learning the language is valuable because it makes you aware of the labeling and classifying systems used in the culture. An American who hears the word "green" may well visualize the color of grass, for example. But a Japanese person may have the color of the sky in mind, because the Japanese designation for the spectrum ranging from our *blue* through our *green* is all the same in Japanese. If this seems strange, think of the vast range of clashing colors that we call, collectively, *red*.

The point here is that *words* represent classification systems. These systems or breakdowns of things and ideas can be sliced in several different ways. Consider the idea, *slice*, for example. A slice of pie in the United States usually means a wedge-shaped piece. But the word "slice" could mean, more literally, a parallel-cut piece. What would you call such a piece? It wouldn't be a wedge, but is there another word? Here and there a "slab," but usually just a slice. So "slice" means *slice* unless it concerns pie, in which case "slice" really means *wedge*. We know that. It's our language. Others have to learn our peculiar uses; we have to learn theirs. No language—surely not English—is systematic and really logical.

Thousands of these examples can be demonstrated in any language. They reflect the way the views of the universe typical within each cultural tradition are reflected in the communication of ideas.

Scientists use the term "taxonomy" to refer to any rigorous classification system. In order to assure cross-cultural clarity in the natural sciences, internationally accepted classification systems have been designed and adopted. The Swedish botanist Carolus Linnaeus, for example, created the binomial system of scientific nomenclature in 1753. It is still in use as the basis for communication among the world's scientific scholars.

No such world-wide schemes of classification exist for the rich

realms of human experience. Every language on earth reflects variations in the ways various people and groups have come to see and
think. Knowledge of the language is the only key to these subtleties.

Recognizing Ideational Differences

Closely related is the awareness of ideational differences. Some of
these differences occur among people using the same language, but
they occur far more often across languages. In reference to the first,
consider "soda." In some regions of the United States, the idea is ice
cream afloat in flavored carbonated water. In other places, especially the Northeast, it means a bottle of pop. In a more technical
context, its idea is something compounded of sodium. "Theater" is
another example. For Americans its meaning includes the place to
show a motion picture. For Britishers this latter is always a
"cinema."

Especially when words look alike or sound alike across two languages, the temptation is to assume that they mean the same thing.
Learning the language can help you avoid such pitfalls, the intercultural equivalent of hanging your bathing costume in a W.C.—
the "water closet" of British tradition (otherwise known as a
"toilet").

In the literature of research on language and the human mind,
the particular language a person uses and the way that person *thinks*
about things are shown to be closely related. The widely accepted
"Sapir-Whorf hypothesis" says that one's language provides the set
of categories and organizing principles through which the person
comprehends all experiences.[2] In other words, language controls the
processing of experience. Thus the meanings of experience are not
simply culturally different from one person to the next, but they are
linguistically determined. The language of thought is real language;
it sets up the label systems and the relational patterns through
which one "makes sense" of experience.

Thinking in Another Language

The deepest satisfactions of language learning come when a person
is capable of thinking in the context of the other culture. One need
not think the same thoughts, in the sense of holding the same values,

but intercultural effectiveness is facilitated when a highly competent level of language skill allows a person to conceive ideas and
communicate them in a way that is synchronous with those of the
people of the host culture.

Those who achieve this lofty plateau are very much valued and
sought after for their services as "bridge people." They are the people who make the world manageable and workable for the rest
of us!

REALISTIC MOTIVATION

Unfortunately there are few shortcuts to language competency. And
of all the bits and pieces of good advice the most valid is this: _do it_.

Perhaps the happiest discovery that an American can make is
that a foreign language can be fun. The fun comes less from the
learning than from the using. When those stilted phrases and utterances of seemingly embarrassing sounds are accepted as meaningful
and responded to in intelligible, consequential ways, all of a sudden
learning a language becomes rewarding.

When the language is being learned in a location where it is actually used in the marketplace and on the streets, this happy discovery comes much earlier in the experience. The _anticipation_ of use,
for many people, is insufficient motivation.

The difficulty of language learning can be forbidding for almost
anyone. Much time and effort must be invested before it begins to
be rewarding. It is easy to feel sorry for yourself and decide that "I
just don't have much language aptitude." Take courage! Almost everyone feels this way at one time or another.

One should never use "if I can learn the language" as a self-
screening test to decide whether or not to go into overseas service.
The dynamics of "if . . . then" work better the other way around. It
isn't "if I can learn the language, I will go," but "if I really want to
go, I can learn the language." It seems overwhelmingly evident that
normal children can and do learn functional language to a highly
effective and practical level within about five years. The desire to be
able to hear with comprehension and to speak expressively toward
consequential ends is motive enough. No infant has to be persuaded
to try.

Adult learning of a second language is a different process, but it
is not so different as many people have convinced themselves. In the

classroom, a foreign language is just another subject—one with unusual potential for embarrassment and frustration. It demands a great amount of work without providing many practical rewards. Further, adults in a basically monolingual society tend to use negative self-persuasion: I-think-I-can't, I-think-I-can't. . . . Little children don't tell themselves they can't, and so they *do*. Adults who tell themselves they can't often turn out to be accurate prophets.

Self-persuasion and self-deception of this sort are exacerbated by the evidences that emerge from formal classroom attempts to learn the language. Because these discouraging encounters are so predictable, many experts recommend that language learning ought to be delayed until the sojourner is in the situation where the language can be immediately useful. Then the natural motivations and rewards of language use can take over, displacing the artificialities of test grades and encouragement from an instructor.

PREPARING FOR LANGUAGE LEARNING

The advice to delay language learning until moving to the field should not be taken to mean that nothing can be done about language skills during preparation. The best programs for intercultural orientation include units on "language acquisition."

Language acquisition programs can include many different varieties of experiences which, taken together, "open up" a person for more effective language learning. In effect, they raise the adult's aptitude for language learning. Some of the emphases and related exercises follow.

Learning to Hear Sounds

Because we hear and think in terms of familiar sounds in our mother tongue, we tend to ignore subtle differences in sounds, assuming them to be unimportant individual variations. There are significant differences between the English word "encourage" and the French word "entourage." In their written forms, however, we tend simply to note the "c" in "encourage" and the "t" in "entourage." We *hear* this contrast as a significant difference, too, but the fact that a different syllable is accented is a more important difference. It is difficult to illustrate this problem in print, but it is one of the keys to becoming "opened up" for language learning: to trust *hearing* more than seeing. Those who tend to "see print" with their ears need to break the habit.

Just two or three hours of training under a language acquisition specialist can produce a remarkable change in aural (hearing) sensitivity and discrimination. It doesn't really matter what languages are used for the exercises or what language the learner intends to learn on the field; the first task is to *hear* more discriminatingly, and to learn to trust the ears rather than relying on the visualization of the printed word.

To explore the difference between an aspirated and a nonaspirated consonant, try saying "puff" the ordinary way, pushing out air while sounding the "p." Now try it without the push of air. It will tend to become "buff," but hold it carefully to a "p" sound. Listen to yourself. Now shift back and forth, "*p*uff-puff-*p*uff-puff. . . ." Test yourself by holding a lighted match four inches or so beyond the lips. The aspirated "*p*uff" will blow out the match. Practice until you can say "puff-puff-puff . . ." without blowing out the match. Listen for the difference the aspiration makes. Being able to hear such subtle differences is a skill you need for good language learning, and it *is* possible to develop this skill.

At the level of language use, listen closely to the different ways people around you sound when they say a common word, for example, *and*. Learn to hear *ayund*, *ann*, *un*, *ayun*, *en*, along with other variations. Right where you live and work now you can begin tuning your ears to language learning.

Making New Sounds

Actually, the problem here is less a matter of making new sounds than it is accepting the legitimacy of new sounds as language. The sounds of English are acceptable, of course, but can a cheek-click be language? (As in "giddy-up horse," followed by the clicking sound made with the tongue fixed against the palate and all the unvoiced sound occurring resonantly in the extended cheek.) In fact, both this cheek-click and the tongue-roof click are necessary linguistic sounds in the tribal languages of southern Africa.

The very thought of saying something with such mouth-sounds is embarrassing to some people. Thus there are inhibitions to be overcome as well as skills to learn. The so-called tonal languages, especially Mandarin, in which rising and falling musical pitches or toned hums form the background sound for certain syllables, are difficult for Americans to imitate. A few hours of training can break this barrier by drawing attention to the many ways we already use pitch and tone variations. An emotional "Wow!" uses just this sort of tonality. We do it all the time. "Aw, c'mon now" can be said at least a half-dozen different ways by varying the tone pattern. Try it. Controlling the tonality changes the meaning considerably. Practicing such shifts of tone aloud can help to break down the inhibitions and correct the mistaken impression that English doesn't already make use of those devices of language.

Specific languages require special skills. Several languages use the glottal stop, for example. In Hawaiian the double a(aa) is the written equivalent of a pair of *ah* sounds separated by a glottal stop, often shown as an apostrophe: *a'a*. Not just *ah-ah*, this effect calls for closing the *throat* (not the mouth or tongue). Can an American do this? It may seem alien to English but it isn't! We commonly use the glottal stop to express a negative—*u'uh*—and as an expression of negative or rejecting dismay—*u'oh*. Try saying *u'oh* over and over. Notice how the throat closes down between the two vowel sounds? You are using the glottal stop. And you knew how already! So applying it to new uses should be a manageable task.

Going Beyond the Code

Formal teaching of a foreign language—should we call it mis-teaching?—causes many language learners to think of languages as equivalent code systems. Thus for the word "rabbit" in English there must be an exact equivalent in Dutch or Greek. The learner becomes frustrated when a word such as the English "bunny," to mean a cute, cuddly little rabbit, doesn't have an exact equivalent word in the new language. For such a person, "little rabbit" doesn't quite say it; there must be a word-for-word code. Oh? Sorry about that. Not even very closely related languages such as Spanish and Portuguese are coded copies of each other.

A series of "freeing up" exercises can be useful to show that alternative ways of saying something, even within the same language, are legitimate translations of an idea. "The effort you put into language-skill preparation will pay good dividends" is essentially the same as saying, "The results of work on language-learning skills will

prove to be worthwhile." Two ways of saying the same thing—
that's what translation means.

Learning the Idioms

Idioms are an important part of any language, but idioms in a second language often seem to the newcomer to be a sort of nuisance.
One rarely thinks about the idioms in one's own language. It isn't
that we close our eyes to them (there's one) so much as it is a matter
of taking them for granted (there's another). Try to make yourself
aware of the dozens of idioms that you use in ordinary conversation.
This will help in two ways: first, you will be better able to accept idioms in the language you want to learn; second, you can attempt to
reduce your use of idioms in order to make your English more understandable to people for whom English is not a native language.
Start with these: cut corners, rise to the occasion, feel for others,
turn over a new leaf, pay the piper, hits the spot, shoe on the other
foot. Notice that idioms are phrases that mean something different
from the literal uses of the words.

The capability of expressing ideas with a different "bag of idioms" and a different flavor of approach is an experience to be appreciated. You can learn to value idioms as the *color* of a language.
Clever ways of saying things—and thinking of things—await you in
a second language. A skilled coach of language acquisition skills can
help with these matters and thus make the on-field language learning a more pleasant and efficient process.[3]

Appreciating Another Mode of Expression

The *sound* of another language is a kind of music. In one's ears and
aesthetic appreciation it can become a pleasing experience. Listening to poetry and songs in the language one is planning to learn is a
valid preparational experience. Language is more than technique; it
is flow, rhythm, tone, and life!

A FONETIC EKSERSIZE

When the world's soccer hero Pele announced that he might marry
the Brazilian model Xuxa, half the newspaper readers in America

stumbled. Gzu-Gza? Zhu-Zha? Ksu-Ksa? Help! How in the world do you pronounce "Xuxa"?

Ah, *Shoo-Sha*! What a beguiling sound to ears tuned either to Portuguese or to English. It helps to know that *x* is often used in Latin America (and Brazil) for the "sh" sound. It is commonly used as the signal that a word has been brought into Spanish or Portuguese from an indigenous Indian language.[4]

Thus when a menu in Rio lists *abacaxi*, you can at least pronounce it: "ah-bok-uh-SHEE." And, if you learn by doing, order some and you'll receive a chunk of the grandest pineapple outside Thailand. But if you want some pineapple in Lisbon, you will need to know that home-country Portuguese uses the more Spanish term, *piña*. In South America the Brazilians, at least, leave the local Indian name on it—after all, that's where the pineapple started.

This tendency to mix in words from the languages of indigenous populations accounts for some of the regional variations in a language. For example, *Mexico* is not what a Spaniard would consider a good Spanish word; the conquistadors didn't take the name *to* Mexico, they accepted it and brought it back to Europe.[5] Try the *x* with the "sh" sound. Then go to "Mexican" (Meh-shih-cahn) and "Mexicano." Slip from there into the anglicization: "Chicano." Get it?

The letter *x* is the most chameleon-like letter in the Romanized alphabet, and it can be fun to discover how many sounds it represents. In the Romanizing of Bantu languages it denotes a tongue click. The Spanish don't like to *see* it, so it becomes the "h" sound of the Spanish *j*. The newest Romanized form of Chinese also uses it for "sh" in some words but not all.

To gain a more flexible sense of the relationships between sounds and print, create for yourself some alternative spellings so that you can "hear" from more than one approach to the visualization of a word. You can thus loosen up your phonetic framework and learn to hear better. Especially since literate people will habitually try to relate printed forms of words to what they hear, and vice versa, you can at least become more flexible about the matter.

BREAKING FREE

Becoming competent as a language learner demands breaking free of the presumptions that come from one's first language. Since *no* language is used as a world standard to which all other languages must be compared, there are no "standard" uses of letters of an alphabet for given sounds. Even the "standard" phonetic alphabet and symbols used internationally in linguistic research are a collection of arbitrary equivalencies that vary somewhat in actual practice, depending on the first language of the individual researcher.

If in the Russian language, for example, the letter *P* is chosen to represent the "R" sound, it's their business, not ours. The Russians don't use the *R*. They use the *P*—it's as simple as that. If, in the development of languages and the borrowing of symbols from one another, the Irish had wanted to let the letter *B* in certain uses represent the sound "V," they were free to do so; and, as do the Russians, they made their choice, as in the popular name Siobhan (Shuh-VON). They also borrowed the English idea of letting the *B* represent the English-sound "B" as in Balbriggan.

How crazy, one might say, that one letter can be used for several different sounds. How do you know which to use? Once again be reminded that users of English—of all people—have no right to make this criticism. Consider the different ways we sound *F*—and interchange the symbol *PH*: often a fitting and em*ph*atic *f*ocus *of* laughter. Or note the various uses of *G*, even in the same word: *garaging*. How crazy, indeed.

Thus it isn't so unreasonable that CCCP is the Russian equivalent of USSR. The Russian letter *C* is the phonetic equivalent of the English *S*, and their word for *Soviet—Cobetckhi—*sounds much the same. This shouldn't seem at all strange to a speaker of English. Although our primary phonetic association with the letter *C* is "hard" as in *carrot* or *concrete*, we use the "soft" sound too, as in *cent* and *census*. The Russian Cyrillic alphabet uses *C* almost exclusively in this "soft" sound.

The "when do you use which" problems of English spelling are horrendous, in comparison with virtually any other language of the Western world. The letter *C*, as we use it, could be abandoned forever, replaced by the letters *S* and *K*. Why do we need it? Another way to simplify would be to throw out *S* and use *C* for all sibilant uses, such as *centc* (notice that *coundz* has a different plural-form-ending—sound it out!). This would leave poor old *K* with a clearer role in life. As it is now, though *K* is apparently the "hardest" sort of *C* sound (*calculate* would become *kalkulate*); the *K* is ordinarily asked to play a meaningless role: *know, knife, knowledge,* and the like. Talk about absurd!

The Russians have been onto this one for several centuries. Their crocodile can't be mistaken for a *srossodilly. Krokodil!* Right on the nose. Even when they borrow words from English, we can read them more precisely as *they* spell them than as we do once we break free from our English presumptions. *Nonkonformizm, kredit, tranzistor, populizm, krizis.* Because they don't like to end words with the "n" sound, you might trip over *eskalatsiya* or *sekularizatsiya*, but for practice on this ending, try mass *mediya!* Not bad.

FREEDOM FROM SPELLING

Freedom from the presumptions of one's first language is the first freedom. Freedom from spelling is the second. To those who never learned to spell their English well enough to trust themselves without a dictionary, freedom from spelling may sound like a very good idea. The point of it, however, is not that spelling is unimportant—indeed, written language with erratic spelling is chaotic—but that spelling to "sound out" a word is a language-learning crutch that can lead to a lot of trouble. Being dependent on *seeing* a word in order to learn it is a serious liability.

Language is first and foremost a matter of sounds. Words are meant for the tongue first, for the pen second. The damage that is done by making introductory learning of any language a matter of paper, pencil, and silent reading is incalculable. There may be other important learnings that are distorted by turning them into school subjects, but surely language is a prime victim of this process.

When a child is capable of virtual mastery of the structure and vocabulary of the "mother tongue" by the age of five, it should be apparent that something is wrong when it takes teenagers and young adults three or four years in a school's foreign language classes to become competent and confident enough to use a language in simple conversation. Part of the problem is the written form of the language. Language learning should start out just as it does in real life—with the *sound* of language.

A major reason why the dependency on written language interferes with language learning is that people tend to "sound out" words based on their own accustomed uses of letters and combinations of letters. There is simply no way to learn a foreign language by looking at it! Read it? Of course you can learn to *read* a foreign language by looking at printed pages, and many people do. I'm reminded of times overseas when I wished that I could get a taxi driver to *write* what he was saying so I could see if it made any sense in terms of my reading knowledge of a language in which I had little or no conversational skill. It's not valid to say you have learned a language simply because you can read it; you haven't really learned it unless you can *hear* it and speak it. The written part, important as literacy is, comes more under the heading of coding and decoding than it does of language use.

When you are in an emergency and want to scream for help, you may know full well that *au secours*! is what the French would expect to hear. But it doesn't help much to know how to spell it. You might as well scream, "dot-dot-dot, dash-dash-dash, dot-dot-dot," as to let go with "Ow see-course!"

STRANGE SOUNDS

The human voice is capable of an enormous range and variety of sounds. No one language uses them all. In every part of the world there are local notions about what sounds are polite and impolite, pleasant and unpleasant, friendly and unfriendly. A newcomer in any culture has some adjustments to make in getting accustomed to the strange sounds of formal language and the even stranger sounds of informal language—signals, calls, appreciation, ridicule, warning, and welcome. It is hard for Americans to show appreciation for tasty soup in the proper oriental way; noisy slurping is one of our "no-no" taboos.

Consider our low whistle of relief and the different whistle that signals the "wolf call" of too-forward appreciation. Consider the "Bronx cheer" and the several situations in which it is acceptable. Think about the cheek-click that sometimes accompanies a wink. The finger snap that is used as an auxiliary sound to catch attention of a child or a waiter. (In Brazil a sort of unvoiced hiss is the way to catch the attention of the waiter: "Psseeoo.")

Communication with animals is a strange subdivision of informal language. There is the special pair of cheek-clicks to encourage a horse to get underway. The growling sounds used to signal a symbolic scrap while rough-housing with a puppy, the lip-popping to talk to the goldfish, and on and on. Ours is a world of many sounds; we are not limited to formal language. Becoming conscious of how many sounds one already uses and accepting the fact that they are actually informal *language* represent big steps toward language-learning competency.

For so many, the stubborn refusal to imitate strange sounds

when the language teacher tries to help and the unwillingness to "sound foolish" and copy a name or word in its true form can be huge barriers blocking good language acquisition. A classic illustration is the stubborn insistence that an *R* is always pronounced the American way, even though in Brazilian Portuguese, for example, the "r" has a substantially different standard sound. Some Americans will stubbornly continue to say "*R*io de Janeiro" for months after discovering that Brazilians *never* do. "Hee-o d'Janayhu" is just too strange—a violation of what one has learned at home to do and not to do with particular letters of the alphabet.

COMMUNICATION WITHOUT WORDS

Nonverbal communication is more generalized than language— *much* more generalized. Similar facial expressions the world over signify pleasure, displeasure, consternation, curiosity, disdain, sadness, and other emotions. Many people make their way into and safely out of all sorts of overseas situations by a "sign language" of gestures and facial expressions. It works remarkably well.

If you ever happen to take hula lessons in Hawaii, you will learn that every move has a meaning. And for every meaning and event in the story there's a right way to shake, to sway, to twist. If you are an "insider," you not only know what the nonverbal signal is, but you also know when it is being done just right—or wrong.

Certain nonverbal signals have the same meaning in many cultures, especially signs or signals that are based on a "picture" of the event or activity intended. Thus to invite someone else to take a swim, a single flowing gesture will usually suffice. But if the person you are inviting seems to be confused, or to doubt your intention, you will notice some quick movement of facial muscles—a creasing of the forehead or a very slight sideways tilt of the head. So you follow through immediately with a pantomime of swimming. At this point you interpret the response and behave accordingly.

A smile usually means yes—in many cultures it is saved up for just such an affirmation. Americans, especially those from the South or Midwest, tend to overuse the smile and sometimes conclude that the local folks are rather cold and indifferent. Some Americans are virtual walking "yes signs" and greet everyone on the street by smiling, causing the local folks to cast down their eyes, in the local equivalent of "I wonder what he or she wants?"

Since facial expressions and pictogram-style sign language work so well for so many situations they are sometimes trusted a little too far. There are subtleties in the right way and the wrong way to express a certain thing. Spending some time in India will cure you of depending too much on your own interpretation of their nonverbal communication. Indians have some very set ways of saying things in nonverbal form and, though the gestures are similar, the meanings can be very different from what Americans might assume.

Hey, Mom, They Shake Wrong

A small boy, seated at the dining table of an American family hosting several foreign students, was fascinated by the gently animated ways of a man from the south of India. The Indian man was not saying much, but he offered a running string of nonverbal feedback to all those who were talking. The small boy's wide eyes were matched by an equally open mouth. Finally he could contain himself no longer: "Hey, Mom, he shakes all wrong," he exclaimed. After a moment of embarrassed silence, the interpretation emerged. Others at the table who were also having their first close-up experience with a person from India had noticed it too: every agreement and affirmation of what was being said was accompanied by a small side-to-side tipping of the head. The basic side to side movement was very similar to the Western sign for "no," but it was being used to say "yes." And this nine-year-old spotted it.

It is well to remember that in matters of nonverbal communication, things aren't always what they seem to be. But don't let that stop you from trying. Nonverbal communication is as close to an international language as we will ever get.

HEARING COMES FIRST

When Americans learn a new language, they want to *see* it, not just hear it. Unfortunately, that is almost the worst thing a beginning language learner can crave. An oral-aural method is likely to be much more effective, especially at first. Hearing and speaking skills should be given greatest attention. In many ways, the preferred pattern is similar to the sequence of learning one's first language: hearing, imitating, comprehending, speaking, in that order; then comes reading, after a good headstart with the other skills. Don't be too eager to get into the reading of your new language. Get an "ear" for it first; then your reading, especially your silent reading, won't drive you into badly formed sounds.

The possibilities for realistic and satisfying language learning are far greater when that language can be heard and used daily. But what can be done during the preparation period before going overseas? Even missionary preparation programs typically tend to approach language learning as a classroom chore.

In the more up-to-date preparation programs, language orientation is taught as a combination of background skills: the linguistic realities underlying language, the skills of transferring things and ideas into sound, and the skills of comprehending sounds—especially new sounds.

Dwight Gradin, language-learning specialist at Missionary Internship, advocates intense emphasis on the skills of hearing with comprehension. His classroom exercises are largely listen-and-act drills. He delays emphasis on speaking the language; that can come later, after a firm foundation in hearing with comprehension has been developed. In fact, the tasks of oral speech production can wait until the sojourner gets to the field.

Gradin's major concern is that the language learner not become overloaded.

> When a language learner is under the dual pressure to develop two skills at the same time (listening and speaking), anxiety goes up and comprehension comes down. But if at the initial stages of language learning, one is under no pressure to speak, he is free to give total concentration to listening. Anxiety is lessened as a result.[6]

This position has a substantial following. James Asher observed that the task of producing alien sounds has a tendency to reduce or interfere with one's capacity to listen well in the struggling early stages of language learning. Thus Asher and those who have developed language-learning methodologies based on this finding argue that *listening* should be the skill most emphasized in the early stages of learning a second language.[7]

In application, the approach asks the learners (individually and in groups) to hear and act upon a variety of commands: "Lift both hands." "Lift your right hand," ". . . left hand," ". . . the book." Simple commands are used at first, always awaiting the hearer's acting upon the command. Of this technique, Gradin notes,

The command form is, in most if not all languages, the simplest gram-
matical form. Spending a lot of time at that level (not discussing or de-
scribing the form grammatically but actually practicing it by carrying
out commands that are given) gives learners the opportunity to do a lot
of listening—in the context of doing. Learners are not forced into
counter-productive activities of pronouncing the alien utterances. En-
ergies are focused rather on listening and doing. Anxiety is reduced
while comprehension leaps forward.[8]

Asher's techniques, sometimes called "Total Physical Response
Comprehension," are to be utilized for ten to twenty hours, or until
learners are able to say the command phrases and respond appropriately to the language instructor, demonstrating their readiness to
add oral speech to the structures of comprehension already gained.

Other techniques make use of cassette recordings that can be listened to again and again until the sounds and their patterns begin to
seem familiar. Most do-it-yourself learners tend to underestimate
the amount of repetition that is necessary in order to acquire this familiarity.

LANGUAGE WITH GLUE

Tom and Elizabeth Brewster are widely recognized for their basic,
direct, and effective approach to language learning.[9] The basic assumption in the Brewsters' method is that language must be learned
from *people* rather than from books and audiovisual devices.

From this point onward, there is far more action than theory in
their approach. Language learning with the Brewsters' method occurs in environments where the language can be used *immediately*—overseas or in ethnic centers within major cities in the United
States, Canada, or Mexico. The newcomer's first job is to become
established on the scene so that others in the surrounding community will recognize his or her presence and purpose and therefore
will be available as conversational partners from the first halting attempts. Next the learners are expected to slow down their American
lifestyle enough to be able to spend leisurely time with, and to be
available to, the people whose language they are learning.

From here, they add GLUE, an acronym for Get, Learn, Use,
and Evaluate.

G—Get a Text for Today

The learner memorizes a few sentences which can be used in a real-life encounter planned for later that day. The "text," as it is called, must communicate something of reasonable interest to the learner and to one or more of the local folk with whom he or she intends to converse that day. The text is usually two to five sentences, a body of ideas that hangs together and that can be concluded politely—not by helplessly walking away. Whenever possible, the text is expected to lead to some practical consequence or specific goal, as in making a purchase or asking for help or advice.

This example of an early text shows that it has been selected for both current and future value. It relates to a real need and simply informs the hearer of this need:

> *Hello.* [polite greeting]
> *I want to learn. . . .*[Arabic or whatever]
> [More sentences can be inserted here.]
> *This is all I know in. . . .*[Arabic]
> *Thanks for listening.*
> *Goodbye.* [polite leavetaking][10]

The process of learning can be explained in the text for a later day:

> *Here is how I am learning. Each day I learn something new. Next, I practice it. Then I spend my day talking with people. I am enjoying learning your language this way.*[11]

At first learners' spoken texts are concerned with explaining their presence, getting around the area, establishing relationships, making purchases, and telling about themselves. This approach to language learning is in sharp contrast with the more common academic approach of delaying the realistic use of speaking until after the development of a substantial reading vocabulary.

L—Learn the Text

No apology is made for the necessity of using a hear-imitate approach. After all, what is language? Is it not an activity of coordination among the tongue (*lingua*), the ears, and the mind? Before

going into the conversational community, the student must carefully learn and practice the text for the day to build confidence.

U—Use It a Lot

The text is chosen to be used not once but many times. The field experiences each day consist of several or many encounters, in each of
which the text is used.

E—Evaluate and Envision

The daily habit of evaluating and replanning gets language learners
into the important practice of "closing the loop" from planning, to
action, to planning again. This process assures that within a relatively short period of time the learners will be able to open up and
actually begin to learn from what they hear spoken back to them in
these language-using encounters. It is hoped that the "opening up"
will occur before ritualization of rote language sets in. Thus the encounter becomes the powerful teaching moment, even more important than the initial step of getting a text.

The Brewsters' strategy is one example of a learning-by-doing
approach based not in some limited-time classroom lesson but in the
unlimited workaday, walking-around world.

HUMOR AS HAZARD

Even after a learner has moved fairly well into the use of a new language, certain basic problems will persist. Thinking and dreaming
in the new language are sure signs of progress. But even at that
stage, handling humor may be elusive.

Humor doesn't translate well. As any old-timer can tell you, the
last thing to fall into place for any intercultural sojourner is deliberate humor.

All human beings sound just about the same when they laugh.

Laughter and the valuing of humor are features of cultures. But beware—what is funny in one culture may not be so funny in another. And how to handle humor in one situation differs from how to deal with it in another.

Some humor depends on quirks of language. Puns, for example, cannot be translated. Consider "When the lightning bug backed into a fan he was absolutely delighted." When a group of Americans indulges in punning, the other-nation participants in the conversation will be instantly excluded.

Other humor depends on the lore and history of a people. The way things are perceived in a given society is largely a product of what the people have come to see as their background and heritage. Thus what may be funny to an American might seem like utter nonsense to a Britisher who lacks the information commonly known among the "insiders." ("Since George Washington was the father of the nation, aren't you glad that wooden teeth aren't inherited?")

The way people like to think of themselves and their pet exaggerations of their values and internal differences is another source of nontranslatable humor: "What's the difference between Republicans and Democrats?" "About four years—four *light* years." "When fifteen Baptists get together for a meeting how many denominations are there?" "Fifteen."

It doesn't take a lot of intercultural experience to see that there is just no way to take those three types of humor to Mexico with any likelihood of more than a polite smile in response.

Humor doesn't export well, nor does it import well. Americans sometimes try too hard to "get it" when the punch line flies right by them. It can be very embarrassing when someone in the party insists on rehearing the story so that he can find out what he missed. This boring person is usually an American who has fairly good knowledge of the local language and thus seems to think he or she is entitled to "get the point" of every funny story that the host-country friends are telling. Some funny thoughts simply will not budge from their original cultural locus. It's best not to ask! And in *every* culture, humor loses appeal if its repetition is demanded.

As expatriates learn the hard way—and as many visiting dignitaries who are called upon to make impromptu speeches never do seem to learn—it is wise not to count on funny stories to enthrall an audience. It may work back home, but overseas it's best to get to the point, cut the humor, and smile a lot.

CONCLUSION

Language is the key to quality in the overseas experience. Especially in relationships with the people of the host nation and in making the best of travel and lasting friendships, language learning pays big dividends. It isn't easy, but it will likely be easier than the typical American may fear.

FOCUS FOR SELF-EVALUATION

The importance of understanding and speaking the language of the host country suggests that preparation for overseas service should include some basic language acquisition skills. Chapter 7 has provided suggestions for the best ways to get started. It has also called attention to some of the major issues of concern for adult learning of language.

Reflection

As I think about language learning, these thoughts come to mind: _____

_____

_____

_____

Review

1. Speaking only English will limit a person to dealing only with

    a. _____   b. _____

    c. _____   d. _____

2. Name three of the skills needed for efficient language learning.

    a. _____   b. _____   c. _____

3. Name four advantages of knowing the local language.

    a. _____   b. _____

    c. _____   d. _____

Commitment

I am prepared to acknowledge the importance of language learning if it will help me in these ways:

1. _____

2. _____

3. _____

8

Your Job and Its Context

GOING OVERSEAS to work places a special responsibility on the so-journer. It is not only a matter of living effectively in a new environment; the quality and effectiveness of doing the intended job is also at stake. One's competency to do the job at the intended level of productiveness has usually been assessed by the employer or sponsor before making the assignment. Then comes the important task of developing intercultural skills so that the overseas context does not seriously inhibit one's competency.

THE FOUR FACES OF READINESS

Four areas of readiness for overseas employment should be assessed and enhanced: orientation to the purposes of one's assignment, orientation to the procedures of the organization, orientation to others, and orientation to oneself.

Orientation to the Purposes of One's Assignment

With respect to the reasons for being overseas, one must take into account the purposes and expectations of the employing organiza-

172

tion. The purpose isn't tourism; of that you can be very sure. Too often the romance of an overseas assignment becomes an end in itself, even for a missionary.

Are you clear about the expectations? Have you discussed the job description and the intentions of your employer thoroughly enough that the potential ambiguities and frustrations can be anticipated? A recent study of 2015 overseas workers from Sweden found that intercultural problems were most likely to occur when "the parent company did not define the employee's role clearly or the local company did not perceive this role clearly. . . ."[1]

No matter how the misunderstandings about job performance arose, this factor was seen as a significant contributor to the decision of one-third of these overseas Swedes to leave their assignments and go home early.

Do you have fundamental misgivings about the worth of what you are expected to do? Do you think of your employment tasks as imposing on your freedom to enjoy and take full advantage of the intercultural experience?

Are you inclined to cross your fingers and hope your purposes and the purposes of the job will somehow fit together? It is far too great a chance to take. Talk it through with your organizational supervisors. Are you hoping to figure out the point of it all after you get there? Too late. On the field you should be ready to evaluate the problems as they are encountered and recommend adjustments, when necessary, to your organization. It may be too late then to start figuring out why you are there.

Orientation to the Procedures of Your Organization

Most organizations with experience in overseas operations will not send a newly employed person overseas until he or she has had several months of experience in the "home office" or some unit located in the United States. Every organization has a "personality" just as surely as every person is unique. Problems arise when the overseas employee makes mistakes in communication, procedures, or tasks in order to learn about the organization. Not only is this wasteful, it is demoralizing. "Culture shock" is sometimes simply *job* shock.

Can you do the job that is expected of you? Can you do it in the United States? What will be different about doing it overseas? Have you spent time with others who have done this sort of job overseas?

Have you asked for a temporary assignment to visit some site overseas where someone is doing the job the way the organization wants it done?

Are you willing to be accountable? Do not assume that distance will get you "off the hook"; when supervisors get peeved with a worker 5000 miles away, they get *really* peeved. The organization is putting a lot of money in you, your preparation, and your career development. They have a right to expect something in return. You need to have a clear understanding about what it is. Job expectations are a matter of mutual responsibility. You have a right to ask for clear definitions. Your employer has a right to expect you to be accountable.

You owe it to yourself to think through these matters very carefully. They are all part of being prepared. No one has a greater stake in your orientation than you do. Being well oriented is a matter of getting yourself faced in a particular direction so that the consequences of any movement will contribute to worthy and intended outcomes of your overseas assignment.

Orientation to Others

Success or failure in the overseas assignment will not depend on some abstraction called "culture." Most intercultural problems can be traced to interpersonal problems. It could even be said that overseas sojourners don't *encounter* problems of this sort, they take them along!

How do you look at other people? Do you look down? Look away? Look above? An adult in an adult world should be respectful toward others, avoiding the tendency to put down others to bolster his or her own sense of power, but not condescending to putting on a cloak of false humility. Perhaps *love* says it best. How are you at loving other people? How do you handle people you resent? People you fear? People you see as incompetent? In your office or work place how does this show through?

Do you have to control things? In the overseas situation being "in charge" can present more problems than it does at home. Do you like to have things come out the way you planned and anticipated? Ease off. You have to learn to live with outcomes that are different from your expectations. It helps if you can learn to enjoy surprises! Do you like to be able to see everything in reasonable orderly terms? Watch out. This one will get you nothing but grief.

Orientation to Self

How do you see yourself? Can you identify the personal motives that have brought you to this point? Do you know why you are going, in terms of what you expect to gain from the experience?

Are you running away from something? It won't work. Are you able to control your fears and anxieties? You *must*; if you haven't learned to handle these concerns in the home scene, you surely will find them to be worse overseas. Do you see yourself as making a big sacrifice by going overseas? Not only is this likely to be inaccurate, it also suggests a condescending attitude. You may need help thinking it through.

JOB EFFECTIVENESS OVERSEAS

A study of 160 overseas technical advisors and 90 spouses was carried out by two outstanding researchers, Frank Hawes and Daniel Kealey, under the sponsorship of the Canadian International Development Agency (CIDA). It became one of the most exhaustive studies of intercultural competency and overseas job effectiveness ever conducted. The subjects were Canadians assigned outside their home country in all sorts of tasks ranging across research, conservation, technical and higher education, health, and engineering.

Over one hundred variables were examined in an attempt to understand job-related effectiveness in overseas situations. The main objective was to find the ways that intercultural adaptation related to job effectiveness. Responses to the opinion questions revealed the following:

As seen by people of the host nation, effectiveness of the sojourner relates to two matters: (1) intercultural professional interaction, socially and on-the-job, leading to successful transfer of skills and knowledge; and (2) personal and family adjustment.

As seen by the sojourners, effectiveness relates to five matters: (1) professional competence (performance of tasks, duties, responsibilities); (2) interaction with local culture and people; (3) personal and family adjustment; (4) social adaptation to other expatriates; and (5) adaptation to the physical environment, including the limitations in housing, services, entertainment, climate, or other conditions that might cause stress.[2]

The fact that both host-country persons and the Canadian expatriates place emphasis on the matter of intercultural relations and skills is important. The difference seemed to be that for the host-country respondents, it was *inseparable from professional interactions*, whereas for the Canadians, professional competence was a separate and topmost concern.

> The best predictor of overseas effectiveness was "Interpersonal Skills," followed by "Identity" and "Realistic Predeparture Expectations." Regarding transfer of skills to nationals, it was found that ineffectiveness of the assistance personnel was attributable to their inability to engage in intercultural interaction.[3]

The isolation of the Canadians into a social life of their own was attested to by the fact that only 10 percent of the available social time was used for intercultural activities. "The message is clear: there was very little interaction taking place between nationals and Canadians." Given this fact, the authors tend to conclude that Canadians were not likely effective at the task of transferring skills.[4]

The conclusions drawn by Hawes and Kealey emphasize four interrelated elements of overseas effectiveness:

1. *Personal/family adjustment*, including satisfaction with living overseas, engagement in enjoyable activities, adjustment as a family unit, and successful coping with day-to-day life.
2. *Intercultural interaction*, including experiences with local people and making local friends; learning the language and nonverbal communication system (gestures, interpersonal space, postures, appropriate eye contact, etc.); factual knowledge about local culture in reference to such matters as politics, history, current events, economy.
3. *Task accomplishment*, including technical background, job commitment, and achievement of daily tasks, duties, and responsibilities. A less tangible achievement is that of transfer of specific, concrete skills to local people.
4. *Transfer of skills and procedures*—"software"—the global know-how by which people manage, control, operate, and maintain the complete system of a technological field. In the CIDA perspective, transfer of technical knowledge and skills is the ultimate goal of technical assistance programs.

Taken as a whole, this research indicates that the sojourner who is most likely to be effective in transfer of skills possesses three global characteristics in addition to technical expertise:

First, the *interpersonal orientation* lends a certain curiosity and natural respect towards others. The person is ready to listen to others, to get to know them, and to seek to understand their world view. Second, *a sense of identity* lends confidence in interaction with nationals. The person can remain open to experiencing local people and culture without feeling threatened by the differences or desiring to abandon his own identity in favor of theirs. Third, the person has a *positive but realistic expectation* about life in the host culture, akin to saying, "I know this won't be easy, in fact it's probably going to be difficult for me and the family, but we intend to do the best we can, and we'll be OK."[5]

PROMISES, PROMISES

Commitment to do one's work well goes a long way toward making the overseas experience successful. Job competency is as important abroad as it is at home. As missionaries used to say, "It takes more than a trip on a ship to make a missionary."

The point is sound. Whatever a person is before going overseas pretty well predicts what he or she will be overseas. The drama (and sometimes the trauma) of the move to a place that is significantly different does, of course, constitute a sort of punctuation mark in the flow of life; but it rarely transforms a person. And it is even less likely to magically turn weaknesses into strengths, avoidances into willingness, and fears into eagerness.

"Oh, they'll be okay after they get into the new situation," is the sort of fingers-crossed prediction that overseas personnel officers usually live to regret. If there are problems, they should be dealt with before going overseas. If new skills will be needed, it is best to get at least a confidence-building head start before adding the extra tasks of making the intercultural adaptations on the job and in one's lifestyle.

Some people approach their move overseas as a sort of king-sized New Year's Day: All sorts of resolutions are stored up to be undertaken "after we move to Rome" or wherever. In some ways this is a good idea, but if overdone it leads to disappointment. For example, it is useful to make a short list of the commitments one is willing to make to start off right and to be faithful to the very highest standards of which one is capable. Such promises, if realistic, are commendable. The expatriate who really is responsible to himself or herself, the family, the job, and to the people of the new culture is the person who will get the most out of the experience.

But if the list of commitments includes job skills that really should have been learned earlier, or if it includes matters of fundamental change in personal style or personality, there are disappointments ahead.

MODERN VERSUS TRADITIONAL

In one way or another, everyone from America exerts a sort of Americanizing and "modernizing" effect wherever we may be. For businessperson or missionary, it seems to be part of the job. If you don't want to emphasize this consequence of doing your job—or if you do intend to do so—it pays to understand the tensions between modern and traditional values.

Though it may get in the way of an effective effort on your part, there will be people who see you and your lifestyle as their ideal and model. Many people want the "things" of the Western and modernized world. The motivation for technological modernization is profound in every "have-not" nation. The vision of an easier life and the fascination for gadgets have universal appeal. Before World War I, the United States was largely an agrarian nation, supplied and stimulated by the eastern seaboard industrial centers. The war pulled hundreds of thousands of farm boys into the outer world—Baltimore, New York, London, Paris, and the like.

In today's shrinking world there is no need for a war to produce this effect. From Kalimantan to Ketchikan, once they've seen television, they want it. Once they get television, they want everything that's on it! Without doubt, television is the most powerful technological force for cultural change the world has ever seen.

Only a naive romanticist would talk in terms of slowing down these processes and influences. It is as reasonable to put the world's smog layers back into bottles. These forces of modernization are at large, and they will shape our future.

Social criticism must be addressed to what we can control of what happens in the world as a result of our decisions. We cannot decide what should be shown on Indonesian television, except indirectly as we may be able to affect what is on ours. Whatever Americans accept in their own media will relate to Indonesia's future—if the Indonesian telecasters ever run out of *I Love Lucy* and *Dragnet* reruns! We are not forcing the world to drink Coca-Cola or watch television. The people of the world do it if it is there to do. One can only hope that Americans will become a little less aggressive in promoting such products.

Things as Common Ground

To come to terms with the ways your overseas assignment and your lifestyle inevitably will affect the people of the host country, specific case material helps. An outstanding collection of such material has been published by Herald Press, representing the Mennonite position on missionary and humanitarian work in Latin America.

Daniel Hess raises a devastating question: "When people of two different cultures communicate with each other, what are the people talking about? . . . *things.*"[6] The pervasiveness of things—the materialistic core of common interest, drinks, smokes, cars, armaments—is the impoverished common ground between two very different agendas. If either society is interested in values of greater consequence than things, they rarely get equal attention.

SELLING POISON

The ethics of selling poison to the unsuspecting, or to those who connive to harm others, is one of the gray areas of international trade. In our own society we establish limitations on what can be bought and sold. In the case of beneficial but potentially hazardous products we establish legal restrictions on buying and selling. Milk, for example, in most of our states must not be sold after a designated number of days of its production. Certain "life-saving" drugs may not be sold at all except under the direct control and responsibility of a physician. Dated products that can become unsafe or lose their potency are strictly regulated.

Then sometimes they are sent overseas. In two important areas the lack of international control and the difficulty of industry's policing itself have led to occasional abuses: the armaments industry and the pharmaceutical industry. As people in these industries are quick to remind us, there is nothing *illegal* about what they do overseas. In the armaments trade, the major customers are other sovereign nations which, of course, would insist on their right to buy what they need wherever they can get it. Thus, with a shrug, the American producer of war machines will calmly insist that if these nations couldn't get the armaments from us, they would be driven into the arms of the Russians and their industrial satellites.

Among many Americans, both here and abroad, the issue of nuclear arms proliferation is lively. The expatriate American needs to know where he or she stands on these matters. It pays also to realize that the issue is generally debated more emotionally overseas than it is in the United States. Be aware that people who have lived closer to war than North Americans have generally have stronger feelings about war. Don't walk into an argument ignorantly! You need to know what you are talking about.

If armament sales are considered perfectly legal, then it can be said that marketing of pharmaceuticals overseas makes Americans healthier. It provides a market for products that are about to be out of date under U.S. regulations, and it provides an outlet for products that are outlawed in the United States.[7] To avoid taking a loss on a product that is found to have serious side effects, pharmaceutical companies may ship the product to one of the nations that has a hands-off approach to drug safety. The manufacturers thereby save money that they can put into "research to benefit humanity."

Research is yet another issue: Because of the restrictiveness and tight regulation of experimentation with human subjects in the United States, it is much easier to conduct quiet experimental programs in countries where drug and chemical companies are less likely to be hampered by anything more serious than the need for treating some government health official to a night on the town (or better) every now and then.

Are these accusations fair? Investigative journalists from this country and elsewhere have checked out these accusations. Disclaimers and protests from American companies are vigorous and persistent. But the evidence persists and withdrawals are rare.

Even more important than whether or not these allegations can be proved is the fact that they are the common stuff of attitudes about Americans and American industry among many of the people with whom the expatriate will be working. It can be helpful to know what people are thinking about you and your country, even if they are too polite to bring it up.

THE THREE WORLDS

Whenever one is employed in an international career, some jargon and ideas about how today's nations fit together into "one world" will be encountered. It can be useful to know what lies behind the terms.

Journalists and some political scientists use a handy "three worlds" system of categorizing sectors of influence. The First World, largely the western nations including westernized nations such as Australia, New Zealand, the Republic of South Africa, and Japan, is generally associated with the capitalistic free enterprise system. In general, the Western world (in contrast with the Eastern or oriental world) embraces the nations most clearly influenced by ancient Greek culture. The philosophies and arts of Hellenistic Greeks are the major source of the Western world's culture. The people of Europe, North America, and urban Latin America hold values that are classical Greek in origin.

The Eastern world includes the Orient and Asia in general. Because of the political influence of Russia over the nations of Eastern Europe, these nations are sometimes included in the generalization.

"Eastern nations," as used today, means anything beyond the Elbe River—East Germany, Poland, Czechoslovakia, Romania, Hungary, Albania, Bulgaria, Russia, and points east, to and through the Orient. Then one starts listing the political exceptions: Turkey, Finland, the Arab nations, Israel, Iran, India, Sri Lanka and so forth. And after this come the touchy matters of Japan, Thailand, Malaysia, Hong Kong, Taiwan, the Philippines, Indonesia, South Korea, and so forth. Clearly they are oriental but not really Eastern nations. By now, many of these—Japan, urban Korea, and, of course, Hong Kong—show strong influences of Hellenistic thought, via England, the United States, and other "Western" nations. Formal education, Western style, has wrought substantial cultural transformations, at least among the people who have had access to it.

The idea of an East-West dichotomy was, from its earliest use, a simplistic generalization to distinguish European from non-European. After World War II two great events began to make this East-West dichotomy less useful. First, the Cold War—pitting Washington and London against Moscow—led to a drawing of new and firm lines. As the lines hardened, the idea of "Eastern" became equivalent to "Communist" (Marxist-Leninist), especially after 1949, when Mao Tse-Tung ended up on top in China.

The second postwar event of importance in this matter was the emergence of a potent bloc of postcolonial nations. It didn't take long after the Dutch were gone from Indonesia, the French from Indochina, the English from dozens of places, and the Belgians from their huge central African holdings for these new governments to find their voices and rush into the United Nations General Assembly as full partners.

It was during these years that the term "Third World" was popularized. It was coined and first used formally in 1952 by the French demographer, Alfred Sauvy, to draw a parallel to the "third estate," the commoners of France at the time of the French Revolution. As used in the United Nations, the term did not mean third in order, as in "third best" or "third rate." Indeed, quite the opposite. It was proudly claimed by those who didn't want any longer to be taken for granted by the controlling powers of the worlds, East or West, which hitherto had presumed to think in terms of two worlds: us and them. To the diplomats of those nations today "Third World" is a good term because it asserts that theirs is yet another bloc of power, not seeking to enter into the East-versus-West controversies (though they do so with unfortunate regularity) but fulfilling a separate agenda with a distinctly different end in mind: avoidance of domination by the Eastern or the Western power giants.

The mockeries of this sort of nonalignment are by now notorious, including such examples as Castro's Cuba and Moscow's newer satellites in Africa, especially Angola and Ethiopia, each of which is still asking to be considered nonaligned except as part of the Third World. Nonetheless, the term survives and if there weren't such a term today, one would have to be coined.

The "three worlds" idea is useful for comparative purposes. It can provide a framework from which to project viewpoints. No one has offered a clearer comparison of these viewpoints than Ron O'Grady, a protestant minister from New Zealand. From his book, *Bread and Freedom*, we can gain insights from the several perspectives. O'Grady's procedure is to compare both the self-understanding and the understanding of the other two worlds as these are typically held in each case. The material following is selected from his comparative analysis of the ways that human rights issues are viewed in the three worlds. It is generalized to focus attention on the ways the people of each set of nations view themselves and each of the others.

The View from the First World

How the People of the Capitalist World See Themselves

The capitalist world sees itself as the defender of liberty and the upholder of rights and democracy. . . . Particular stress is laid on individual liberties, which are protected by constitutions and a liberal interpretation of the rule of law. The right to hold and express minority views, to possess property, to have a fair trial before one's peers, to have freedom of expression in public media, and the rights of fair electoral procedures are all jealously guarded within the First World.

How the People of the Capitalist Nations View the Communist Nations

Since the communist revolutions have not had the full approval of the majority, the people are repressed and denied their rights under communism. Communist rule is dictatorial and the single party state denies the possibility of dissent. . . . The refusal to allow political dissent has led to imprisonment, torture, exile, brainwashing, character defamation and forced confessions. . . . The flow of refugees seeking asylum in the West [is] proof that communist society is repressive of human dignity. . . . First world churches reflect their national ethos. There is the belief that . . . communism . . . [is] inimical to Christianity and deliberately restrict[s] religious freedom. The inference is sometimes drawn that those churches which survive in eastern Europe have done so by compromising their beliefs—a view which is encouraged by refugees.

How the People of the Capitalist Nations View the Third World

There is ambivalence in the western understanding of the third world nations, because there are extensive historical links as well as the ever-present desire to retain western influence over the non-aligned nations lest they become communist. Even so, the liberal conscience of the West is angered by some blatant human rights violations in [many of these nations]. . . . Since a number of third world nations are important trading partners or sources of raw materials, the protest at government level is often muted.

The View from the Second World

How the People of the Communist Nations See Themselves

After years of capitalist and bourgeois rule by persons whose motivation was their own self-interest, the communist revolutions gave back to the people the power to determine their own future. Competition gave way to cooperation, and the rights of rulers yielded to the rights of the masses. . . . [Communist states are the forerunners of the new world society.] This new society will preserve the community rights and spell the end of the competitive systems of private enterprise. . . . If individuals threaten the well-being of the wider community, they must be punished.

How the People of the Communist Nations View the Capitalist Nations

The First World speaks about human rights in a self-righteous manner, but in fact it is the principal offender. Western democracy denies people their rights in both subtle and blatant ways. The competitive system concentrates capital and leads to inefficiency, wastage of natural resources, unfair trade practices, and money manipulation, and the net results include poverty and unemployment. . . .

Loneliness and disenchantment mark the youth of western society, and corruption in high places indicates a basically unjust system. . . . Christian groups in eastern Europe are defensive about western church criticism of their role. . . . Western society is often portrayed as a society which has become consumer-oriented and materialistic to the exclusion of the Christian virtues of compassion and community.

How the People of the Communist Nations View the Third World

If a criticism is made, the background portentous presence of the western world is castigated. [Many third world nations are] puppet governments, kept in power by American aid and armaments. If the rulers become oppressive, this will be interpreted as a way of retaining power for the capitalist system. The non-aligned nations are to be encouraged to take part in the world Soviet revolution.

The View from the Third World

How the People of the Third World Nations See Themselves

The Third World, especially in Africa and Asia, is conscious of its difference from either the First or the Second World. Much of its cultural heritage dates back centuries, and [it] has developed independently of the Graeco-Roman traditions of the West . . . [and has resisted] the competitive individualism which marked the 19th and 20th centuries in western Christian nations. . . .

The rulers will often return to their traditional history and claim, for example, that they are seeking African answers or an Asian-style democracy. It will sometimes be claimed that the people understand an assertive leadership better than western-style freedoms. The intense concern for economic development is overriding. Third world leaders who recognize that they are taking unpopular and stern measures will justify the stand by claiming that some lesser rights must be sacrificed in order to achieve economic growth.

How the People of the Third World Nations View the Capitalist Nations

Third world nations are irritated by first world accusations of human rights violations, because they claim that the First World has violated the basic rights of developing nations for centuries. They look back to the exploitation of the colonial era as the root of many of their current economic ills. . . . Through multinational corporations and the control of capital flow, the western nations have a stranglehold on third world economy.

The Third World reacts strongly when it is criticized for the same things which take place in the First World. They claim that a western society which can produce a Watergate and industrial bribery is in no position to criticize corruption in third world nations. . . .

There is the suspicion that the capitalist nations use their intelligence services and their economic strength to keep the third world nations in a continual state of poverty and, therefore, dependence.

How the People of Third World Nations View the Communist Nations

At times communism, both in Europe and Asia, has aroused the anger of third world nations for its influence on, and support for, revolutionary groups within the borders of an independent nation. . . .

To many third world nations the communist bloc is considered to be just as exploitative as western capitalism. They have seen the same desire to purchase natural resources and convert them to manufactured goods which sell at prices no less than those of the capitalist nations. Communism is seen as a form of state capitalism which generates just as much injustice as private capitalism. *

*Adapted with permission from Ron O'Grady, *Bread and Freedom* (Geneva: World Council of Churches, 1978).

Your overseas work, especially in politically sensitive situations, requires a knowledgeable grasp of the perspectives and the biases of others. An inquiring mind and an alert consciousness will anticipate the differing views that "make sense" to people depending on their background.

KEEP A LIGHT HOLD

Don't take yourself too seriously. It's one thing to believe in what you are doing. It's quite another to believe that it wouldn't happen without you. As G. K. Chesterton put it, "It is the test of a good religion whether you can joke about it."[8]

You'll live longer and live better if you chuckle. Many of the things you find yourself doing overseas make very little sense. Learn to laugh about the silliness that comes with the job.

The expatriate is inclined to feel self-conscious about being "different." The common human tendency is to interpret "different" as either "better" or "worse." Many expatriates act as though they feel inferior to their hosts; others seem to see themselves as God's great gift to those poor foreigners. From the mass marketer of soft drinks to the missionary, self-importance is a temptation to be avoided.

TOLERANCE OF AMBIGUITY

Especially in the neat and buttoned-down world of Western business, one gets in the habit of counting on predictability and regularity. In much of the world you have to live with things that don't even make sense. You'll need lots of tolerance of ambiguity. Do you expect others to follow through on agreements? The problem is that, interculturally, the perception of an agreement is rarely a mutually shared matter. You think you know what was agreed, but someone whose background and cultural orientation are fundamentally different will more than likely hold a significantly different notion of what the terms of agreement were.

I remember holding a chartered bus full of American kids on a frantically busy corner in Paris for over an hour waiting for a Parisian teacher who had "agreed" to join the tour at this point. When we finally made contact by telephone, we discovered that the teacher had gone home to bed. He had decided we didn't need him—for reasons I have never understood. In France—and many another place in the world—you learn to shrug at such occurrences. It's an essential coping tactic.

SUMMARY

As you go overseas, four matters become more important than ever before: *awareness*—the degree of sensitive, interpretative consciousness of what is going on around you; *acceptance*—the emotional security and spiritual peace that allows you to see other people in *their* terms, not just yours; *ability*—the competencies and sense of worth that you carry with you; and *accountability*—the sense of well-being and honor that comes from seeing yourself as a responsible person and acknowledging your efforts as part of a bigger picture.

The first two of these matters, awareness and acceptance, respond well to effective orientation training. The third and fourth concerns, ability and accountability, are closely related to your perceptions of the job to be done. It is important to take the needed job skills into the field.

FOCUS FOR SELF-EVALUATION

The major concern in Chapter 8 has been with ways you can improve your job-related effectiveness.

Reflection

1. What part of my job-related activities overseas may be seen as a threat or an imposition to host-country nationals?

_____

_____

2. To what extent do I agree with these possible criticisms?

_____

_____

3. How can I respond to these criticisms?

_____

_____

Review

1. How can I make improvements in each of these four areas?

   a. Orientation to the purposes of my assignment overseas _____

   _____

   b. Orientation to the procedures of the organization I work for _____

   _____

   c. Orientation to others _____

   _____

   d. Orientation to myself _____

   _____

2. What is the origin and the meaning of the term "Third World"?

   _____

   _____

Commitment

On the basis of the Hawes and Kealey research, my own job effectiveness
will be improved if I take these steps during preparation: _____

_____

_____

9

A Consumer's Guide to Orientation Training

You can tell that some people are disoriented simply by looking at them. If the shoes aren't both tied, if the shirt is buttoned crookedly, and if the socks don't match, you may be looking at a person who needs help. Don't misunderstand; some of these folks are quite happy—they just *look* like they are about to misstep off the ledge.

On the other hand, meticulous people with not one hair out of place may appear to be oriented, but one must wonder. The real clues are not in the snapshots but in the moving pictures. Watching children at play, you can often spot the difference. One youngster has watched televised baseball so much that he looks the part as he awaits the action—but every ball goes past him. Then there's the casual kid who may even look uninterested, but when he springs into action, he's on top of the ball every time.

And so it is with orientation. Posturing and expectancy are a very small part of the whole; what really counts is *action*. An orientation training experience that is exclusively organized around information—what you'll need to know—can leave your baggage packed with bricks.

What you need instead is a kit of tools. Tools are active processes, concerned with what you do when this or that arises. Make these concerns the center of your preparation and, better yet, seek out opportunities to practice these skills in advance.

As one practical suggestion, notice the way you relate to unfamiliar situations in everyday life at home—the new cafeteria or fast-food restaurant, for example. How do you decide what to do first? What next? How? Try several new places within the next week or so and pay attention to how you relate to each. Each cafeteria has nuances—where things are located, whether there are orders to be placed or merely things to pick up, whether to remove dishes from the tray or not? What to do when you are done? This is a microcosm of cultural difference. Some people avoid unfamiliar places because they aren't exactly certain how to behave. People return to McDonald's because of its absolute predictability. Such dependence is limiting. Begin your loosening-up process. Go someplace different.

If you are not already a regular user of public transportation—the city bus, for example—try it. Notice what you go through to make it work for you. You will learn quickly enough, but at first you will feel strange and uneasy. The "regulars" are well ahead of you; for them it seems so natural. How can you become a "regular?"

Pay attention to the clues around you. Learn a strategy for dealing with variability. Put that strategy in your baggage. An effective orientation experience can make you more competent in this sort of skill.

WHAT IS ORIENTATION?

Sailors and experienced wilderness hikers have a precise way of using the world "orientation." For them it refers to knowing which way is north. Even more to the point, orientation is being able to tell which way you are headed. The word "orientation" has its root in "Orient" or "East." Its early uses had more to do with knowing where the sun would rise than where the compass needle points, but then as now it has meant to know one's location and direction in terms of the surrounding environment.

An old optimist's slogan says, "I always know where I am; it's what's around me that sometimes seems out of place." With such a positive attitude there is no such thing as being lost. It might be more accurate to say that there is no *admitting* that one is lost. But foolhardy bravado is not to be recommended as a substitute for keeping one's bearings.

In regard to orientation, three different postures can be seen among expatriates. Indeed, the same three postures can be seen among recreational sailors, tourists, and hikers: the anxious, the careless, and the secure.

Each of these three postures reflects a way of relating to the environment and to the orienting resources.

The Anxious Person

You can usually find an anxious person standing at a quiet corner or even in the middle of a swirling crowd, map in hand, head turning this way and that, question marks radiating from every glance. Anxiety is not relieved by the map—in fact, were this person to have a second map, they would both be open and the additional problem of deciding which map to trust would be added to the burden. More burdens this person doesn't need.

An anxious person usually lacks orientation not because of a shortage of information but because of the inability to trust whatever information is available. Anxiety leads to inactivity, a sort of stalemating in the face of competing interpretations. When an anxious person comes to a fork in the road or any other point of decision-making, the tendency is to come to a full halt. Getting started again is always hard. Despite the signs, maps, the recalled advice, and the awareness of the logical preference of one choice over another, the decision is overwhelming.

An anxious person's disorientation requires action, not just more knowledge. Acting upon whatever is already known is the first step.

The Careless Person

Of the three types, this person is most apt to plunge over a cliff at full throttle. The best that can be said is that in matters of orientation, carelessness provides its own reward in naive happiness.

The lack of concern for where the trail may lead or whether the right choice has been made can lead to very unpleasant consequences, even if getting there is a lot of fun. In the forest, on the sea, or in unfamiliar cultural relationships, the cost of carelessness can be far too dear.

A careless person is usually unconcerned when he or she becomes lost. What the careless person needs first is a sober awakening, some sort of jolt that will call attention to the hazards, and, better yet, increase the consciousness of the greater satisfactions that are available to those who know what's going on.

The Secure Person

In the forest, in the desert, or in a foreign culture, "secure" doesn't mean that a person can't get lost. Orientation is something that the secure person works at just as surely as does the anxious person. What makes the secure person different is his or her confidence that it is possible to keep a sense of direction. A positive attitude about recovery if one *does* get lost or disoriented is also basic to security. The secure person tries to avoid becoming disoriented but doesn't *fear* it. When it happens—as it surely will—he or she devises ways to relocate the trail and to rediscover the compass bearings.

A secure person uses information well but also has a keen sense of what sorts of information are more trustworthy. Think of it this way: though maps or orientation manuals may be authoritative, they can be wrong. They may be out of date, or the author or artist may have made some mistake. To discover that an indicated fork in the road turns out to be a three-way choice, not two-way as the map suggests, will disturb a secure person relatively little. The reality is right in front of his nose—not on the map. But the fact that the map says two-way suggests that one of the three forks is either newer than the map or so unimportant as to have been left out by the map maker. The secure person has enough confidence in observation and reasoning processes to make the best of this potential confusion.

It isn't information that creates security, though the secure person seeks out information. What really counts is that the secure person knows what to do with information—information brought along *and* information encountered along the way.

Of these three types, one would surely choose to become the secure person. To do so requires gaining the skills of seeking out and effectively using information. But it also demands the developing of a sense of self-confidence and a willingness to cope with unknowns.

NEEDS FOR ORIENTATION TRAINING

Needs for orientation fall into three categories. First, orientation is generally assumed to be necessary for anyone who is to undertake a new task. For example, the assembly-line worker whose electric drill is to be replaced by a pneumatic drill will need orientation; the new tool is different in certain ways and will require some changes in the worker's techniques and habits.

Second, the person who will be doing the same job, but in a new place or setting, will need orientation. The teacher of first-grade children in rural Michigan will require orientation to the different demands of teaching first-grade children in inner-city Detroit. The job is the same at one level of generalization, but very different in a wide array of specific demands.

A third need for orientation relates to the way employers or organizations want to relate to the employees. This is a confusing area because so many motives are all mixed together, and many of these motives are unrealistic. The basic goal of the organization is to encourage loyalty in its employees. Achieving this objective is difficult. The usual approach—the imparting of information—is of no great value in fostering loyalty. Participants are bombarded with information about the company, its history, its admirable founders and heroes, its accomplishments, unique qualities, and its intentions for the future. Heady stuff, serving to divide the trainees into two groups: the impressed and the yawners. The former group includes the gung-ho loyalists-to-be. The latter group may well include those who could help the organization break important new ground; however, they may be tagged as unenthusiastic, resistant, and potential troublemakers. Thus this type of orientation not only fails to produce loyalty, but it can mistake gullibility for potential loyalty and at the same time can stifle creativity.

The needs of the employer are usually more thoroughly reflected in company-sponsored orientation than are needs of the newcomers. Such orientation is concerned more with what the employee should know about the company than with how ready he or she may be to do the job.

PURPOSES OF ORIENTATION TRAINING

The purposes of orientation training are widely misunderstood. Partly because the majority of orientation training programs are provided from within employing organizations, there is a tendency to emphasize matters of company image, policy, and practice. Employees do need to know such things, of course, but overemphasis can squeeze out other concerns. Quite often orientation training consists of little more than a numbing series of lectures with tightly controlled discussions following each.

Several types of orientation programs should be avoided. These programs are closely related to four inadequate but common ways of looking at the purposes of training for intercultural orientation: (1) as providing information, (2) as helping people survive in hostile environments, (3) as enabling people to "fit in" enough to get the job done, and (4) as a sort of socio-emotional sedative to treat symptoms of anxiety. Quite often a poor program emphasizes only one purpose simply because senior management people are not able to see the worth of a more comprehensive training. In other words, the training staff is not always at fault, even if the program is seriously deficient.

GETTING HELP

Getting help with your orientation to overseas living is wise. So often in life people resist getting timely help. Especially for overconfident individualists, it is taken as a sign of weakness to admit needing help. Such pride can be hazardous—as when one puts off seeking medical help for too long. In emotional and relational matters, the smart action is to get to the counselor before the sky falls.

Today there are many ways to get help in the orientation process. In certain fields where there have been long experience and substantial research—such as religious missions and international business—special orientation programs, managed and taught by competent men and women, are available in many parts of the country. Some organizations and companies still provide their own in-house orientation training for people being assigned to overseas duty.

Not long ago, orientation training consisted largely of lectures and booklets loaded with information—all sorts of facts and figures about the country, its people, history, habits, and customs. Today orientation training tends to be concerned less with country-specific facts—they can be learned quickly on the field. Instead the emphasis is on personal, emotional, and relational skills, one's mental state, and the importance of learning to trust. These sort of concerns have been demonstrated to be far more crucial to intercultural competency than are vast stores of facts.

The trends in the emphasis of preparation for missionary services, for example, reveal that little was done beyond passing along facts, figures, and advice until well into the twentieth century. It was assumed that knowing what to expect was the best preparation for the person going overseas.

As the understandings of human variability have increased, so has the awareness that going from one culture to another requires more than knowledge. The idea of *adaptation* has become more important than the idea of adoption. Being among the Pokot in Western Kenya requires information about what they are like and why; but it also requires an approach to accepting them and adapting oneself to their realities. In earlier times the major choice for the sojourner was assumed to be either to hold onto one's own ways, expecting the Pokot to accept those ways, or to try to adopt the ways of the Pokot, thus becoming a sort of phony Pokot.

By mid-century, intercultural orientation tended to be based on adversarial assumptions: survival in the face of stress and hardship was seen to be the issue; practicing and testing one's capability for accommodating interpersonal stress was seen as the way to get ready. Thus all sorts of stressful can-you-hack-it experiences were at the heart of the training process.

The wisdom of that position was in its forward-looking awareness that relationships between and among people are the major source of difficulty for an expatriate. In that period it became fashionable to recognize that tensions among expatriates could be more serious than tensions between expatriates and host-country persons.

Today orientation training has come to be concerned with enabling a person to engage in productive and functional relationships in the different cultural situation.

Four Necessary Outcomes of Orientation

No matter how one gets the needed preparation, four abilities must be developed:

1. The ability to become more independent of external sources of information and problem definition. This ability can be developed through experiences that require independent inquiry and reasoning. The aim is not isolated self-sufficiency but self confidence in one's ability to find and use information.

2. The ability to deal with feelings created by value conflicts. To gain this ability, one must "get in touch" with one's own reactions, biases, and values while at the same time developing a sensitive awareness of the rights of others to see things differently.
3. The ability to make decisions in stressful situations. Learning to think clearly and keep one's wits during difficult moments is a hard skill to learn. Gaining humility along with self-respect and creative problem-solving skills is the most useful combination.
4. The ability to use one's own and others' feelings as information. Close and continued contacts with others provide the best situations in which to learn this. Orientation, therefore, usually includes small-group and interactive dialogue sessions wherein one can learn to handle interpersonal relationships with greater sensitivity and perceptive awareness.

TWO WAYS TO TEACH CULTURE

Two approaches account for most of the deliberate efforts to teach culture. Each has its own particular emphases and uses its own methods. Two rather different assumptions about the desirable and undesirable outcomes are represented. Whether the subject is American Indians or urban Russians, either approach may be used, depending on the teacher and the type of educational program. Even if the subject for each of two training programs is "How to live and work in Saudi Arabia," one program might use one approach and the other program might use the other.

The first approach, along with the associated viewpoints and assumptions, *Paradigm I—the informational approach*, is the classical approach. This approach is well established in its formalized traditions and deeply indebted to classical approaches to schooling.

The other of these approaches, *Paradigm II—the experimental approach*, is both newer and older. It is modern, in that it puts greater emphasis on experience, yet such an emphasis has its roots in antiquity. One of the earliest travelers and movers of family and goods was the patriarch Abraham who, according to the book of Genesis, "sought a city." His behavior and activity as an international sojourner were more of the sort we assume to be valid in Paradigm II. He packed up and went forth. He was very much into experimental learning!

All over the world I have watched the ways children in schools for expatriates are prepared to deal with people of another culture. Usually a combination of the two paradigms is used, but the dominant tendency is toward Paradigm I. Schools tend to reduce all important learning to book-type forms of literature and to rely on teaching models bounded by four walls and marked by clocks.

For me, the most satisfactory situations for helping people become effective learners of culture have been the Michigan State University three-week workshops in Hawaii. Using the human and physical resources of the East-West Center, and, even more important, the whole population of Oahu as a culture-learning laboratory, remarkable development has occurred in a relatively short period of time. The back-and-forth praxis of experience and reflection stimulates the learning. We engage in activities in the field in the afternoons and evenings—deliberately going out in pairs and small groups to make discoveries or to test hypotheses. We talk to people, ask questions, note their questions, try out food, dances, music, make new friends, and visit churches, temples, and shrines—all in order to relate to people. In the seminar room the next morning, we engage in "reflections processing" as a whole group, trying to make sense out of what has been encountered in the previous afternoon. Day after day the learners gain a sense of commitment to the learning process. They are not just acquiring information but are gaining skills which can be carried into future experiences of continued cultural learning.

Through it all, the greatest satisfactions come from discoveries by the learners that there is more about *themselves* that can and should be learned. It is this emphasis which confirms that culture learning, especially when taught in Paradigm II, has significant value in helping people become more humane and competent human beings.

Table 9–1 compares the two modes of teaching for culture learning.

TRENDS IN ORIENTATION TRAINING

Like many other forms of education, orientation training has a history and has undergone change. Tracing the history of the major approaches to training, Gerd Seidel identifies three phases: *information* (1968–71), *training* (1971–74), and *learning* (1974–81). He reflects on what these changes have wrought in our present-day

TABLE 9-1. Two Paradigms of Approach to Teaching for Culture Learning

	The Learners	Preferred Outcomes	Evidences of Orientation	Essential Content

Paradigm I	Interested
	Curious
		Knowledge
		Awareness
			Recall of information
			Sophisticated:
			  suspicious
			  on-guard
				Culture-specific facts
				Familiarity with artifacts

Paradigm II	Committed
	Active
		Coping skills
		Self-understanding
			Seeking encounters
			Trusting
			Accepting
				Active field experiences
				Readings of background/
				  history of things
				  observed
				Contextual discussion

view of the methods and content of orientation programs. He concludes that such programs aim to assist participants in the following ways:

> To attain a practical working knowledge of a particular foreign language
>
> To acquire management and interpersonal skills in an intercultural setting
>
> To achieve a better understanding of their own culture as a basis for increased sensitivity to an understanding of the culture assignment
>
> To accept and to be tolerant of values, beliefs, attitudes, and behavior patterns that might be quite different from their own
>
> To communicate more effectively with persons from other cultures as well as from their own
>
> To develop a more creative and effective approach to problem solving and goal setting by the application of modern management techniques
>
> To acquire the learning skills that will enable the participants to increase their interest in continued learning during the cross-cultural experience, and to provide them with techniques to do so
>
> To reduce problems of adjustment by achieving heightened self-understanding and self-awareness, thus increasing their ability to perform within the requirements of a new cultural environment
>
> To acquire new learning skills that will enable them to become sensitive and to respond appropriately to the subtleties of the new culture.[1]

For many years, natural (and supernatural) selection was assumed to be the basis for intercultural effectiveness. One either had it or didn't have it. It was largely a matter of a "calling." Thus for many missions and international projects there was little or no emphasis on training. A simple assumption reigned: a good spirit and a willingness to "roll with the punches" would see the sojourner through hell or high water.

After World War II, the idea of intensive short-term training for overseas workers became popular. It began with the redeployment of American missionaries and the expansion of U.S. assistance programs and culminated in the early training for the Peace Corps.[2] These training programs were often information-oriented. If one could acquire enough information, it was believed, functioning in a foreign culture would be much easier. Thus Seidel's Phase I can be identified as having its heyday in the late 1960s.

The inadequacy of the informational approach was soon discovered:

. . . The traditional assumption that information-giving will enable a person working in an alien culture to make the necessary adjustments has not proven to be so. On the contrary, too often stereotyping and false expectations result from the transmission of so-called factual information. Such a traditional approach ignores the trainee's own cultural biases, values, behavior patterns, attitudes, expectations, and the problems these might create for him in another culture.[3]

The need for an alternative approach was recognized at the time when the "small-group movement" was at its peak in the early 1970s (Seidel's Phase II). T-groups, sensitivity training, values clarification, and other forms of group-mode amateur psychotherapy were being advocated for virtually every ill of society. Why not for intercultural training? The Peace Corps tried it, the Armed Forces tried it, and, within limits, it worked. At least this training approach worked much better than had the informational approach.

In the euphoria, the need for substantial information was almost ignored. As is so typical in educational change, the pendulum had moved from one extreme to its opposite.

Now we are in a unifying phase (Seidel's Phase III), seeking a balance between information and skills which must be learned through activities.

The emphasis has now shifted from personal awareness of general behavior and attitudes to the self-examination and improvement of specific abilities and skills, such as the accurate perception of others, listening ability, acting on feedback, and so on, and to the analysis of how these variables affect the cross-cultural situation. . . . In addition, attention has been paid to improving the quality and integration of the various parts of the training program. Great efforts were made to create an optimal learning climate for the participants during the training procedure. The approach is now trainee-centered rather than trainer-centered and focuses on problem-solving rather than on the memorizing of facts, although relevant informational content is considered important. However, the focus is more on the process of learning, to prepare the participants for continued learning on the job.[4]

Table 9–2 indicates the shifting emphases in the quest for more effective approaches to intercultural orientation training.

NEW GUIDELINES FOR
INTERCULTURAL ORIENTATION TRAINING

Some people today are suggesting yet a fourth phase in the development of intercultural training, one which may move even further

TABLE 9-2.   Three Phases of Development in Orientation Training Programs

	PHASE I (1968–1971): *Information*	PHASE II (1971–1974): *Training*	PHASE III (1974–): *Learning*
General goal	To prepare participants and their families adequately to live and work in a new cultural environment.	To prepare participants and their families adequately to live and work in a new cultural environment.	To prepare participants and their families adequately to live and work in a new cultural environment.
Content	Area orientation studies about host country; information on project; information on living conditions; administrative details.	Improvement of behavioral skills; emphasis on personal and cultural awareness and "learning how to learn"; emphasis on process of learning rather than content.	Information-giving and skill development; improving special abilities and skills; providing the trainees with tools for analyzing their situation; problem-solving.
Methodology	Information-giving approach; traditional lecture/reading approach; one-way communication.	Variety of "human relations" training techniques; T-groups, sensitivity training; simulation games.	Integration of a variety of learning approaches; participants are creating their own learning, corresponding to their needs and interests; task-oriented.
Assumption	Information transmission of facts is sufficient for the individuals to adapt successfully to the new culture.	Changing of behavior and attitudes is necessary in preparing trainees for an overseas assignment.	Program should offer a variety of cognitive and affective activities, enable the participants to identify optimal ways of learning and give support for, integration.

SOURCE: Adapted with permission of the publisher from Gerd Seidel, "Cross-Cultural Training Procedures: Their Theoretical Framework and Evaluation," in Stephen Bochner, *The Mediating Person: Bridges Between Cultures* (Cambridge, Mass.: Schenkman), 1981, p. 186.

from the technical language of anthropology into an emphasis on contextual philosophy and the processes of *knowing*.

> Because the term *culture* is so difficult to define and because the primary purpose of the sojourner is to accomplish something other than the systematic study of behaviors, beliefs, and mores of another group, the introduction of the term *culture* and perhaps all its attendant terminology becomes cumbersome, confusing, and constricting for all save the technician in the area of anthropology.[5]

This concern is reflected in a series of guidelines intended to undergird an approach to culture learning that is not fixated on terminology and propositions from abstract scholarship but instead is concerned with learning to perceive and interpret experience. Such training would necessarily involve an emphasis on the circumstances in which learners exist at the time of their training rather than attempting to project into a future context.

Eugene Lamoureux suggests three major guidelines for this next phase of the development of orientation training programs:

1. Eliminate all technical terms and concepts which limit or impose themselves upon the particular experience in question. The teacher should be sure that every concept that is introduced clarifies and does not inhibit understanding.

2. Emphasize the relational and interpersonal aspects that are undeniable and inescapable in every human encounter, whether intercultural or other. Constantly remind the learner that such behaviors as good manners, appropriate dress, and signs of deference are of paramount importance when dealing with strangers *anywhere*. A review of the prospective sojourner's current understanding and practices of etiquette would be helpful, for example. Also, a field trip and subsequent lecture-discussions conducted by a qualified "bridge person" (a member of the host culture who can use the sojourner's language with fluency) might drive home more forcefully that the "culture" of a particular group of people does not exist so much in the artifacts, museums, shrines, or parks as it does in the *minds* and *behaviors* of the people of the host country.

3. Some training in what might be termed the "interpretive or hermeneutical" skills of learning through interpersonal situations should be introduced. For example, by means of case studies, videotapes, field experiences or "discovery through interviews," learners could be taught to move toward an open, questioning, and flexible method of inquiry, with a constant moving from object to ground and back until, in the words of Charles Taylor, the

student ". . . arrives at a good explanation, one which makes sense of behavior." This is much to be preferred over the concept-to-judgment and the belief-to-valuation style of approach to culture so common today.[6]

At the most practical level, Lamoureux's advice suggests that the learning of categories and labeling systems, so dear to academic hearts, is not very important. Thus, instead of forcing specific things, people, and events into a scheme drawn up and labeled *before* the encounter, the better way is to free up the observation skills and the motivation to *talk about* experience, interpreting along the way as one's own life history suggests. Through such a process one learns to acknowledge one's own past as the perceptual grid through which the new experience is processed. Of course, that is exactly the way it works *in any case*, but an academic approach to culture may have, in Lamoureux's view, the effect of masking this reality.

ORIENTATION TRAINING:
A Meddlesome List of Problematic Programs

This list of descriptions is offered in the good-humored hope that such programs can be either avoided or substantially improved. Sometimes alert participants can have a constructive influence on an orientation training program in which they are enrolled. If you can see the dangers or dead ends coming, you may be able to help to steer the learning experience around them.

CATEGORY A. PROGRAMS FOR INFORMATION

Programs in this category emphasize the importance of knowing, in the sense of being informed (or having once been informed). Whether or not the information is learned in a context which will make it apparently useful or readily available is not always regarded as a major concern.

A1. The Memorize-Everything-You-Will-Need-to-Know Program

This most common type of orientation program is built on an admirable and often valid assumption: If a person knows enough about what lies ahead, anxiety will be reduced and competency will be increased. This is not always the case; information is important, but it isn't everything. Only rarely is all needed information adequately learned in advance. In aviation training, "ground school" preparation makes sense before getting into the pilot's seat for the first time, but it is no substitute for experience with the real thing. Further, some things just don't lend themselves to classroom learning. Few would suggest a "ground school" for bicycle riding.

A2. *The Osmosis Overload Program*

A longer version of the informational orientation program is based on the widely held view that if a little is good, a whole lot will be better. This program is usually provided in a resource center where an impressive document file and library are available to the trainees. The purpose, of course, is to encourage and facilitate selective reading from this vast collection. It is important that every participant be thoroughly impressed that there is much to learn and plenty of material from which to learn. Going into an intercultural assignment unprepared is unnecessary; just get on top of the literature.

Ah, but there's a rub: The major effect of all this array is to overwhelm and frighten the participant into a premature frustration. Surely no one can handle such an avalanche of information. So what happens? During much of the orientation program the participants sit in a daze within this information tank, talking to each other more than reading, and through it all hoping to pick up some help, possibly through osmosis.

What is needed far more than a rich array of literature is a well-selected set of readings that will respond to the real needs of the learners. Participants will be able to identify some things they really do want to learn; other things will have to be pointed out to them. Learning is not an osmotic process; it demands both active participation and competent guidance.

CATEGORY B. PROGRAMS FOR DEFENSIVE PURPOSES

Programs of this sort are based less on the needs of the trainees than on the needs of the company or organization. An adversarial posture is implied in such programs, because the employee is to be sent out on a sink-or-swim basis; the major purpose of the training is to reduce the liability to the company or organization if the employee should sink.

B1. The We-Told-You-So Weekend

This program is usually short, consisting of several manuals to read, topical lectures to endure, and various company dignitaries to meet. The apparent purpose is to discharge the moral responsibility of the company so that the employee will never be able to say, "But no one ever told me about this."

In many respects the We-Told-You-So Weekend is an informational experience, but with the added threat that from this moment onward, it isn't the company's fault, no matter what happens.

We-Told-You-So Weekend is almost exclusively focused on what the trainee will need to do in order to make the company look good. Personal and family needs are usually touched upon only enough to establish just how much the company is prepared to help with arrangements, costs, and other physical matters. It should be very apparent that an employing organization that presumes to cram an intercultural orientation program into two or three days isn't taking its employees and their needs very seriously. In such an approach there is a kind of cold, clanking rattle: "It's no longer our responsibility—we've told you what you need to know. From here on it's up to you."

B2. The Whatever-You-Do-Don't Program

The major purpose here is to give lots of excellent advice so that people don't get into trouble. The grandfather of all such programs was the originator of that memorable intercultural advice: "Whatever you do, don't drink the water." Though his name is lost, his influence lingers; this type of program is a sort of living memorial. There are still plenty of such programs alive today.

Two problems arise in such a program: knowing what not to do hardly provides an adequate orientation; worse, a person who is full of the what-not-to-do sort of wisdom is likely to become overconfident, putting too much value in what will almost surely be hollow information.

Whatever you do, don't carry your passport on the street. So?
Leave it in your hotel room?

Whatever you do, don't drive your car when there is water over
the road. So? Abandon it?

Any catalog of what-not-to-do will, of course, offer some worthwhile tidbits. Don't touch a Muslim with your left hand. Important
advice: the left hand is not polite! Traditionally, Muslims avoid using the left hand for anything except as a wash-up device for toilet
purposes. Another: if you cross your legs in such a way as to show
the bottom of your shoe, many Asians will see it as a sign of disdain.
So don't do it.

Advice of this sort—"don't do it"—has limited value. Turn it
around to the positive: keep your feet down, preferably on the
ground, and when sitting cross-legged, tuck them in.[7]

There *is* a need for culture-specific warnings about gestures,
body language, verbal expressions, and the like, most of which you
might otherwise never find out until too late. And many of these
warnings will come in the form of negatives. Here are some classics:
Don't say "bloody" to a polite Commonwealth person. Don't make
the "okay" sign; it's obscene in much of the world. Don't point with
a finger. Don't pat a child on the head—unless you're among the
Maasai who not only pat but spit on the child's head to give a special
blessing. Don't sit until invited. Don't eat raw vegetables or un-
peeled fruit. Don't eat inadequately cooked meat. Don't offend
your host by refusing food.

Fine and dandy. But what do you *do*? Notice that after you get
beyond bad words and obscene gestures the really important items
deal with things you'll have to know about in terms of taking some
alternative action. That's what orientation should be concerned
with—what *do* you do?

CATEGORY C. PROGRAMS FOR AGGRESSIVE PURPOSES

Putting orientation into harness for the forward movement of the
company and its purposes makes a refreshing contrast. In these programs the purposes of orientation are made to serve the employee
just as the employee is expected to serve the company or organization. Although such programs can be manipulative, they generally
are straightforward, with well-stated objectives and a reasonable
measure of respect for the needs of the trainee, so long as those needs
can be met in ways that are good for the company.

What is apt to be lacking is a matching respect for the "target people" and their culture. The fact that the people of the host country are "different" is assumed to be regrettable but tolerable.

C1. *Pitching Practice*

In this program one learns how to do the company thing in the "foreign" context. The purpose is to provide an acquaintance with the altered rules of the game in the particular assignment overseas. The problem for the expatriate is seen as a matter of adjusting this and that, even as a good coach must help the pitcher get back in shape at the beginning of the season. For salespersons, manufacturers' representatives, as well as social welfare and missionary folks who see themselves as "change agents," this means getting the pitch straight—or at least concealing the curve balls. What pitch works best with these people? How can we get them to buy into our thing? (It will "help" them, of course.)

At one level, these questions are refreshingly honest and open— no beating around the bush. No need to be something we aren't, no reason for letting "their ways" become our ways. The issue is how to get our message across; and, of course, that requires a bit of understanding of their viewpoint and values. But there's no use overdoing it. After all, we won't be there forever. Let's get just enough practice with our pitch that we can win the game and get on to the next.

Is there another level? Unfortunately, no. Pitching Practice is limited to the bull pen.

C2. *Chameleon Camp*

Hardship and survival skills have been part of military training since the Romans—and before. The logic of Chameleon Camp is reasonable enough: People have to learn to fit in; it isn't enough to talk about it—you have to do it. So far, so good. The overt purpose of orientation training programs of this sort is to develop experientially the skills of "fitting in." The underlying purpose, though, is much the same as in Pitching Practice: We have our agenda and we need the skills to fulfill it among people who are "different."

The skills of "fitting in" present a moral dilemma: Should one attempt to appear to be what one isn't? Isn't the very process of

changing one's appearance, habits, and communicative style a matter of subterfuge? What are the justifications?

The answer given at Chameleon Camp is the standard alibi for
intercultural contacts by cultural aggressors: "They will be better
off because we have helped them (or told them, or whatever)."
Many people who are otherwise intelligent and highly moral will go
through Chameleon Camp without addressing the question, "Why
are we doing it?" In Chameleon Camp the emphasis is on the price
we must pay to get the job done, the adjustments *we* must make,
and the efforts *we* must put forth. There is something about effort—
especially sweaty exertion—that masquerades as moral worth. We
are putting ourselves out a whole lot—isn't that enough? Why do
you ask about *them*? After all, it's *us* we have to think about. We are
here to improve our fitness. Then *we* will go help *them*.

Help them in what way? That's the moral question. The rest is
all technology.

Chameleons change color to fit in. They fit in to be less noticed
by their predators—and by their prey.

Orientation for intercultural competency deserves better than
Chameleon Camp.

CATEGORY D. PROGRAMS FOR NAIVE PURPOSES

Some programs appear to have no purpose at all. Perhaps they
don't, at least at the explicit level of intended outcomes. They seem
more to be a sort of induction ceremony, more ideological than tac-
tical.

The purposes that can be inferred and deduced from what actually goes on are naive. Thus the criticism is directed toward the underlying assumptions rather than toward the methodology or personnel.

D1. The Nothing-to-It Program

Like a revival meeting or a cheerleaders' contest, this sort of program goes right for the emotions. The tactics are to puff up the
trainees in terms of importance of the job to be done, the honor of
being selected, and the invisible but oh-so-readily-available "inner
strength." Thus what happens is often quite hollow—a great deal of
drummed up enthusiasm but not much development of skills.

Such a program is often a waste of time. No doubt an emotional commitment and a sense of self-confidence are very important, but if these are built on anything less than a solid footing in reality, they will be quickly vaporized in the heat of the stress that lies ahead for the expatriate.

The message seems to be, "There is really nothing to it; after all, if you can make it in the United States, you can make it overseas—all it takes is a little extra self-confidence and a strong determination." The best response is to laugh out loud. If the person telling you these things is a humorist, your laughter will provide a fitting reward. If not, the person is a fool and deserves your laughter even more.

D2. *The Staying-Out-of-It Program*

A carry-over of the ideology of missionary activity in an earlier era, staying out of controversy has a great deal of appeal today. Especially among those who are overwhelmed by the conflicting viewpoints on the United States' involvement in world affairs, this new revival of the "know-nothing" stance on political issues has great appeal. Now and then one runs across an orientation program—especially for missionaries or for medical personnel on relief or refugee support assignments—in which the major theme is something like the following: "Remain neutral; do not get involved in political matters. You will be accepted and respected by both sides because you are neutral."

Great idea. A bit dated, of course, but that alone doesn't make it wrong. What's bad is that it doesn't take into account today's complex world of political tensions and challenged authority structures. Those pretty notions about neutrality can get a person into a lot of difficulty. It's better to come to grips openly with the fact that the presence of *every expatriate has a political meaning*. The very fact that the host-country government will grant visas to Americans to do certain types of work is a political statement.

A government may recognize and commemorate on its postage stamps the long history of a missionary organization in its country. Such an "honor" may be seen naively as "acceptance." But it can also be the sure kiss of death for that mission when that government is overthrown. At the individual level, sojourners today are kidnapped and killed. It is not wise to believe that a neutral strance is an adequate protection.

The advice to avoid overt political statements and politically-oriented commentary on local and larger issues still holds true. The warning against encouraging (or discouraging) host-country friends to take political stands still holds. Indeed, the most reprehensible act of an outsider is to encourage people of a country to get themselves killed. The second most reprehensible act is to dissuade such people from making statements and taking stands on issues of justice according to their sense of moral honor.

Take it from one who has lost good friends in the undeclared wars of Latin America, the fact that a threatened person has maintained contact and identity with you, an American, has a political meaning—for you and for that person. If your friend should be "made to disappear," you will go through life wondering about the degree to which your friendship played a part. And you may sometime come to wonder if you are next.

Don't be misled, "Staying-Out-of-It" is often thinly disguised amorality.

BEFORE TACO BELL

What *should* be built into a good orientation program? Practical experience, for one thing, along with plenty of opportunities to discuss its meaning and to seek insights. These are the major ingredients. How they are arranged depends on the creativity of the program planners and the responsiveness of the learners.

Activity-based orientation training can be enjoyable. Certain sorts of experiences work best if you encounter them as a group and then come away together to discuss them.

Because Michigan is the winter home for many Mexican-American agricultural laborers who finish the migrant-year cycle in Michigan orchards, Mexican restaurants have been common here for twenty-five years or more. For a long time they weren't popular except among the Chicanos. Until the last decade's rash of new franchises of the pseudo-Mexican cuisine, Mexican food was anything but stylish. Before they became popular we included a noontime Mexican meal in the less elegant part of the city as a regular feature of one of our orientation programs. It seemed to open the participants' eyes a little wider. For many a young person headed overseas, this was the first encounter with a "foreign" menu, waitress, and decor.

Our standing request was that the waitresses should speak only Spanish and offer only the Spanish menu. This was no simple "taco stand"; the food was very unfamiliar and the names even less reassuring. Coping with it was, for most of our monolingual trainees, an experience very much like what they would encounter in their first days overseas.

For some groups it clicked. They got into the spirit of it, loosened up, and worked together to figure things out. Through nonverbal communication—mostly an on-the-spot re-invention of childhood sign language—they managed to decipher the menu and order. They discovered that coping can be fun—especially if it is a group venture. But now and then we would spot a withdrawn, panicky paleface needing help. And we would unobtrusively signal a nearby reveler to "adopt" this poor soul.

In those days before Taco Bell arrived, even a Mexican restaurant could induce culture shock. But more important, it provided an appropriate field experience which could become substance for the discussions in our orientation seminars.

Good orientation programs also include substantial encounters with up-to-date facts and figures. Insight without data can be nonsense.

COUNTRY-SPECIFIC INFORMATION

Thorough orientation requires two kinds of preparation: (1) gaining the outlook and skills that will be needed regardless of one's particular destination overseas and (2) becoming informed about the specific country and people. The emphasis here on the first set of learnings should not be interpreted as minimizing the importance of current and accurate information about the particular country. Being prepared includes a responsible background of country-specific knowledge.

The assumption that country-specific information is the most important concern in preparation is a common mistake. Three strong reasons argue against it. First, there are plenty of cross-cultural skills that will be of use regardless of the characteristics of the particular country for which one is preparing. It is more feasible to learn how to conduct oneself as an effective foreigner than to prepare to become a knowledgeable "insider." Second, an emphasis on country-specific data could easily overwhelm the learner or, at best, unintentionally lead to the notion that the most important concern in preparation for overseas living is the acquiring of a large body of facts. What is most important is not how much you know before you get there but how well-prepared you are to learn *after* you arrive. Third, even if it were possible to collect in advance everything one might ever want to read or hear about a country and its people, no one has the time to absorb it, short of spending a lifetime in the library!

One's expanded understanding of the process of culture learning should be followed up by a self-initiated search for useful country-specific information. Excellent materials are available on all major countries and regions and even on most of the smaller countries. The cost of a basic collection will range from $35 to $60, and it will be well worth the expense and the time to read and study.[8] In any case, this collection and its systematic study should be begun during preparation and continued faithfully during the entire sojourn overseas.

A SAMPLE PROGRAM

How best to put all of this together has been the challenge for professionals in the intercultural training field. Paul Pedersen and Richard Brislin surveyed and evaluated many programs. Their recommendations are represented by the following sketch of one well-documented ten-week orientation program.

1. The trainees were encouraged to participate actively in the planning of their experiences. In a sense, there was no program except as they took part in determining what was needed in order to reach the objectives they had identified.
2. Formal classroom lectures were minimal: small-group interaction and informal interaction were the major modes of instruction.
3. The various elements of the program were integrated rather than compartmentalized.
4. The program was based on *experiences*. Doing things together and individually were seen as the learning experiences: organizing and operating cooperatives, raising chickens and pigs, planting and tending gardens, and learning needed information through inquiry projects.

5. <u>Trainees with useful skills were urged to teach them to others.</u>

6. Emphasis was placed on awareness of the training environment and how the trainees were reacting to it and to one another. Weekly small-group evaluation sessions helped to increase these awarenesses and leadership of the training groups remained fairly constant throughout the program.[9]

DO-IT-YOURSELF ORIENTATION

Even for the person engaged in self-directed preparation with little or no help from a formal orientation program, there are a number of actions to be taken:

1. Work as never before on <u>collecting information.</u> Carefully think through the implications for your own planning and action. Try to look ahead, imagining, for example: "Because such-and-such is the case in this country, I will need to be ready, able, and willing to do this-or-that."

2. <u>Decide now what you are going to think about yourself and about others when you find your ideas and values distinctly in the minority.</u> Try to anticipate possible interferences with your work which could be caused by value conflicts. Write down your most serious concerns about the conflicts you might run into. For each of these make a plan of action: What could *I* do to reduce the conflict or the resulting tension?

3. <u>Get yourself ready for delays</u> and a slower pace of life with <u>fewer accomplishments.</u> Start work now to stem the tide of compulsiveness, if that is a problem for you. One practical exercise is to write out some "alibis" you could send home to explain delays and disappointments. Try to write these in such a way as to avoid putting blame on yourself or on your colleagues in the field—both fellow Americans and host-nation persons. To live with a slower pace, you need to learn to be gracious, not peevish, about it.

4. Begin now a vigorous campaign to see other people's points of view and sense their feelings. In other words, try to become sensitive enough to the feelings of others that you can estimate their probable or apparent response to *you* in the context of your daily or periodic encounters.

These four undertakings should put you well on your way to attaining the competencies you will need overseas—among your fellow Americans and those of other backgrounds.

FOCUS FOR SELF-EVALUATION

In Chapter 9 you have been given a look at what orientation is and how it can be gained or improved.

Reflection

What would I have to do to make an orientation training experience worthwhile? _____

_____

_____

Review

1. What are the major features of a good orientation training program? __

   _____

   _____

2. What is the major hazard in negative advice? _____

   _____

   _____

3. What is meant by getting help? When is advice better than discovery? _

   _____

   _____

Commitment

With reference to the following important matters, I intend to take these steps to be the sort of person overseas who will

1. *Trust.* _____

   _____

2. *Inquire.* _____

_____

3. *Learn.* _____

_____

10

The Humanitarians
Those Who Go to Help

EACH SOJOURNER has some reason for being in the "foreign" country. Business people are there to make a buck. Government people are there to assure the maintenance of official and procedural relationships. Missionaries are there to "be a witness" or, in plainer terms, to make converts. Relief and humanitarian workers are there "to help," especially in times and situations of privation and hardship—and they want to feel that their help makes a difference.

Not only must the well-oriented expatriate be comfortable with her or his own reason for being there; knowing the way others perceive and value one's mission is also important. In a world marked by international and intercultural tension, one must understand the political effects and meanings of one's work in the eyes of others. Clarifying one's own values and recognizing one's motives for entering a particular line of service is a good place to begin. It is not enough to take for granted that a kindly act and an "honest" motive will lead to understanding and appreciation. The outsider has one agenda; those to whom he or she relates in the host country may have a different agenda.

THE LOGIC OF KINDNESS

Much of the tension between people can be traced to the relationships that have resulted from their acts of giving or receiving. The tendency is to assume that if one's motives are pure and if the act is kind in the eyes of the giver, then the results will be good. Not always so!

It is easy enough to think of situations in life wherein people are hurt by acts of pure but naive kindness: the blind man helped across a street he didn't want to cross, presugared tea for a diabetic guest, and hosing the dust off a neighbor's car when its windows are open. "Oh, but I thought you would like that!" It is half an apology, half a judgment. Somehow the fault must be transferred to the receiver; somehow the "kind act" must be justified. Beware: there are kind acts that cannot be justified. No act is an end in itself. The relationship fostered by the act is every bit as important.

Four motives account for most acts of kindness. On the basis of one or more of these motives and the consequent thought processes, the giver determines his or her actions toward the receiver.

1. The Golden Rule

Doing to others what one would want done toward oneself demands more than asking, "What would *I* want?" The difficult part is *empathy*. "What would I want *if* I were in the other person's situation?" Since it is very difficult to *feel* from someone else's viewpoint, the Golden Rule tends to become a simple alibi for making judgments on a self-pleasing basis. It isn't enough to assume that the receiver would want something the same way in which the giver wants it or wants to do it.

2. Sharing from Abundance

Whatever one has in oversupply is what can or should be given. This logic is a good motivator, since the "embarrassment of riches" often points to some feasible sorts of sharing. But it can be absurd. Consider the massive stupidity of sharing from our nation's number one oversupply: nuclear armaments—or military resources in general. And our wheat surplus is useless as a tool of famine relief in rice-eating Asia.

Yet there are other forms of our abundance which we seem unwilling to share. Church people, for example, are notoriously unwilling to give funds to missions to hire host-country persons. Instead, even larger amounts are given to hire, transport, support, and retire Americans who are willing to take their skills overseas. Especially in the case of technical skills already available among national persons, this practice is a major factor in mission inflexibility and high costs.

We should *offer* from our abundance but only *give* that which the receiver sees as valuable. Down with the "missionary barrel" and the legendary used tea bags! And a resounding "bah, humbug!" to "mutual assistance" contracts that demand markets for American overproduction as the price for needed items of aid.

3. *Human Compassion*

When we become aware of "substandard" conditions in which other people are living, an emotionally loaded motive takes over. Whether it is out of a sense of embarrassment, a feeling of guilt, or simply a compassionate concern, we seek ways to make the other people's condition more like ours. The major problem is in the way we assess needs for others. What is *really* substandard and what isn't? From anyone's viewpoint, something in every other person's condition is substandard. The happy family man sees the bachelor as living in substandard conditions. The servant may see the cold and friendless life of the rich master as substandard.

On the intercultural basis, human compassion can lead to faulty acts of kindness. Because of profoundly different views of the world, outlooks on life, and value systems in general, intercultural assessment of need is very difficult. Both secular aid agencies and religious missions fall into this trap. Many stories are told of frontal attacks on polygamy "to improve the substandard conditions of women," on burial practices "to conserve farmland," and dietary change to include some largely unavailable or unpalatable source of protein. Sometimes earthquake-blighted Indians have to wait patiently while Americans and Europeans make their houses and villages "earthquake-proof"—never mind that no one can tolerate the temperature extremes created by the lovely new corrugated metal roofs.

It isn't easy to keep compassion in line with logical reason. We tend to see how life might be made better in our own terms—more comfortable, free from pain, hunger, and disease—but those are *our* comforts, *our* pains, *our* hungers, and diseases. We can help people see the possibilities of change and of alternatives; they must make their own decisions about what conditions they want to change, in what direction, and with what resources.

4. Life Is at Stake

Because the human family shares a viewpoint about the value of life itself, we act most compulsively and least respectfully where we see people in grave difficulty. It is too easy to *assume* agreement about what to do about life-at-stake issues. When we act on our own view of how best to perform a rescue, we are least likely to heed advice and warnings. Whether it is flying "relief supplies" to the starving children of Nigeria during the Biafran uprising—with or without permission—or well-drilling projects in the Sahel, we must get on with it! Saving lives seems, for most of us, to have its own justification.

EVALUATION OF ACTS OF KINDNESS

Evaluating an act of kindness should take account of the particular logic underlying the act. For example, if the "Golden Rule" motive is evident, the major issue to be examined is the degree of empathy. If it is the "sharing from abundance" motive, the major issue is the appropriateness of the abundant commodity. In the "human compassion" motive, the major issue is whether or not the viewpoint of those who are being "helped" is allowed to shape the means used to act out the compassion.

The "life is at stake" motive presents some special problems. Simultaneously it is both rational and emotional. Evaluation is particularly difficult. Religious motivations, especially the concerns to save the lost, usually adopt this logic; objective evaluations of such efforts are rare. The need for salvation—whether spiritual or physical—seems to be adequate justification. And since no one likes to affix a monetary worth to a life or a soul, no matter what the costs, the efforts are always deemed worthwhile—at least by the outsiders.

All acts of kindness, no matter what the motive, need to be put to the test of relationship-building; but the saving of lives is especially hard to submit to this test. Consider the grateful-for-life reaction of the rescued nonswimmer. Profound gratitude causes the

blinded, burned, and smoke-saturated victim to overlook the wet
and harsh over-the-shoulder lugging by a firefighter. The medical
literature has often reported the strange psychological dependency
and childlike adoration of the patient for the surgeon. Acts of rescue
seem to be self-justifying and not to require further evaluation. Perhaps so; but what if the one who has been rescued is, because of a
new dependency relationship, hindered from normal development
as an interdependent human being? Improbable? Consider the matter of the forms of "relief" that cause profound dependency. Do not
even our own national and state patchwork programs of welfare
and unemployment compensation in some cases suppress the normal
tendencies toward fulfillment and social contribution? It is one
thing to try to help people, but when one inadvertently prevents or
reduces their capability to get back on their own feet, one may not
really be helping.

A HUMANE RELATIONSHIP

The best guidelines for defining purposes and carrying out joint activity across cultural lines are based on the concept of reciprocity.
The give-and-take of reciprocity assumes that a humane relationship is one in which both or all partners give and receive. If the parties to such an arrangement are able to be open and honest about
what they expect to *gain* and what they want to feel good about, the
quality of giving increases substantially.

Here is a set of ten guidelines for reciprocal relationships:

1. Both partners must want to work together.
2. Both partners must identify and profess their own motives.
3. Both partners must honestly confess their own needs and
   vulnerabilities.
4. Both partners must respect and share their resources.
5. Each partner must put concern for the other above self-con-
   cern.
6. Each partner must carefully avoid making the other dependent.
7. Both partners must respect each other's capability as a
   helper.
8. Each partner must be willing to be helped.

9. Each partner must value the worth of community effort above the worth of individual effort.
10. Each partner must experience growth through giving while receiving.

RELIGIOUS MOTIVES

The special problems of intercultural religious motives and purposes require special attention. Since so many people in overseas assignments have religious motives as primary or secondary reasons for being overseas, it seems reasonable to address these matters in their own terms.

The matter of religious values affects all of us, whether we are aware of it or not. Americans and people from certain European countries seem more uneasy about religious matters than is typical of most of the world's peoples. In most of the world, religion is taken for granted. But where religions clash, religious values affect history.

Religious tolerance is just as much a matter of intercultural concern as is any other matter of values. The religious sojourner, therefore, will need to be especially thoughtful of the ways in which religious activities and statements serve to build or to destroy trust. In general, it can be said that integrity, openness, sincerity, and patience are the virtues that make one's religious convictions seem worthy of respect. Conversely, blatancy, bigotry, harshness, or even secretiveness can work against one's hopes to share religious beliefs across cultural lines.

Above all, the intercultural sharing of religious ideas, if the ideas are to be taken seriously, must take place within a relationship of trust. As an outsider, one has even more to overcome than among one's own people. Being an American does not make for religious credibility.

Then, too, there is the crucial matter of being able to act consistently with one's professed values and beliefs. Nothing damages the credibility of a witness so much as inconsistency. Although religion is concerned with spiritual matters, religious people cannot be oblivious to physical and social aspects of human consciousness and experience. In fact, concern about spiritual matters usually becomes more evident as one shows that other matters of need are also important. The spiritual essence at the core of humanness exists within wholeness that includes intellectual, social, emotional, moral, and physical aspects.

RESPECT IS TWO-WAY

If there is anything a religious person likes to see respected, it is his or her religious beliefs and symbols. It is unfitting for such a person to show any less respect for someone else's religion. Tearing down another religion in order to make one's own stand taller is not only futile but, as history shows, it is counterproductive.

The tendency to belittle a different religion is, in part, rooted in one's view of truth. The assumed right to attack falsehood is transferred into the realm of religion and thus it becomes fair game to disparage any other grasp of truth. The result is sure to be more offensive than persuasive. Those whose view of their own mission is to persuade others should be especially aware that respect must work both ways.

If one's own faith rests on shaky premises or if one's convictions have only subjective and experiential groundings, someone else's convictions and faith may be a directly competing threat. In such a case, one's impulse is to argue or to cover the ears and close the eyes. But watch out: closed and resistive convictions are hard to share!

If, on the other hand, one's faith is grounded in objective substance, it will stand up well to contrast and conflicts. There will be little need to avoid discourse and dialogue. It follows, then, that a religious position that is open and hospitable will have the greatest probability of being persuasive.

Americans and Europeans are familiar with the idea that a person can have no religious beliefs. In most of the world, this idea is seen as nonsense. Religion, in the sense of some fairly specific way to account for and relate to the spirit world, is as much a part of life as is physical health. *Health* and *religion*, then, are comparable abstractions. For most of the world's population, arguing that a person is able to ignore religious concerns is like arguing that one can escape health concerns. No way.

The ceremonial aspects of any religion seem like superstitious and meaningless rituals to outsiders. Protestants, especially those from the less liturgical traditions, often disdain the incense and "idols" of Catholicism (or even those of the Episcopalians). Such "excesses" are seen as fair game for criticism. But the practice of closing the eyes while praying, a Protestant custom, is no less a ritual act.

Christians are often put off by the repetitions and the background noises of Buddhist worship. When does the service start? Why don't they all get together and sit down? They call this worship? I've seen more worship at the county fair! And so it goes.

That which is different is assumed to be inferior. That which is inferior is, of course, wrong. To replace the inferior with the better way is why we're here; whether it is diet, health care, educational methods, or especially religion. If this train of thought is allowed to control one's behavior, the chances for positive influence are seriously reduced.

Respect has to spring from a heart of concern and compassion for the integrity of human beings. At no point can a spirit of humble thankfulness become a club with which to hurt others. Even one's enemies are to be loved, not just tolerated. Further, if one's life is going to have any sort of positive impact on others, it is necessary to get close enough to them and to the ideas that are important to them in order to be able to build bridges of trust and relationship. Zeal alone provides no grounds for mutual respect.

PAUL: A MISSIONARY AS BRIDGE BUILDER

The Apostle Paul is often recommended as a "model missionary." His travels and ministries, as reported in the New Testament's *Acts of the Apostles* and through his own thirteen or fourteen preserved letters, constitute a remarkable body of early intercultural experience. Educated in the best of both the Hebrew and the Hellenistic traditional forms, Paul was remarkably well versed in matters of culture and, particularly, the influence of culture on religion. His sensitive awareness is evident in dozens of encounters, and is nowhere more convincing than in his sermon and dialogues on the Areopagus.

No place were erudite scholarship and academic debate more respected. Nowhere on earth, at the time, was debate for the sake of debate more allowable than on the little peak called Areopagus in the heart of Athens, the cultural center of the Greek and Roman civilizations.

If there was ever a place where you could dump your agenda all over other people, this was it. Paul could have impressed people as a scholar—he had the credentials and the competencies—or he could have based his appeal on the issue of truth itself—what it is and how one knows it. The Greek debaters and scholarly sages would have loved that. They might have tried to disprove his contentions and might have challenged his sources, but at least they would have listened.

Paul may have felt exactly these motivations and concerns. Surely his commitment to a monotheistic view of the universe (from his Jewish and his Christian values) was offended by the proliferation of gods, memorials to gods, and altars of all sorts that cluttered the walkways up that hillside.

Whatever his feelings at the time, his respect for people and his skills as a bridge builder came to the fore. Instead of criticizing and attacking, he started with a conciliatory and gentle observation, carefully crafted to build an honest linkage based on a shared value: "Men of Athens," Paul declared, "I see in every way that you are very religious. As I walked through your city and looked at the place where you worship, I found also an altar on which is written, 'To the Unknown God'."[1]

Paul then proceeded to invite his Athenian audience to become acquainted with this unknown god—"The God who made the world and everything in it. . . ." He raised a question about their idols, but even this was less a matter of abrupt challenge than it was a rational and unemotional question for them to ponder. The premise of the question even served to wrap a warm embrace around his Athenian hearers, putting himself into a "we" relationship with them. "Since we are God's offspring, we should not suppose that God's nature is anything like an image of gold or silver or stone, shaped by the art and skill of man." Paul then built on this base of common ground a straightforward claim for the Gospel—he was a respectful builder of bridges, but he was not trying to deceive or manipulate:

> God has overlooked the times when people did not know, but now he commands all people everywhere to turn away from their evil ways. For he has fixed a day in which he will judge the whole world with justice, by means of a man he has chosen. He has given proof of this to everyone by raising that man from death![2]

Among these learned and experienced religious debaters of Athens, the mention of resurrection caused some to laugh, but others said, "We want to hear you speak about this again." To discover that even a handful of skeptical Athenians were willing to come back for more is startling. It attests to the care and concern that Paul showed; he found a common ground and built a bridge, and then he passed his message—with respect, allowing people the freedom to walk away and to come back for another conversation if they wished.

This dramatic illustration from one of the earliest Christian missionaries provides a commendable example for all missionaries today. It is neither necessary nor wise to approach people in an aggressive or offensive manner; it is far better to build a bridge of communication through one or another common ground. You have to know what is on *their* agenda if you are going to relate yours to theirs.

The lesson of patience also should be noted: Instant decisions are rare indeed. People aren't easily convinced on matters that fundamentally change the way they look at life. With the Apostle Paul, be thankful for the few who will come back later to talk again.

THE SCOPE OF RELIGION

In the nineteenth century, certainly, religious motives included concern for the physical and social needs of people—especially people who were hurting because of calamity or deprivation. This concern has been revived across almost all of organized religion since World War II. Many of the missionary activities of the so-called modern missionary movement[3] have been noted for the schools, hospitals, literacy, and other humanitarian services that have accompanied the more rudimentary quest for converts.

The worth of people and the integrity of their society are always at issue when a missionary's motive is simply to change people's opinions about deity or the hereafter. This sort of small vision is more a caricature of mission activity than it is a reality. In general, it has been religious missionaries far more than other expatriates or conquesting entrepreneurs who have taken an interest in the welfare of people and devoted themselves to the upgrading of the quality of life. For some missionaries these practical matters are simply a logical consequence of a spiritual transformation; for others, they are seen as a balanced accompaniment of a spiritual concern—in the sense that the emphasis on spiritual matters can only be communicated with meaning and integrity if it is within the context of the whole condition and welfare of the person: physically, socially, intellectually, emotionally, and morally.

The tendency of missionaries to let themselves be overwhelmed with the practical and so-called nonspiritual matters has led to dissension. Those who see a legitimate concern for the social and physical needs of people can find themselves in sharp conflict with those who believe that any diversion from the seeking of spiritual objectives is a threat to the integrity of a religious mission. Mission organizations and individual missionaries have tended to be pulled toward one extreme or the other on this issue. In general, the evangelicalism of the nineteenth century accepted the "whole person" perspective and embraced all sorts of institution building and social action as a legitimate part of the missionary enterprise; but the coming of fundamentalism, a twentieth-century innovation within Christianity, caused a long period of withdrawal from social and humanitarian causes in the interests of a more doctrinaire approach to the Gospel. In this latter view, the Gospel is seen as a propositional position about the person and work of Jesus Christ; the crucial issue is acceptance or rejection of this position—more specifically, of a specific body of statements represented in a creed.[4] The social consequences of conversion are expected to affect one's moral and physical approach to one's culture. But to accompany the appeal for spiritual conversion with this or that social activity is to be avoided because it might weaken or divert attention from the main issue of the Gospel: accepting Jesus Christ as one's personal savior.

THE NEW HUMANITARIANS

After decades of resistance to anything that smacks of social action, even conservative sectors of Christianity are today in the forefront of world-wide relief and development activity. After more than a half-century of hair-splitting about how much of what sort of social action is appropriate, Christians are coming together around the practical implications of the Gospel. Thus, the expansion of relief and development organizations and the increased support of humanitarian aspects of "mission" work have substantially increased the number of Americans in that sort of work overseas.

For conservative Christians the major question has been, "What will you do with Jesus?" The centerpiece of their theology has been the redemptive acts of God in the person and work of Jesus Christ. Thus the prime focus has been on the cross and the Resurrection—

"for there is no other name under heaven given among men by which we must be saved."⁵ For conservatives, the emphasis has been salvation by faith in the name of the Lord Jesus Christ. None of this has changed. The increase in humanitarian activity is not a shift as much as it is an addition—many would say that it is a return to the approach of earlier Christianity. George Marsden has described how American Christianity was split over the issue of social reform as a reaction to the influence of radical European theology in the early twentieth century.⁶ By subordinating the motives of compassion to an anxious isolationism and preference for verbal debate, much of the initiative and vision was lost for a time.

Christians today are moving out of the "age of anxiety" into a concern for the broader meaning of the Gospel. Today's consciousness of the Gospel includes a fundamental concern for the whole condition.

THE "FAVORABLE YEAR OF THE LORD"

Substantial principles underly the renewal of concern for physical relief and social justice. When John the Baptist sought words to express what God was going to do through the Messiah, he reached his arms wide and embraced both judgment and transformation.⁷ He identified the Messiah with fulfillment of the long-term promises of the Scriptures as well as with a then-and-there social reform.⁸

In no way were John's practical references to justice and social reform set aside by Jesus Himself. In what must surely rate as one of the half-dozen most dramatic incidents in Scripture, Jesus revealed His true identity in His home town, Nazareth, by reading from Isaiah (61:1–2):

> *The Spirit of the Lord is upon me.*
> *Because He anointed me to preach the Gospel*
>   *to the poor.*
> *He has sent me to proclaim release to the*
>   *captive,*
> *And recovery of sight to the blind.*
> *To set free those who are downtrodden,*
> *To proclaim the favorable year of the Lord.*

With the curious attention of the whole community on Him, He closed the scroll, handed it to the synagogue attendant, deliberately sat down—back among them, no longer standing above—and said, "Today this Scripture has been fulfilled. . . ."[9]

People today are becoming more conscious that Jesus said, "*Today*" and "has *been* fulfilled." Today's world is *in* the fulfillment. It is ongoing—not someday, somehow, but here and now.

Evangelicals have never lacked respect for the Old Testament, but they have been weakened by internal schisms and debates over such issues as the techniques used to create the world and the refining of predictive timetables for the "last days." As a result, the emphases on social justice and the needs of the poor have been somewhat neglected. The Biblical references to the "favorable year of the Lord" have never meant anything other than the requirement for periodic social reform including, indeed, *centering on* redistribution of wealth to redress the evils that occur when the rich get richer and the poor get poorer. Where, even today, is the evangelical church that preaches this "favorable year of the Lord" with the same fervor that it preaches the Second Coming of Christ?

Some sectors of evangelical Christianity may still have difficulty taking seriously the social implications of the Gospel of Jesus Christ. Nevertheless the emphasis is shifting in the direction of Jesus' own example of humane and healing concern for people.

THE TERMINOLOGY OF INTERNATIONAL ASSISTANCE

Although the presence of people from a strong nation carrying out service and administrative roles in a weaker nation is as old as recorded history, the twentieth century has added much to the practice and the terminology. Because in these recent decades the practice of overt colonialism has come to its final hours—even prosperous Hong Kong reverts to China in 1994—the general feeling is that in terms of relationships between "have" and "have-not" nations, it's a new ball game.

The new ball game has a very different set of rules and a whole new vocabulary. Going, going, gone are the colonial governors, the kings' emissaries, and the centers of administrative power in far-off colonial offices. London, Paris, the Hague, Brussels, Lisbon, Madrid, Rome, and Berlin no longer call the shots. Certainly the economic manipulations of such power centers as Wall Street and Houston, along with London, Tokyo, Paris, Zurich, and others of the world's money markets have an enormous influence on what happens in *all* nations, but the political climate is postcolonial.

The words used to describe the status of nations constitute a vital vocabulary for the expatriate. One doesn't say "weak nation, strong nation" out loud; the sensitivities and pride of the postcolonial peoples are such that sometimes they bristle at even such a useful term as *developing nations* or increasingly, at the time-honored standard of American economists and assistance specialists, <u>less-developed countries.</u>

This latter term, LDC for short, is assumed by many to be simply based on evident fact: a nation is either more developed, as in the Western industrial nations, or less developed, as in Central America, most of Africa, and much of Asia. The problem, however, rises out of two complaints: first, the matter of comparative standards—can you really divide the world that neatly? How should Turkey be classified? Mexico? Argentina? Malaysia? What about that great conundrum, the People's Republic of China? What measures can be applied to determine the extent of dependency of a *less-developed country*?

The second problem is even more profound because it is qualitative, not quantitative: Who is to say what constitutes development? The economists point to statistical indicators of productivity, per capita income, and other averages and ranges. Philosophers, on the other hand, point to indicators of the quality of life—far more subjective and elusive matters but, for many of us, more vital and to the point.

Is a happy peasant less developed because his family has no television receiver? Any reasonable person would say, "Of course not!" <u>Happiness, peace, sufficiency, and honor are far more important than physical things.</u> This argument is not very debatable. But it conceals an important issue: To some extent, there are *things* that figure into the formula by which the quality of life is defined. For example, sufficiency of food is a measure of the quality of life. If a nation is overpopulated or underdeveloped in its agricultural, food processing, and food distribution systems, then quality of life is adversely affected. If a nation is profoundly dependent on external resources for maintenance and survival, the very dignity of its citizenship suffers. In such cases people know they can't control their own destiny; it is in the hands of international cartels and banking consortia.

Surely *less-developed country* is a useful term, but it is becoming less acceptable because of its emotional connotations and its threat to people's collective pride.

The term *emerging nation* seems to be easier for people in such

countries to accept, as long as the term doesn't get confused with
new nation. People in a postcolonial nation are quick to remind outsiders that their nation is not *new* so much as recently freed from the
external powers that interrupted their ancient nationhood. Especially in Africa, this argument doesn't hold up well against historical evidence, but since it is an emotional debate, facts are not likely
to settle it.[10]

HAVES AND HAVE-NOTS

Economics is more important than political ideology. To some extent, ideology arises from economic conditions; but issues of wealth
and poverty, power and weakness are based in ownership and control of land and resources. The crucial issues in Central America, for
example, have to do with power—the power that arises out of privileged land ownership and the resultant servitude of the poor. Some
people persist in seeing international tensions in terms of political
lefts and rights. Others see things in terms of race—hence the
"North versus South" rhetoric in which all the white dominators are
assumed to live north of the Equator and all the "colored" races live
to the south. These are less useful generalizations than the "rich versus poor" distinction.

   Clearly, there is a difference in *every* nation between the aspirations of the "haves" and those of the "have-nots." The latter want
something and intend to take steps to get. The former have a vested
interest in the status quo. To them, *change* itself can be a dirty
word. On this same criterion the posture and political actions of nations can be predicted. Thus the United States, for example, as one
of the wealthy nations, tends to view social unrest and strife within
any other nation as a threat to the status quo; the presumed basis of
resolving such tension is to restore the power of the side least likely
to work for change. Notable exceptions to this model have occurred;
for example, the United States took a chance on the Sandanistas and
withdrew support from Somoza in Nicaragua. Similarly, our government took a chance on popular reform in Iran and pulled the
props out from under the Shah: Khomeini emerged.

ACCELERATED DEVELOPMENT

The terminology for what is happening within a nation is another
part of the vocabulary problem. The term *developing nation* im-

plies that some nations are developing and some nations are not. While it might be alleged that some nations are not developing, according to some preset criterion, it is not a distinction likely to be admitted as fact or accepted emotionally. Thus all nations are in one way or another, as their own people see it at least, *developing nations*. Surely Japan is a developing nation, but not in the same sense or at the same stages of development as Jamaica. The term is one of the least precise generalizations.

The real issue is whether a nation is seeking to accelerate its own natural processes of development by intensifying its own activities and resources and by seeking external assistance. Natural processes, of course, are slower and less predictable. Nothing in the social order stands still very long; it either moves forward or it slides backward. All of humanity is in some state of development flux.

To some extent and in limited ways development can be accelerated. Especially in matters of technology and commerce, change can be wrestled into place. The social dislocation resulting from such change usually works its greatest hardships on the rural poor.

Consider Brazil's widely heralded decision to reduce its dependency on foreign petroleum and thus substantially improve its international balance of payments. Marginally profitable farm land, from which impoverished *Nordestinos*, the peasants of the Northeast, were scratching out a marginal diet, was suddenly claimed by huge farming corporations for growing sugar cane. The scheme has worked well in terms of the objectives of the national government, producing fuel-grade alcohol from sugarcane, but the by-products have been further reductions in the land available for providing the meager food supply and fewer opportunities for the *Nordestinos* to seek a livelihood. Massive, highly mechanized cane farms afford relatively few jobs. Who thinks about the human disasters of accelerated development? Indeed, only a few daring persons have even written about these problems, including Denis Goulet, Paulo Freire, Dom Helder Camara, and Gustavo Gutierrez.[11]

THE WHEEL OF CHANGE

Carping about backwardness becomes a habit for many sojourners. Even in terms of a society's own notions of progress, the processes are slow and often painful. Progress takes time, resources, and a vision. That vision is sometimes communicated by a symbol. For Herbert Hoover it was "a car in every garage."

The wheel bears an intriguing relationship to social progress. The principle of the wheel and the use of the fixed-axle wheel, as in cart, wagon, chariot, and the like were taken by early social historians as evidence of advancement. Those who used the wheel were thought to represent higher forms of civilization than those who didn't. The American Indians, for example, were seen as primitive partly because of the way they pulled their small children and their goods behind horses, on a sort of drag-skid contraption made of poles; the French gave the rig a name: *le travois*. The first Europeans to visit Japan thought they had stumbled onto another such "primitive" situation because the Japanese didn't use wheeled vehicles. In fact, wheeled vehicles were known in Japan, but were reserved for the Emperor's ceremonial use. In the profound respect for nature so characteristic of the Japanese, wheels were seen as destructive of trails and a major cause of erosion, and so they had been banned long before.

When Gandhi established his *ashram*, a working community tied close to the land and to peasant ways, he literally and symbolically began to turn the spinning wheel that would spin out the end of the British Empire. This strange little skinny brown man was hard to take seriously at first, because he seemed too much like a David with no stones in his sack facing Britain as Goliath. What had his homely Indian spinning wheel to do with colonialism? Gandhi's grasp of history and the nature of human beings was so well developed that he was able to pick exactly the right symbol of independence and progress. Gandhi understood that progress always involves a reviving from the past which then energizes the step ahead. The folk-style spinning wheel of India's past was the symbol that energized history's largest successful nonviolent emancipation.

Understanding colonialism is essential for the expatriate. It is so easy for the outsider to set in place again the very processes that have enslaved people before. It does not require a mean spirit or a vicious plot to become a colonialist. More often, colonialism results from well-intentioned generosity, from pity, from efforts to share. But underneath all these humane person-to-person motives are some powerful economic forces—call them facts of life. Gandhi was profoundly committed to nonviolent social change. As a devout Hindu he was more committed to nonviolence than to change, however, and when change brought about violence he used every ounce of his enormous charisma and many ounces of his meager body weight in fasting and moral persuasion. He is the only person in history credited with stopping a civil war by fasting.

He was a mystic; yet he grasped the economic realities. Though he respected and even loved the British, the effects of their century and a half of control in India were clear to him. Gandhi understood colonialism not just in terms of the oppression of those colonized but in terms of the motives of the colonizers. He could respond at an insightful level because he understood the values at stake.

As is typical of every colonial relationship, the colonial master is motivated by some combination of these needs:

1. Sites for military and naval bases for use in maintaining and extending control
2. Markets for manufactured goods from the homeland
3. Sources of raw materials, commodities, foods, and minerals for the homeland, especially to supply the manufacturing sector
4. Sources of cheap labor, available for transfer to other points in the colonial network or homeland, particularly to fill the bottom rung of menial, high risk, and distasteful employment, and, depending on political allegiances, for the military.

SILENT SULLEN PEOPLE

India and its position as the "crown jewel of the empire" are rich with object lessons about colonialism. These lessons are there for all to reflect upon, as valid today as when they were experienced by such persons as Gandhi and, earlier, Rudyard Kipling.

Kipling was part of the very system he criticized. British domination of India was over a century old when Kipling, the expatriate, became an editor of the British newspaper in Lahore (North India, today Pakistan).

Now, a full century later Kipling's writings endure, both because of their historical value and period charm and because Kipling's inner consciousness rebelled at what he found himself engaged in—and enjoying. In his self-criticism and in his capacity to change himself we find strong moral lessons.

Kipling's writings suggest that being part of a colonial system— even being a little cog in the larger machine—demeans and drags a person down to mean and depraved levels of behavior just as surely as does a drug addiction. Colonialism's tendency to degrade both the colonized and the colonizers is still the great tragedy of social exploitation—as the Russians are learning in Afghanistan and as the Israelis are learning in Lebanon.

History shows that Kipling's kind were scattered throughout the British Empire: thinking, educated people, many with finely tuned gentility and sensitivity who, finding themselves in a tyrannical and inhumane system, adopted various means to insulate their consciences. Some few worked against the colonial system, but others, like Kipling, put a sort of second ledger inside some enlightened corner of their souls and kept track of what they were learning about themselves. Fortunately for us, Kipling's conscience was committed to ink on paper. His poems, especially, show a compassionate spirit and an awareness of the ultimate folly of the British colonial system.

For Kipling, as for colonialists everywhere, the ultimate terror was "silent sullen people." Colonialists are typically outnumbered in fact and tend to be paranoid and anxious about potential revolution—whether small-scale or large. The lack of communication and the slow stare of those one encounters on every street are, indeed, frightening. For expatriates today, especially those who find themselves in a neo-colonial enterprise of some sort, whether an economic exploitation of land or industry or an attempt to impose foreign values in religion or lifestyle—the "silent sullen people" become a private nightmare.

The arrogance of presuming that any people should take charge of the destiny of other people is at the heart of colonialism. This arrogance is still practiced today, although on nowhere near the scale the British imposed on much of the world until recent years. There are corporations in Latin America that practice colonialism, determining by some assumed right that they should control the destiny of others. There are missions that operate in this way, based on the even more hazardous assumption that their imposing on others is willed by God. There are governments that control the destiny of their own people, asserting that their authority comes from Allah. Secularized societies do the same when they impute to a Marx or a Mao a timeless and infallible truth. Power-mad generals do it in Latin America and elsewhere when they put themselves forward as "saviors" of the nation. Rich land-holding individuals and baronial families do it to thousands of peasants whose obligations for rent and taxes are coupled with restrictions on what they can plant and to whom they can sell. Oppressed people in these situations are little different from slaves whose destiny is bought and sold. No, indeed, colonialism is not dead. Kipling's verses carry valid and timely warnings.

The poem that follows is the source of the phrase, "the white man's burden," which has become a common way to refer to the presumed contribution that the "advanced" nations can make to the "backward" people of the world. Its every line reeks of arrogance and its ultimate ironies; it challenges the "generous" spirit that supposedly accompanies the willingness to become an expatriate.

Beware; this viper still lurks along the trails through foreign forests. *Colonialism is not dead.*

> *Take up the White Man's burden—*
>   *Send forth the best ye breed—*
> *Go bind your sons to exile*
>   *To serve your captives' need;*
> *To wait in heavy harness,*
>   *On fluttered folk and wild—*
> *Your new-caught, sullen peoples,*
>   *Half-devil and half-child.*
>
> *Take up the White Man's burden—*
>   *In patience to abide,*
> *To veil the threat of terror*
>   *And check the show of pride;*
> *By open speech and simple,*
>   *An hundred times made plain,*
> *To seek another's profit,*
>   *And work another's gain.*
>
> *Take up the White Man's burden—*
>   *The savage wars of peace—*
> *Fill full the mouth of Famine*
>   *And bid the sickness cease;*
> *And when your goal is nearest*
>   *The end for others sought,*
> *Watch Sloth and heathen Folly*
>   *Bring all your hope to nought.*
>
> *Take up the White Man's burden—*
>   *No tawdry rule of kings,*
> *But toil of serf and sweeper—*
>   *The tale of common things.*
> *The ports ye shall not enter,*
>   *The roads ye shall not tread,*
> *Go make them with your living,*
>   *And mark them with your dead.*
>
> *Take up the White Man's burden—*
>   *And reap his old reward:*

The blame of those ye better,
The hate of those ye guard—
The cry of hosts ye humour
(Ah, slowly!) toward the light:—
"Why brought ye us from bondage,
"Our loved Egyptian night?"

Take up the White Man's burden—
Ye dare not stoop to less—
Nor call too loud on Freedom
To cloak your weariness;
By all ye cry or whisper,
By all ye leave or do,
The silent, sullen peoples
Shall weigh your Gods and you.

Take up the White Man's burden—
Have done with childish days—
The lightly proffered laurel,
The easy, ungrudged praise.
Comes now, to search your manhood
Through all the thankless years,
Cold, edged with dear-bought wisdom,
The judgment of your peers! *

And still they wait . . . to weigh *your* God and you.

CHANGING CHANGE AGENTS

Perhaps the popular and pseudo-scientific talk about "change agents" is only a symptom, but whatever the cause, a new form of colonialism is emerging even among those who fly humanitarian flags. A preoccupation with achievement of one's own "intended objectives" leads toward a manipulative and sometimes downright pushy attitude toward other people.

In the old colonialism, the military (bluntly called *conquistadors*—conquerors—in the Spanish language), merchants (traders in whatever was profitable, not excluding human life itself), and missionaries were hand-in-hand partners. Though often critical of each other, these three groups needed each other. The military made it

*From *The Portable Kipling*, edited and with an Introduction by Irving Howe (New York: Viking, 1982), pp. 602–603.

possible, the merchants made it worthwhile, and the missionaries made it legitimate. More often than not it was an unholy alliance. The missionary presence, for example, often sank to the low calling of a sort of "presence of the church"—a political rather than religious involvement. Concern for God's justice and mercy was squeezed off the agenda.

In the more recent "modern missionary movement," dating roughly from the late eighteenth- and early nineteenth-century movements of English, Moravian, Mennonite, Reformed and Free Church, Scandinavian, German, Swiss and Dutch Protestants, there has generally been an aloofness both from commerce and from government—especially from the military—and for good reason.

During the last two hundred years mission effort has been focused more on individuals, in an extension of the cultural bias of western Protestantism toward individual and personal accountability before God. Even when ministering among intensively communitarian, family, and tribe-oriented societies, the habit has been to preach the Gospel in individualistic terms.

Then along came the postwar wave of new communication technologies with their preoccupation with measurable results. Major sectors of the modern missionary movement have adopted the philosophy and orientation of this essentially pragmatic trend. Missionaries saw themselves less as proclaimers and companions in the walk of faith and more as "agents of change." Their worth was less in their persons and their presence as witness to the beneficence of a merciful God than as strategists who could count converts. Originally a movement to counteract lethargic and purposeless missions, the Church Growth movement has been widely influential and, to some extent, identified with the quantitative emphasis of "strategists of change."

Herein lies a dilemma: The purpose of any humanitarian effort is to make changes—*for* and ultimately *in* the lives of people. The life of a drowning person needs to be changed; make no mistake about it. The life of a starving child needs to be changed. The sinbound life of a wretch out of fellowship with God needs to be changed. But when one undertakes to bring about such changes, questions of worthiness, purity of motive, and the rights of the needy to remain needy if they wish make the waters murky, indeed.

In this era of more deliberately structured and motivated "change agents," the whole idea of intentional change, whether motivated from *outside* or from the *top down* within the society, has taken on a bad name. It's almost useless to try to argue that change is needed—even on humanitarian grounds. The voices of naturalistic preservationism will respond with the unfeeling, if not mindless argument that things will take care of themselves and that even unselfish help is not welcome. "Leave them alone" has become the official answer in so many cases. Surely this is an overreaction to pushy change agents. We can only hope that a humane and gentle touch may once again come into favor.

The issue may be more a matter of orientation and style than of purpose. Analysis of the life of Jesus Christ reveals a person who was change-oriented, but at the same time very person-oriented. He responded to people in terms of their own diagnosis and analysis of their situation. Jesus gave people hope, through which they felt more inclined to identify their needs and seek change, but He did not *impose* change on people. Nor did He shrewdly contrive to get people to think as He thought—to see things His way. His style was straightforward, sometimes blunt, but always respectful. He never changed the subject; in conversations with people who sought Him out, He allowed the other person to introduce the subject and the objective. Hardly the description of a manipulative "change agent."

Change agents and their sponsors tend to be self-appointed, and this can pose grave dangers to the people targeted for being changed. If your job description or your view of yourself is wrapped up in a particular set of outcomes, and especially if those outcomes are to be changes in other people's beliefs, values, or behaviors, your role shrinks to that of a salesperson, or worse, a pusher. Human beings should never be seen as objects to be operated upon or shoved around like checkers on a checkerboard. Whatever is done with others, legitimately, is done *with* others—not *to* them.

A VERY PRIVATE MATTER

A brave person is one who speaks and acts to defend human rights in his or her own country. A foolhardy person is one who speaks and acts to defend human rights while in someone else's country. This paradox is easier to grasp when the difference between deportation and execution is understood. A person who speaks out against a government while a guest of that government will probably be deported. Furthermore, when a hothead speaks out or acts in protest while in someone else's country, his or her friends are also likely to suffer the consequences. The likelihood of getting one's associates and friends in serious trouble should be a deterrent to misplaced "patriotism" of the expatriate.

This problem, of course, is much more serious in Kenya than in England. It is so obviously an issue in countries such as Ethiopia, Korea, the Philippines, the Republic of South Africa, Russia, Kampuchea, and Nepal that one's friends will simply fade away if any tendency to be carelessly outspoken becomes evident.

Expatriates who build close affiliative relationships over a long period of time have special difficulty with this issue. Just how far should they go to show solidarity with their national colleagues? The question has no easy answer that will work in all cases, but the following guidelines can be recommended.

- Keep a loose hold; be ready to back off when commitment to any issue, policy decision, or affiliation shows signs of embarrassing or overexposing your host-country counterparts.
- Take cues from the mainstream of the opinions and judgments of local persons, not just from a handful of loyal friends who wouldn't dream of offending you.
- Accept the fact that a backing-off or even a "moratorium" on your operations isn't necessarily permanent. Many a shrewd person or organization has returned to service on location after a relatively short withdrawal for cooling off.
- Differentiate the idea of loyalty and the commitment to faithfulness from the temporary matters of safety and visibility. Act on the latter.
- Explain the situation (to yourself and to others) in terms of realities, but avoid "heroics." Play down the political angle and stay away from attributing blame.

The experiences of postcolonial Africa still provide sober reminders that expatriates—missionaries, especially—can get into a great deal of difficulty over the matter of inappropriate solidarity. In Congo/Zaire and more recently in Rhodesia/Zimbabwe, the winds of revolution blew in the windows of many a dismayed white household—especially in frontier and remote outposts. Recognizing that the approaching storm would bring bloodshed and death to Africans who appeared too cozy with the whites and, possibly, to the whites themselves, many a trembling voice asked the whites to go away—at least for a season. For freedom-loving Americans and British this was as a red scarf to a bull. Their pride and honor—and property—were at stake. All sorts of communications were sent. Self-serving in part, they proclaimed a righteous commitment to stand by their African brothers and sisters. They even justified their continued presence by claiming to be witnesses against the "spiritual instability" of Africans who, after many years of faithful affiliation with Christianity, were now asking their white Christian colleagues to leave. What else could this mean but a resurgence of paganism? A good shot of political science should be a requirement for overseas service today!

There is nothing unfaithful about going home in order that one's friends may be less in the line of fire. More often than not in times of tension and insurrection, the people who have close ties to those who are foreign or racially different are most apt to be marked. Villages built up around missionary medical outposts or schools are sure to be prime targets. Ironically, the outsiders may be spared, but the local people who have "curried their favor" are often the first to taste violence.

In troubled times the wise expatriate will remain quiet about local political issues—even in a relatively free country. Even the morally valid support of freedom and truth should be handled quietly. In conversations, at work and especially at parties or social events, it is important—very important—to refrain from remarks that could be held against one's friends. As in wartime, the walls have ears. Many Americans are so unaccustomed to speaking for anyone but themselves that they can inadvertently get many others in trouble in a society wherein the words of one person are taken as judgment against all those who associate with that person.

Private encouragement of one's friends is always in order; but even here it is important to remember that in a less free society, encouraging a local person to take a stand or to act out a conviction of integrity could be, in fact, encouraging the person to risk imprisonment—or worse. Such matters should be very private, very honest, and enlightened by a realistic awareness of "the facts of life."

FOCUS FOR SELF-EVALUATION

The importance of sensitive concern for the motives and feelings of others has been emphasized in Chapter 10. Special concern has been given to the issues of religious differences and the contrast between narrow and broad definitions of the purposes of missionary outreach and humanitarian assistance.

Reflection

As I see my purposes overseas, I anticipate the following possible points of conflict with the purposes of the host-country people with whom I will be working: _____

_____

_____

Review

1. What is the value of the "bridge-builder" approach?

    _____

    _____

2. What would be the basis for reciprocity in what I expect to do overseas? What do I want to gain from the experience? _____

    _____

    _____

Commitment

Of the practical implications I see in Chapter 10, I am most ready to commit myself to the following: _____

_____

_____

_____

_____

11

Planning the Move
You and Your Family

AT THE PERSONAL and family level you must deal with anxieties and doubts of many sorts. The ordinary American preoccupations with health, safety, communication, mobility, food, and bathrooms will emerge to block your thinking about more important matters. These concerns must be confronted, and you must find a basis for dealing with them rationally lest they become debilitating anxieties. With some of these you will need help—professional help.

You must sort through your purposes for accepting an intercultural assignment. Readiness depends on far more than ability to list the meritorious reasons for going. What, exactly, is important to you? What are you assuming about the worth of the assignment—for you, for others, especially for your family? What outcomes would make you feel satisfied? Are there "failures" that you could not accept?

All of this must fit within carefully drawn plans. The practical level of physical arrangements is where you can do the most to assure a comfortable and orderly experience. All sorts of suggestions will come your way as you prepare. How can you sort out the good advice and follow it? As you get into the active preparation phase, there will be an overwhelming mass of concerns, curiosities, and practical things to handle. One way to bring some order to a potentially overwhelming situation is to sort out different types of tasks.

DETAILS, DETAILS

The variety of details—arrangements, processes, filing of this and that, sorting out what to take—is enough to discourage all but the most stalwart. Each person's situation is unique; nevertheless some general guidance may be helpful. The basis for development of a personal checklist follows. It is organized around the people you will need to see—and a few other matters:

Doctors. Health records; dental records; glasses prescriptions; international inoculation record form; discussion of allergies, foods, emergency plans.

Lawyers. Wills for each person; custody arrangements in case of death; power of attorney for actions that must be taken while you are overseas. If your tax situation is at all complicated, ask for advice on the latest procedures, especially for federal and state income taxes.

Merchants. Suspension of charge accounts or arrangements for shop-by-mail; clearing all outstanding debts or arranging payments.

Chiefs (bureaucrats). Passports, visas; absentee voting arrangements; postal change-of-address forms.

Insurance agents. Home and car while overseas; household effects en route; arrangements for payments; validity of insurance for cars shipped overseas; record of insurance claims.

Bankers. Arrangements for deposits; accounting for checking; savings plan adjustments; traveler's checks; transfers of funds by bank draft to an overseas branch of a major bank.

Real estate. Find tenants for the house, decide what furnishings to leave in place.

Photographers. Passport photos, extras for permits and visas (at least 20). Try to talk the photographer into letting you take the negative.

Schoolmaster. Formal records or transcripts for the children; samples of recent work in each subject.

Other. Storage of household treasures, breakables, heirlooms, and idiosyncracies—the renters won't want to contend with the weaver's loom you have in the dining room or the disassembled 1938 Packard you keep in the basement.

Shipping. A real headache, no matter how you do it—get advice from at least three good sources, then plan carefully.

Carry with you only the minimal essentials. The must-have-soon items should go air freight; the rest can go by sea. Make sure the packing is done carefully: it will be handled by several sets of semi-accountable caretakers before you ever see it again.

Schweitzer's Piano

How do you decide what to leave behind and what to take overseas? There are no easy formulas. Most people find that they have left behind a number of basic items that they do need after all. Electric blankets and small appliances, for example, should be taken along if the voltage is compatible. But what about hobbies and "nonessentials"?

The great Renaissance man of foreign missions, Albert Schweitzer, gave his life to the people of Africa. His ability to meet the human needs and to adapt himself to the lifestyle of the people of rural Gabon is a matter of record. His training and talents as a musician, theologian, philosopher, and physician went with him to Africa. He never denied who or what he was, but his compassion ruled the whole of it.

Albert Schweitzer dedicated his life to the poorest of the poor, but he never asked for sympathy, nor did he concede that he had given up anything of value. In fact, he took with him the things that meant the most to him. Recognizing the futility of maintaining a pipe organ in such a climate, this world-class organist took an upright piano for which he designed a pedal-board, equivalent to that of a pipe organ, so that he might keep in shape for the concert performances which were a regular feature of his "furloughs."

Whenever people speak of leaving behind important things in order to sacrifice themselves to others, I think of Schweitzer's piano. If it's that important, take it with you, especially if it's a vital aspect of your wholeness as a person. It's far better than feeling sorry for yourself.

Video Cassettes—The New Support System

Especially for those Americans who have grown accustomed to the more passive forms of entertainment, the absence of American movies and television is hard to take. In various cities of the world, and especially in the Third World, the favorite "night out" is the weekly first-run motion picture at the American or Canadian embassy or consulate.

Thanks to the enterprising Japanese, a new way to solve the problem of "cultural isolation" is emerging: the video cassette. Among overseas Americans video cassette players have become very popular, and the swapping of video cassettes has become a consuming passion for many.

Local television fare may be pretty slim stuff. After ten hours of *sumo* wrestling, the viewer compulsively gains weight. After ten days of *Dragnet* reruns, even "the facts, ma'am" seem unreal. Protecting oneself against the backwash of early American television can be solved by a compact cassette player and a few hundred dollars' investment in late-model movies to view once or twice and then put into the local trading club.

In this matter as for other appliances and electronic equipment, find out what voltages and systems are in use where you are going. Many items are not interchangeable, though transformers and adapters can help with the problems of matching. (If only there were "social adapters" and "human transformers" to help people fit better!)

In many places, even on U.S. military bases overseas, video cassettes are almost the only game in town. But personally, I find this development disappointing. I'll miss the time to talk, play games, practice musical instruments, and do things actively as a family which for so long has been an important advantage of the TV-less overseas assignment.

GATHERING INFORMATION

One of the most practical guides to obtaining and using information is the *Trans-Cultural Study Guide* published by the Volunteers in Asia, a group which specializes in helping people find rewarding volunteer service opportunities. They recommend going through a number of books and pamphlets during preparation and photocopying, clipping, sorting, and selecting a few of the best to take to the field. Once on the field, they suggest an intensive local search of libraries, government bulletins, census data, policy statements, and the like.

To augment this search for printed material, the Volunteers recommend holding conversations and interviews, and recording useful bits of information in a pocket notebook. They also strongly urge
identifying "bridge people" who can help to *explain* information.

Their system is informal, but they do recommend keeping specific files. They suggest the following categories of information:

Economics. Jobs, family incomes and budgets, agriculture,
  manufacture, monetary and trade styles, social welfare, income levels, GNP, natural resources, foreign trade, balance of
  payments, foreign aid, tourism.
Politics. International posture, national structures, provincial
  and local structure, the state and the individual, integrity and
  corruption.
Social structure. National unity or fragmentation; ethnic, economic, and class structures; city, village, and town distinctions; family and individual roles and relationships.
Roles of men and women. Responsibilities for children, marriage and child-rearing practices, economic considerations,
  community considerations.
Religion and beliefs. Membership organizations, informal ad-
  herency, beliefs and practices, religious symbolism and expression, religion in the community's life, history and trends,
  influences of foreign religions.
Music and art. Types and uses of music, types and forms of art,
  architecture, history of forms, especially internal and external
  influences and trends.
Food. Forms of protein, fats, carbohydrates, standard diets,
  sources of food, taboos about food, public food, cooking
  styles, food budgets.
Education. Structure of system, types, administration and fi-
  nancing, facilities, curriculum, motives, historical background, evident effects.
Communication. Forms, freedom and censorship, control of
  media, access and feedback, content, motives, media-use
  habits, evident effects.
Health and welfare. Nutrition; water supplies; delivery systems
  of health care; disease patterns; folk medicine; healers and beliefs; effects of illness on social structure; social, legal, and political aspects of health care; family planning; ecological considerations; housing; clothing; worker safety.[1]

If the children in the family are old enough, they can help in the locating and filing of information. This help is realistic and practical and also serves the psychological purpose of making each person feel involved in preparation for the move.

THIRD-CULTURE FAMILIES

Ruth Hill Useem has maintained a career-long involvement with the overseas family. Motivated by motherly and grandmotherly empathy as well as by her disciplinary competencies as a sociologist and cultural anthropologist, Useem has spent hundreds of hours conversing with and interviewing expatriates in many parts of the world, especially India and Southeast Asia, and studying the schools where their children are being educated. The term "third culture" is her own. Not to be confused with the term "third world," Ruth and John Useem use "third culture" to identify the values, styles of life, and patterns of interaction that are created and maintained by persons who cross societal boundaries as representatives of some sponsoring organization.[2] Thus they are to be distinguished from refugees, tourists, and immigrants. Their period of residence outside their country of citizenship may be as little as a year or two, or it may be for a lifetime.

These people often have more in common with others who are also from the expatriate community than they do with people of their first culture or with natives of the land where they now live. They are becoming a culture of their own—a *third* culture. Thus the expatriate American family may have more in common with the Dutch family down the lane in Kuala Lumpur than either family has with the Malaysians among whom they live and work—and they surely have less in common with tourists from the Netherlands or from the United States. Even when they "go home" on vacations ("home leaves," "furloughs," and "holidays" are the more likely words among third-culture people), they find that this estrangement has even cut into their family ties and old friendships. Such people of the "third culture" are often identifiable by their restless eagerness to get back to the field. The overseas location has become the only place they really feel "at home"—among others of the third culture.

This is particularly true for many of their minor dependents who have spent most of their lives in the third culture communities.

THE "NONWORKING" SPOUSE

Much of the research on intercultural adaptation has been conducted among overseas workers. Spouses and other family members are often less accessible to the researchers, so they tend to be overlooked or, at best, represented indirectly by the "working" member of the family. Therefore the research tends to focus on the tasks of intercultural adaptation to co-workers and to the lifestyles of persons who have relatively structured roles to play. In fact, the problems of those in the household who must create their own agendas and schedules are at least as great—quite likely more difficult.

School-age children, of course, will have the schedules and requirements of school to use as a sort of skeleton on which to build an overseas lifestyle, but for wives and mothers, or for an unemployed husband accompanying a working wife, the adjustments required are almost overwhelming.

Many things must be approached in ways that bear little resemblance to "back home." In each country—and in each region within a country—the circumstances will require a unique approach. A few matters can be expected to be more or less similar in any overseas location—grocery shopping will need to be done more frequently than is necessary in the United States, for example. Any shopping list will require more stops—there are fewer "general stores" and more specialized shops and markets. Milk and meat, for example, are rarely purchased in the same place. Vegetables are better in the early-morning farmer's markets than in the food stores. The food stores have far fewer packaged convenience foods, and frozen food is less widely available and less safe. Beyond these predictable generalizations, almost everything else will need to be discovered in the situation—just be ready for many variations.

Even in some seemingly modern cities, overdemand on scarce resources will result in delays for banking transactions, telephone connections, and utilities. At certain hours of the day electricity may be unavailable or "browned" so much that motors should be switched off to avoid burning them out. Then there is the water. Sometimes. When water service is intermittent, it is also likely to be contaminated because of backflow during outages. This typical problem rather than the source or treatment of water is the major reason why the safety of drinking water is always an important question. Should you use a filter? Boil it? Use bottled water? Any solution takes time and effort. Such matters add up to a sizable load, usually falling on the shoulders of the "nonworking" spouse.

Managing the thousand and one extra chores and the nuisances of life in a different culture becomes a heavy agenda. Having only one spouse employed outside the home is the typical pattern overseas. Thus a good marriage requires teamwork and complementary efforts, not just taking turns with the same duties and chores. In the United States today this team approach to marriage and family is becoming less common, perhaps because it is less necessary. Overseas, the old-fashioned team effort wherein each person makes unique contributions is more necessary for a pleasant life together. Young families can find great satisfaction in making the necessary adjustments. The burdens, if accepted, negotiated, and carried with respect and responsibility, can produce strength for individuals and for the family as a whole. Each member of the family will have to be involved, but inevitably the "nonworking" spouse will carry the heaviest load in reference to the household responsibilities.

CHILDREN OVERSEAS

When children are involved in the overseas move, there are special problems and greater anxieties. Uneasy parents can compile quite a list of worries about their children. Many of these concerns will turn out to be less difficult than expected.

In every family the overseas sojourn will be good news and bad news, but as far as the welfare of children is concerned, the good news is likely to outweigh the bad news. For a start, consider the stress on the family unit as a whole. The move itself is likely to be quite stressful. There's no doubt about it, any move is hard. Packing things up, giving away things that have meanings for the children far in excess of their value in the adult world, leaving friends and family far behind, facing the unknowns of neighborhood, housing, schooling, and new friends of a different sort—all these are understandable sources of anxiety or unhappiness, and they aren't easy to face. But children are likely to be less perturbed and more resilient than their parents. Parents often worry on behalf of their children about things that the children themselves take in stride. So look at the bright side: children who grow up in intercultural environments can gain a global perspective that will have a lasting influence on their appreciation and acceptance of other human beings.

The lives of families in contemporary *American* society are stressful. Many long for the magical power of turning back the calendar to a simpler and quieter time. It is an open secret that an overseas move almost surely offers such a chance to step into a less complex and less stressful time. For the family which makes the transitions and handles the necessary adaptations, the pleasure of family solidarity lies ahead.

Ruth Useem tells of a flight from Saigon during that late lamented war, accompanying some American teen-age young people to "refuge" in the United States. Ruth's seatmate, obviously perturbed, finally explained that she was not as upset at leaving her missionary parents behind in Vietnam as she was apprehensive about the life she faced in a Chicago suburb, where she anticipated daily encounters with rampant lawlessness. The irony of this situation tells a deep and true story. With her family, even in a war zone, life overseas had a security and calm about it that was more to be desired than the pleasures of Chicago's Babylon.

Children raised overseas are often strong on resourcefulness and creativity. They tend to be able to entertain themselves instead of demanding that others keep them entertained. Because they have grown up with less, they become more self-reliant. They have learned early in life that unknowns are not to be feared and have developed remarkable coping skills. It is no surprise, then, that they rarely need anyone's sympathy, protection, or direction when they return to the United States. Like any expatriate, they will need time to adjust, but coping is their specialty—stand back and watch them take hold.

A generation ago it was popular to point out the remarkably high frequency of MKs* in *Who's Who in America*. No recent studies have been published, but those who have spent several years overseas more often than not report that the experience has been valuable.

Schools overseas tend to be more demanding. An almost paranoid anxiety on the part of overseas parents to make sure that their children will be able to climb onto the right rung of the educational ladder when they "go home" has resulted is a whole network of overseas international and American schools serving expatriate families. The curriculum in these schools is not only academic, but almost elitist in its presumption that every child is to be made ready for Princeton or Yale. Even military families feel the pressure to see that the schools on U.S. bases overseas are "tough" and "college prep."

*"MK" is a fond and familiar short form for *missionary's kid*.

The students, at least those who can handle it, benefit from this intellectual pressure; but it is the out-of-school factors that are likely to be more consequential. Especially for the children who learn early to speak the language, use local transportation, and get out on their own with other young people, the potential for social development is almost limitless.

If one or both parents are having a hard time coping with the new culture, the tendency will be to restrict the child's exploratory spirit, to overprotect, and to isolate. In such cases, serious problems often result.

In many ways, children can lead the way for the rest of the family's cultural adaptation, if given half a chance. For example, the youngster may turn out to be the family's best translator—children tend to learn language rapidly in the course of play and friendship. Or the child may be the "excuse" parents give themselves for investing in travel and sight-seeing within the country. Fine. Whatever the causes and effects, the finest sort of cultural adaptation seems to occur more commonly among the expatriates who have well-integrated children or adolescents with them.

Overseas families tend to spend more time together—playing games together, listening to the news together. Generally a closer, smaller, and more intense circle of friends is developed than is common in the United States. Thus involvement as a sort of extended family is quite typical among people who are, in fact, unrelated. This pattern leads to several happy ends and one or two that are not so happy. Among the former is the much greater willingness to take in each other's children overnight or on weekends while the parents travel together. For many new expatriate families this practice represents a radical departure from the more "tied down" lifestyle "back home."

The dark side of this picture is the tendency to become too involved in one another's home and family affairs. Real problems can occur, especially among supposedly like-minded people who live too close to each other. Notorious among missionary families who live in confined "compounds" of clustered houses or apartments is the tendency to scrutinize each other's laundry line for telltale signs of high living.

Establishing clear ground rules about who reprimands whose children for what sorts of activity is advisable. The sort of closeness that can occur among expatriate families can be constructive and satisfying, but in all sorts of matters it requires social structures, agreements, and controls not generally needed in the American life-style. And here's more good news: the processes of working out those agreements and negotiating those misunderstandings tend to build character—in adults as well as in the children. Back home a family might simply "drop" another family in the face of tensions and mis-understandings. But overseas, there aren't so many potential re-placements for one's good friends; so you tend to seek a ground for redressing grievances and rebuilding damaged relationships. What a valuable contrast with today's throw-away society! The result can be children with a greater sense of fidelity and trust.

The Reassuring Experiences of MKs

In a recent review for a prospective-missionary magazine, Cliff Schimmels reflected on the research about children of missionaries and on his own experiences as a teacher of American youngsters in schools for MKs.

> The most frequent finding of the research is that MKs are usually aca-demically advanced over their counterparts in the United States. They have better study habits and are more widely read. They also have a better mastery of academic tools such as reading, writing, and math facts. There is a good possibility that your child will have an academi-cally sound education while you are serving on the mission field.[3]

Educational advantages and opportunities are the first category of concerns on almost every list compiled on the topic of overseas children. The anxiety about education seems most pervasive of the concerns of overseas parents—or at least of parents considering the overseas move.

The other major concern of parents deals with social adjust-ment. It should be obvious that being in a different culture, espe-cially becoming part of a "third culture," will create some adjust-ment problems when a youngster returns to the United States. Cultural stress is a two-way street.

To reduce the likelihood of a difficult transition back into life in the United States, parents on overseas assignments of three or more years should bring their children back to the United States on regu-lar intervals, perhaps in alternate summers, so they can do some "growing up" along with their U.S. age-mates. The overseas family must straddle the cultural gap, keeping one foot planted firmly in each culture.

MKs are usually a little behind in American social development. It is rather obvious that children reared outside the States won't act exactly like American teenagers. One example is the area of boy-girl relations. MKs simply don't get down to one-to-one dating as early as teenagers here. So, if you come on furlough with a 16-year-old daughter, she probably won't know how to flirt as well as the other girls.[4]

Growing up in two worlds is a challenge that not every child can handle well, but resiliency and adaptability are usually such well-established characteristics of the overseas child that parents can count on adequate progress when "catching up" is needed.

Schooling

The concerns about quality and accessibility of education loom large in the minds of parents preparing for an overseas move. They usually find that their fears were groundless.

American-style education programs fall into five general categories. Each type can prepare a student well for fitting back into the formal education system within the United States, either as a transferring student or as a college applicant.

In virtually every major city of the world—at least in every city where there are large numbers of Americans, Canadians, and British folk, there is sure to be at least one *International School*. This school is provided by the expatriate community to serve its children. It is a private school, operated as a nonprofit corporation with a board of directors consisting largely of outstanding women and men of the expatriate community. In a capital city the American or Canadian Ambassador's wife is apt to be on the board, as is the manager of the local branch of Barclay's Bank, the manager of the Ford plant, and so forth. Industries usually provide part of the financial support for the school—their employees wouldn't be willing to take overseas assignments if good schools weren't available.

The U.S. Department of State helps to subsidize schools that have been officially authorized for children of diplomatic corps personnel. But the school's main income is from tuition fees; these can be quite high, because such a school is likely to pay its teachers at least as well as they were paid in the States—that's where most of them were recruited, if the school serves primarily the American community.

If the American community of expatriates is large enough, such a school is likely to be called the *American School*. Again, this is a private school, with or without subsidies from the Department of State, that uses a very American sort of curriculum. In many ways the American School in Rio is like the American School in Tokyo— or anywhere else. They appear to be transplantations of American society in remote locations, with a minimum of differences except that rice may be served in the cafeteria along with the hamburgers.

In some of the best of these schools children get some help in appreciating the culture of the host country, though even this may be largely in the form of a token language class, one or two "culture fairs" a year, and a locally hired "culture learning teacher" whose influence on the curriculum is often minimal. Fortunately, many children and young people investigate their host culture independently outside of school and thus discover where the action is.

Among my young friends in American schools I have known motorcyclists who have backpacked all over Honshu, teenage explorers who have gone from Panama to Buenos Aires on freight trains, hikers who have spent countless weekends during the school year on the country lanes of England, skindivers who can identify the fish off Java better than most marine biologists, and youngsters who have made a game of building their own can-you-top-this collection of photographs from behind the Iron Curtain. The culture learning that takes place outside the school may well be more vital than that which is learned inside.

Missionary dependents often attend a third type of school, the *missionary children's school*. Schools of this sort are often in rural or suburban locations, and many of their students—even six-year-olds—live in campus dormitories or boarding homes. The pupils are mostly from missionary families who are living well away from the cities. Some mission families feel a strong desire to have their children experience a religiously based education. The same parents might choose to send their children to a church-affiliated private school in the United States.

The missionary children's school may be as remote as several thousand miles, as in the case of the Rift Valley Academy in Kenya, where the children of missionary families come from all over Africa. Many a missionary family is thus split by the presumed necessity of sending the children to a boarding school many miles away, visiting them occasionally, and receiving them home again for the periodic school holidays.

A fourth type of education—it can hardly be called a school—is also common among missionaries assigned to remote or lonely posts:

the *correspondence course*. Of these, the venerable leader is the
Calvert course, providing a straightforward curriculum of traditional basic subjects for children who work alone or with one or two
others under the supervision of a parent.[5] Now that home study is
becoming more popular and accepted in the United States as a part
of today's reactionary attacks on public education, it would seem
that the correspondence course or the religious school equivalent,
"Accelerated Christian Education," might become more popular
among missionaries. In the recent past, home study programs have
had little strong support because of the belief that learning is best
approached as a social process, and is best accomplished among others of comparable developmental levels.

A fifth type of schooling accounts for the largest enrollment of
American school children overseas: *The U.S. Department of Defense Dependents Schools* (DODDS). In many ways the DODDS
schools are much like the schools found in towns or small cities in
the United States. Except for their high scholastic standards, they
have little in common with overseas private schooling. The DODDS
schools are public schools, operated with tax funds on a tuition-free
basis, and as such cannot discriminate on the basis of race, religion,
or ability. They are provided exclusively for dependents of the overseas armed forces, however, and only under very rare circumstances
are other students admitted. Since armed forces families rarely
spend even three years on one base, student turnover at DODDS
schools is rapid, and continuity can be a problem.

Teachers are hired in accord with policies of typical American
state school authorities. The regulation and curriculum supervision
of these schools are regional. Each region as a whole is structured
like the school administration of an American city school district under a district superintendent of schools; for example, the Pacific District ranges from Midway to Korea.

When the Children Go Native

Now and then a family will decide that the schools of the host country are best for its child. Such a decision should be taken only after
the most thorough and careful consideration.

In English-language regions, such as East African cities or Singapore, there are outstanding private schools—most of which follow a
British-style curriculum—to which unusually bright American stu-

dents might be admitted. Such an experience would be more intensively intercultural than attendance at the local American school, and as such could be very stimulating. But, by American standards, it would also be very demanding, requiring more homework and often more classroom days and hours in the week. Further, transferring from such a school back to a school using an American-style curriculum would create a variety of problems in sequence of courses, level of accomplishment, style of test-taking habits, and lifestyle itself.

Where the language of instruction is not English, a compounding problem is introduced. The language of one's schooling has a profound effect on one's life. Many, if not most, young people tend to prefer going on into higher education in the language of their previous schooling. Thus a high school experience in a Francophone African private school is more likely to be followed by university enrollment at the Sorbonne in Paris or at the Lavalle Université in Quebec than at Texas Tech.

Parents who encourage their children in this direction should be prepared to cope with the emotionally difficult discovery that their offspring have "gone native" and may prefer to become citizens of the host country rather than to return to the United States. This possibility is by no means certain. Among the most intriguing families I have known are several whose children have gone to local schools in Nairobi, Paris, Geneva, and elsewhere. Within the families of which I am aware, no child has ever renounced American citizenship, though some have dual citizenship because they were born overseas. About half of them reside in other countries today, as missionaries and as international specialists in business, government, and education. Their contributions to a world of intercultural understanding are commendable.

ASSESSING YOUR READINESS

How can you know that you are ready to go? Having gone through the preparational steps is one thing; being ready to go is another! Some sort of self-assessment is in order. It isn't someone else you must convince; it's yourself.

In many of life's more important transitions what really counts is how you relate yourself to another person or to a given social group. Marriage is one obvious example. A sure clue that a person isn't yet ready for marriage is selfishness and egocentrism—thinking of one-self so intensely that all others are defined in terms of how they meet one's own needs. Readiness for parenthood is another transition that can be assessed this way. The incapacity to put others first explains a lot of abused children. At a more abstract level, employment readiness and affiliation in a profession can be assessed in similar fashion. A high professional standard of integrity and service is unattainable by those who seek their own selfish ends first and foremost. Litigious attorneys and knife-happy surgeons have become negative stereotypes in our society for exactly this reason.

What egocentrism is in these relationships, ethnocentrism is in intercultural matters. They both refer to being centered on oneself or one's own ways of doing things.

In matters of intercultural competency, the dangers of ethnocentrism cannot be overemphasized. Ethnocentrism is human. It is a natural and reasonable outcome of culture; it is a product of growing up American, or Austrian, or Japanese. It is certainly not unhealthy or unreasonable to think well of one's own cultural heritage; but self-centered narrowness and stubbornness in the presence of people who are different is evidence of ethnocentrism carried to extremes. In general, well-adjusted people seem to be quite happy with who they are and why they prefer what they prefer. But they are neither belligerent nor defensive about it. Narrowmindedness is not an appropriate foundation for intercultural competency.

One need not reject one's own ways in order to accept another who is different. The term *ethnocentrism* refers to a tendency to bring everything one experiences in social contacts up against one's own values and outlook and to pass judgment as if one's own ways and standards were superior. Another form of self-orientation might be termed *ethnoradiant* (see Figure 11–1). This concept realistically acknowledges that a person inevitably uses his or her own experiences and beliefs as an initial frame of reference for everything; after all, perception is always a product of one's previous experiences. But one need not remain the center of the universe. Indeed, the beauty of liberation from ethnocentrism is not in any rejection of one's own reality and validity but in the freedom to acknowledge the reality and validity of others. And to do this with integrity, one needs a very substantial sense of self-worth.

Ethnocentrism is generally nurtured by insecurity, and it is maintained from a defensive posture about one's own lack of worth. Like extroverted behavior, giving the impression of being com-

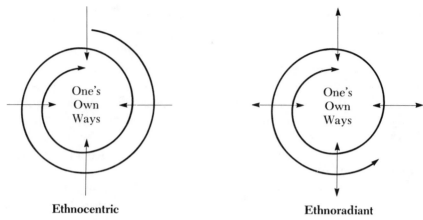

Ethnocentric   Ethnoradiant

Figure 11-1.   Two ways to relate to difference

pletely sure of oneself can be nothing more than a disguise for a sense of inferiority.

GUIDANCE FOR SELF-ASSESSMENT

A few years ago when "culture shock" was the focus of much research, William Redden and Ken Powell developed an instrument they called the Culture Shock Inventory.[6] It was intended as an aid to self-assessment, particularly in regard to people's becoming alert to things about themselves that could become disorienting once they entered a different culture. The eight categories from their instrument suggest useful questions to ask about one's readiness to go overseas. Following each of those categories, self-assessment questions are suggested here.

1. *Reduced Western Ethnocentrism*
   —Would the rest of the world be better off if they did things our way?
   —Do all people in the world hold the same basic values?
   —Do I tend to assume that things that are different are inferior?
   —Does "Third World" mean *primitive?*
   —Is there anything that "high tech" people might learn from people who depend less on technology?
2. *Experience*
   —Have I learned to enjoy being in places where other languages are spoken?

—Have I sought out opportunities to meet foreigners in the United States?

—Do I avoid parts of my own town, city, or state where there are high concentrations of people who are racially, ethnically, or economically different?

—Can I describe the history of any particular ethnic group in the United States?

3. *Cognitive Flex*

—Do I avoid people as friends if their beliefs are different from mine?

—Do I expect to see something today that I have never before noticed?

—Can I explain, to my own satisfaction, why my views are right for me but still perhaps not best for someone else?

—Do I go out of my way to get new experiences or do I stay with things I already know about?

—Do I avoid conversations wherein my values may be questioned by someone else?

4. *Behavioral Flex*

—Have I tried out something lately that someone else suggested?

—Have I learned a particular new skill within the last month?

—Can I list five things I wish I could learn to do?

—Do I see myself as experimental rather than habituated?

—In my family or social group am I one who suggests new things to do or places to go?

5. *Cultural Knowledge—Specific*

—In reference to the country or region to which I expect to go, can I list ten outstanding characteristics?

—Can I name five people they see as national heroes?

—Can I describe a typical diet and pattern of meals among the rich? Among the poor?

—Can I describe five key beliefs in the major religion of their country?

—Am I able to predict the features of this other culture which I am most apt to fear or distrust?

6. *Cultural Knowledge—General*

—Can I name at least five areas of human experience that would be expected to be different across cultural lines?

—What are the various attitudes toward modernization that would be found in various places?

——When in an unfamiliar city can I ask appropriate people
for directions when I need to?
——Can I list five topics which are apt to be poor subjects for
jokes among an intercultural group?

7. *Cultural Behavior—General*
——Do I take specific, thoughtful steps toward understanding
people whose lifestyles are different from mine?
——Do I avoid situations wherein I will have to explain why I
do things a certain way?
——When attending a religious service that is different from
my own do I know what to do and can I feel reasonably
comfortable?
——Do I like to call attention to my differences so that people
will be forced to ask about them?
——In a strange or new situation, do I find excuses to leave?

8. *Interpersonal Sensitivity*
——Does sympathy come easily for me? When others hurt, do I
hurt?
——Do I try to remain objective and not get swept into other
people's feelings?
——Can I usually tell what is worrying members of my family
or close friends even before they tell me?
——Do others tend to confide in me for one reason or another?
——Do I like to get into situations where other people come to
depend on me for emotional support?

FOCUS FOR SELF-EVALUATION

In Chapter 11 many concerns—both practical and emotional—associated
with an overseas move are identified. A number of suggestions have been
offered. Which of these suggestions will you follow?

Reflection

1. My greatest uneasiness about moving my family overseas:

_____

_____

2. Things we must discuss as a family:

_____

_____

Review

1. What is meant by "third culture"?

_____

_____

2. What types of schools are available for children of expatriates?

_____

_____

_____

_____

_____

Commitment

In order to make the overseas experience a positive one, I need to take care of some matters very soon.

Things I must arrange before I go: _____

_____

Things I must take overseas: _____

_____

_____

12

Living with
What You Find

BEFORE LONG, the newness wears off and the newcomer is tempted to make a list of all the things that need changing. If only they did things here like they do back home!

Getting accustomed to new ways and strange resources requires patience and skills. The tourist is usually protected by the insulation of artificial accommodations: food, housing, and transportation designed to fulfill Western expectations and tastes. The sojourner, on the other hand, very soon is plunged into the mainstream of a flowing current, much colder or hotter than "back home," swirling and bubbling this way and that. It's sink or swim. For example, consider such "minor" details as odors, bugs, and germs.

THE SMELLS OF THE TROPICS

Jasmine and sweet spices. That's the stuff of tourist promotion. In the *real* world, far less pleasant odors await the newcomers. For the family members who have to turn a house into a home, the smells and varmints are a special nuisance. Being alerted and being prepared to understand and deal with them can minimize the jolt.

Experiences back home in America probably include a variety of odors of technological origin. Air pollution, in general, is a machine-age reality the world over; but the American newcomer, especially in a tropical land, may come to welcome a whiff of good ol' diesel exhaust as a relief from the smell of garbage and sewage.

Except for the northern part of Alaska, the United States lies in the earth's temperate zone. Most overseas Americans live in climates that are warmer than what they were used to before. They need to be warned that food will spoil much faster if unrefrigerated. The incubation of weevils and other critters will be hastened in all sorts of grain products. Shoes, belts, purses, and clothing can become mildewed beyond repair in only a week or two if put away even slightly damp in a tropical seaside or rain forest region.

The matter of odors in the environment rarely gets the attention it deserves. Americans are quick to make olfactory judgments; turning up the nose is a typical newcomer's reaction. No one warned them that it was going to smell like this.

Unlike the seasonality of the temperate zone, in the tropics nature is renewing itself constantly. Leaves fall all year, and they rot quickly. Fruit falls from domestic and wild trees. It smells. Because frost lines are unheard of, sewers and pipes of all sorts are just under the surface. They leak and especially in rainy areas drainage and sewage tend to overflow frequently. Water stands in puddles and ponds. Crowded conditions in the cities produce still other odors, and the various smells of nature combine with the smells of burning coal, wood, or charcoal fires. These, combined with the distinctive odors of pungent cooking, can give the nose alone enough jolts to account for mild culture shock.

Being completely prepared for these encounters with strange sensory experiences is out of the question. The best you can hope is that being forewarned will make you more comfortable with your reactions. You *will* react—especially at first. But hold on! You'll get so used to it that you may even forget it. Perhaps the ability to forget to let it bother them is the reason so few old-timers think to alert you about odors.

BUGS

To listen to some overseas Americans, one might think that there were no bugs in the United States. Especially in the northern half of our country, the winter cold is an ally against household pests. Thus if reasonable habits of cleanliness are maintained, the human popu-

lation stays more or less on top of the bug population. But in the
tropics, those who hate cockroaches and their many cousins are going to have to take steps to discourage or destroy the unwelcome
boarders.

In every cubic meter of topsoil and in every pile of junk stacked
beside or partly under the house, there are enough creatures—if
they were united in purpose—to evict the human occupants by
dragging them bodily through the doorway while they sleep. Bugs
are a fact of life. Cockroaches are politically neutral, or perhaps naive. They indiscriminately annoy Americans, Russians, Africans,
Asians, Latin Americans, Republicans, and Democrats. Remember
this, lest you become paranoid and assume that some subversive plot
of global proportions underlies the quiet invasion.

Some creatures invade and destroy the very chair one sits in—
others attack the floors and the walls. These, especially termites and
carpenter ants, are almost impossible to resist effectively except
through lethal fumigation. Bug sprays only touch the edges of the
problem. You have to enlist heavyweight help.

But there is some good news about the much more common
complaint—roaches and other kitchen bugs. Given a very careful
regimen of neatness and a month or so of teeth-clenched determination, you can get these uninvited guests to move away or face star-
vation. It's the only way.

If there are children in the home, it will be especially difficult,
because the children's snack crumbs and half-eaten cookies will undermine your whole campaign. So even before you go overseas,
start to work on the children's food habits. *Eat at the table* is rule
number one. *Wipe up promptly* is rule two. The children have to
learn to help on these two matters, especially. The third rule, *seal
everything edible*, can be accomplished best if you take with you a
supply of two items: wide-mouth plastic canister jars, large enough
for a box of cereal or a bag of rice; and resealable freezer-weight
plastic bags. Make sure that at least a few of each of these go into
your accompanying baggage, since you will want to start your anti-
insect campaign as soon as you move into your residence.[1]

Insects seem especially impervious to angry words and they seem
to relish the late-night races that diligent householders occasionally
stage. So few lose their lives in these contests with brooms, stomping
shoes, swatting newspapers, and assorted missiles that roaches seem
to think of aggressive Americans as the sponsors of a nocturnal
Olympics. They thrive on it.

Starve them out. It's the only way. Tightly cover the sink drains at night, take out the garbage twice a day, leave no crumbs, and keep everything edible sealed or in the refrigerator. Then grit your teeth until the problem goes away. It might.

REDUCING RISKS

Boiling water for drinking and for cooking is still a valid practice, especially during the first six months to a year while your body begins to establish appropriate antibodies to deal with local strains of microorganisms.[2]

Cautious use of water and the additional precaution of soaking fresh vegetables in a diluted chlorine solution will cut down the frequency of the troublesome diarrhea that afflicts most newcomers. The old traveler's advice still holds: "Don't eat anything you haven't peeled yourself." For homemakers these extra chores are a terrible nuisance, but unless you have a cook who has had long experience working for American families, you may want to oversee or attend to these matters of health and safety yourself.

In some regions it is wise to cook meat slowly and thoroughly. This precaution is bad news for the person who likes a rare steak, but the incidence of meat-carried parasites as well as the local conditions of butchering and marketing meat should be taken into consideration.

With almost all these matters, the human body can be expected to develop resistance over time. The old-timers among the expatriates may take few precautions and get away with it. They become dangerous people when they give bad advice to newcomers: "They told you to Clorox the vegetables, eh? We used to think that was necessary. Found out we don't need to." In time, you may find the same thing. But stomach cramps can be the reward for premature bravery. Better safe than sorry.

Of the many ailments to which the sojourner is susceptible, internal parasites are the major threat. Amoebae and worms are persistent invaders. They are hard to get rid of once they get a good start. If parasites were restricted to the alimentary canal, that would be trouble enough, but the scary part is that vital organs can become the nesting place for various species. Therefore, periodic checkups with appropriate laboratory tests of blood and stool are strongly recommended.

All of life is risky. Going overseas should be seen as trading one set of risks for a somewhat different set. Just as wearing a seatbelt reduces one sort of common life-and-death risk, special care about food and water, coupled with regular medical tests, will reduce the risk of serious health complications for the overseas American.

STRANGE CRAVINGS

Even as expectant mothers can be counted on to awaken in the middle of the night with irrational cravings for such things as dill pickles and strawberry soda pop, overseas Americans develop surprising tastes for things they left back in the States. Americans in Paris, that gastronomical paradise, have been known to beg family and friends to line their suitcases with packages of gelatin dessert when coming to visit. For many years France banned such "filthy" by-products of animal hooves as being unfit for human consumption.

After delivery of one enormous "care package" to a Parisian-American household, I was thanked with the following words: "What a delight! This will be a treat for our whole family for weeks. But you know—it's so odd—I never thought much about Jello one way or the other before we came to Paris." Does deprivation make the heart grow fonder?

Then there's peanut butter. The lowly peanut, a native of Africa, was put through its versatile paces in the United States by George Washington Carver. So peanut butter is as American as apple pie. In many places of the world, even where the peanut grows in abundance today, peanut butter is still uncommon.

One approach to tracing the patterns of Americanization in the world's out-of-the-way places is, as the French might say, "Cherchez la peanut butter." On one solemn occasion I stood in awe and reverence in the dusty shop of a mission school for Quechua children high in the Andes of Bolivia, listening as my host demonstrated the machine that first brought peanut butter into the lives of thousands of Indians (and others) of the Cochabamba district. It was simply a food grinding machine powered by a sizable electric motor, wired to the mission's generator. If peanuts, in any form, were not such a significant addition to the protein-deficient diet of these Indians, it would have been funny. I had to ask:

"How do you keep the Americans in Cochabamba from eating up all the peanut butter?"

"Oh, that's no problem. The Indian students here make plenty for them too."

I knew it. There's no way to keep expatriates away from peanut butter. Even if they didn't eat it back in the States, scarcity makes it better—or something. It turned out that the one place to buy this commodity in Cochabamba was in the mission bookstore.

How do you cope with the absence of familiar foods and the presence of new—and strange—ones?

- Know your own dietary habits and tastes well enough to plan ahead.
- Try to enjoy local delicacies even if they stick to the roof of your mouth until you learn how to eat them.
- Expect to discover a strange craving now and then, but don't let it warp your life.
- If all else fails, check with other expatriates, especially the missionaries. They may know a little bookstore where you can get peanut butter—or cranberry sauce.

"BACK HOME" STORIES

"Back home, we would have thrown away a fish that old." "Back home, a person that drunk would be arrested." "Back home, it felt a lot more like Christmas." "Back home, you wouldn't have to wonder what all they put in the gasoline." On and on it goes.

"Back home" stories are often an unhealthy symptom. There's nothing wrong with a wholesome flash of recollection, especially if it is warm or humorous. Indeed an occasional wave of nostalgic reminiscence about friends, school days, childhood, earlier days with one's family, and other fond experiences is part of a normal life. Being overseas doesn't (or shouldn't) change that. But the nagging habit of constant comparison, of continuously bringing up the ways things were different back home—and usually one means *better*—is destructive. The habit, if unchecked, becomes a style of thinking, and its inevitable result is to make a person even more uncomfortable.

I recall two couples who took a vacation together to a region widely known as a resort and retirement area. At first all four seemed happy enough and were taking full advantage of the attractive qualities of the region. One morning at breakfast the subject was cockroaches.

LIVING OVERSEAS

"I've never seen roaches so big," she said, "and not just one. They're all over this place. Roaches have never bothered me before. But you know, after I saw that creature in the bathroom last night I just couldn't sleep. Thank goodness, back home we have those awful things under control."

And it started. Back home this, back home that—and for two more weeks the discontent built and the trip became miserable. Never again did those two couples take a trip together. And worse, never again did those folks with their fixation on "back home" take an extended vacation. They sat out their lives "back home."

A psychologist might see the "back home" story as only a symptom of a deeper maladjustment. In some cases, this is no doubt true; but like the habit of persistently scratching oneself, sooner or later it produces a sore even if there wasn't one to start with. And like other bad habits, there's no better time to break it than when it first emerges.

CURIOUS NOTIONS OF CLEANLINESS

With a few exceptions, someone who really enjoys Oriental food will like anything on the Chinese menu. But after a walk along a busy, crowded Oriental street, misgivings emerge. When the semi-washed sidewalk tiles become a kitchen and you step over and around the chopping of vegetables, ducks, fish, eels, chickens, and various mammalian parts rarely seen in the polite company of ground beef and pork chops in their fastidious American supermarket wrappings, you wonder who may end up eating the stuff. *You,* that's who! You and, as the saying goes, "China's millions."

Such customs as washing the dishes in oily plastic buckets, rinsing them with a garden hose lying like a booby trap across the sidewalk, and stacking them in buckets at the curb to drain dry may strike the American newcomer as unusual. In the Western world, kitchen procedures are kept out of sight on the assumption that what you don't know won't hurt you. Even in the tourist districts of the major cities, Taipei, Hong Kong, Jakarta, and Kuala Lumpur— to say nothing of the smaller places—such overt displays of bacteriological nightmare are there for all to see. The best newcomer's rule of thumb is, if a restaurant has a sidewalk-and-buckets approach, avoid it. Establishments with running water indoors are usually safer—if you can find one. Ironically, on the *world* standard, Oriental cooking is relatively safer from food contamination than are the food preparation habits of many another region. The Chinese restaurant tends to be the safest place in town in a small Andean or Equatorial African community. Clearly, cleanliness is a relative matter and, for all the difference it may make in our physical well-being, Americans tend to have very high expectations.

Where this most sharply affects the long-term sojourner is in the selection and training of household help. If, as in the majority of cases, you will be hiring a cook or general household maid, ask for and *check* references. A person who has grown up stepping over sliced tripe on a sidewalk may think your dainty ways not worth the effort. Such a person will be a persistent aggravation unless you can specify your standards clearly and thoroughly right at the outset. But since language barriers will be likely to make this difficult, you are far better off with household helpers who have already been trained to American tastes and standards by a previous employer. On some matters you won't want to adapt to local customs.

THE WORLD HAS A CHINESE KITCHEN

Before long, Americans will be able to take their children around the world without a worry about their willingness to eat. Thanks to the persistence of profits, the American hamburger is moving faster than a change agent's fondest dreams. Even in Japan, where beef-eating has never been common,[3] McDonald's puts it within reach of the middle class, and the affluent Japanese middle class buys. It seems unlikely that the same thing could happen in India. So perhaps the hint should be this: If you are hopping around the world and hamburgers are your preferred menu, skip over the vegetarian countries and ask your taxi drivers in all the other spots to take you to the nearest Golden Arches.

Old-timers know a better trick. Learning to appreciate Chinese food and to savor its relatively minor sweet-to-peppery variations from Cantonese to Szechuan puts you in a good position to find something familiar in even the most exotic location.

Chinese restaurants vary somewhat in appearance, and the menu will reflect the availability of local vegetables and meats, especially seafood. Since chicken and pork are Chinese staples and since chicken is among the safest meats to order, you should even be able to keep up your American-style protein intake. Another benefit is that the well-boiled Chinese tea is probably one of the safest drinks you can get even in places where the water is unreliable.

In the most authentic Chinese restaurants, especially in warmer climates, the cooking is done where you can see it—often in the very entrance to the restaurant. Another sign of the genuine article is the abundance of staff—aunts and uncles and cousins by the dozens.

If you really want to have fun, learn to eat with chopsticks before you go overseas. It will identify you as a sympathetic internationalist; even if you are thoroughly non-Chinese in appearance, the likelihood of being treated well is increased.

BIDDING, BARGAINING, BUYING

One of the basic skills that Americans—adults and children alike— will probably need to learn quickly is bargaining. You'll need to do it virtually every day. The prices you will pay for the basics of food, clothing, furniture, and many more items will depend partly on your skill as a bargainer.

Bartering or bargaining is actually a sort of game; it is seen as good fun. Americans may at first be defensive or feel threatened because control of the situation is in the more experienced hands. The game has some very definite rules, and violating any of the rules is almost always a source of embarrassment. Fortunately, the rules are essentially the same the world over. They can be learned in one situation and then applied almost anywhere, with appropriate small variations which can be learned on the spot.

"No, thanks, I'm just looking" is the language of the American retail store. In much of the world, where barter-and-bid systems of commerce prevail, the mere uttering of this great American line is sure to start an almost overwhelming dialogue of bargaining.

Two of the favorite starter lines used on Americans are "What do you think it is worth?" and "How much would you give me for it?" Shrewd market traders, no matter how backward and simple they may look, have a phenomenal understanding of human nature. And they have it sorted out by cultural types. They can see an American coming long before the American sees them. With their shrewdly chosen nonchalance or eager deference, they can go after an American's dollars with such skill that the observer can do no less than admire them.

In the typical market outside the United States, your curiosities can become badly frustrated. Rarely are any prices marked, and within the first thirty seconds, usually, someone is after you to buy this or that, depending on what the shopkeeper thinks you're looking at. Whether or not you even speak a common language—the shopkeeper will try several in order to try to get you to talk—the preliminary process goes forward until you finally ask: "How much?"

In one type of situation, the shopkeeper will answer this question directly, as for example, "Two dollars." A typical dialogue will continue like this:

"Two dollars? Too much."

"Good quality! Two dollars."

"No. Too much."

In this situation you *must* look at something else; don't let your gaze linger on the thing you are curious about. You might even turn as if to leave, but don't act huffy or peeved. That violates a basic rule: bargaining must lead toward a friendly agreement, not toward a hostile or threatening confrontation.

About now the shopkeeper will pick up the item and begin a speech about its merits. (If *you* go back to the item or pick it up before he does, the price will still be $2—he knows you *really* want it!)

"OK. So how much you give me for this?"

And here's a crucial moment. Whatever you say next you must be prepared to pay—on the spot. If you offer a ridiculously low amount, he will go into a pathetic "hurt" act; he may even scream at you for offending him. With that, you lose the game and buy at his price to placate him and get him off your back. So it's best to decide right then and there just what you would be willing to pay and bid about a quarter or a third less. In some places other expatriates can tell you what the shopkeeper really expects when he says "Two dollars." Often the asking price is twice the rock-bottom price.

"I'll pay seventy-five cents. That's what it would be worth to me."

"Seventy-five cents? No, no, no. This is good quality, not cheap like most places. Americans don't want bad things. You want good price? Just for you. I like Americans, I have many Americans come here to buy. You know Mrs. Swanson, the Ambassador's wife? She brings all her friends here. For you, one dollar and fifty cents, special price."

Hold your nerve. Remember that the difference between asking price and "special price for my friends" is usually about halfway to the lowest offer he will ultimately settle for.

Most Americans don't like to dicker more than two or three stages, and your shopkeeper knows that. So he will be ready to hear you say:

"No, one dollar and fifty cents is too much. I'll give you one dollar. No more. That's all I can spend on it."

"One dollar? No, no, no. It is worth two dollars!"

Now what? Back where you started? Not really. He *wants* you to say, "Well, then, how about a dollar twenty-five?" But he may be ready to take one dollar. So you had better try it.

"No, one dollar. That is final." (The term "final" or "last price" is somewhat like the last two pages of a Beethoven symphony; it sounds like it's going to stop but it keeps saying "The End" over and over.)

And even then the shopkeeper may balk. So you have to test his firmness, perhaps three times, then slowly turn as if to walk away. If he doesn't budge and you really want the item—and are willing to pay $1.25—say so now. You've probably reached an agreement. But he could, even now, hold out for his $1.50.

This routine is a lot of work just to find out how much an item costs. It can be very frustrating for an acquisitive American. So you learn to "window-shop" without asking.

In a second type of situation, the shopkeeper will insist that you name the first price. This may *sound* more pleasant, but it isn't. In the first place, you are now striking a precarious balance. On the one hand, you risk being "taken" by offering more than an item is worth; on the other hand, you may be scolded—perhaps shouted out of the shop—for insulting the merchant: "You want to cheat me! You think I am stupid? You Americans are all alike. You are exploiting our people. You are not paying fair price. You are son of the dog. Go away. I don't like you." Your mind bursts with visions of thousands of paratroopers; the skies fill with a huge airlift fleet; the Marines trot down the narrow street, bayonets to the ready, double time; the shopkeeper disappears up a ladder to the loft where his family lives; and another American has been rescued from intercultural conflict.

No, that sort of relief went out with Grenada. The best help in this sort of bargaining situation is a friend who knows the value of the thing. He or she can suggest a price for your first bid. But you also need to have a maximum price in mind, because the rules for this type of bargaining are just like those of a typical American auction except that the shopkeeper is both the auctioneer and your competing bidder.

"I'll give you one dollar for it."

"No, no, good quality. Much more. Not less than three dollars."

If you were well advised, your bid was about one-third of the price she will then identify as "what it's worth." If the discrepancy is more than the one-to-three ratio, she is telling you that you started too low.

"Three dollars? No, too much. I will give you one dollar and fifty cents. That's all."

"No. Three dollars."

Now you stall. Wait until she starts down. If you give two prices in a row and she hasn't offered to come down at all, she has you "climbing the ladder" toward her, and she knows your eagerness to buy is greater than your interest in saving money. You have lost. When she gets you up the ladder far enough to satisfy her, she will hand the item to you or start to wrap it. The bargaining session is over. There are two universal rules of bargaining: First, when the shopkeeper signals that he or she has accepted your price, the dealing is closed. You cannot attempt to back down from that price, nor will the shopkeeper push it up. Second, after the shopkeeper agrees to your offer, the deal is settled; the bidder must buy.

Once, in a community market in Addis Ababa, my affluent American curiosity clouded my alertness and, eager to know the value of a particularly well-carved wooden bowl, I asked my companion what he thought the price might be. Thinking that I wanted to buy it, he told me both what he believed its market price would be and what might be an appropriate first-offer price. Without thinking of the consequences, I started talking to the shopkeeper about the price of the bowl. But this wasn't Mobile, Alabama. The shopkeeper had no interest in my curiosity—only in my dollars.

Before long I found out what the value of the bowl was and walked away. Then I realized that my companion was dying several of his thousand deaths and that the shopkeeper was consigning us both to the Amharic equivalent of Hades. The buyer had failed to buy. By failing to consummate the bargain, trust was broken. Such is the stuff of poor intercultural behavior. One fails miserably now and then.

LIVING WITH DOCUMENTS

Carrying documents takes some getting used to! Start with the more familiar: the driver's license. The American Automobile Association (AAA) makes available at small cost an "International Driving

Card." It is essentially a multilingual translation of one's American (state) driver's license, and although it is not a long-term substitute for a local driving license, it serves well as an interim document while the sojourner gets established in the overseas assignment. During preparation time, get one for each member of the family who has a driver's license. After you take up residency overseas you will need to comply with the regulations and obtain proper national, provincial, and sometimes local registrations and licenses. Officialdom the world over takes documents very seriously.

Because documents in general play such an important role in so many other countries, it would be wise to keep the following points in mind.

Always carry some sort of official-looking document with your picture on it wherever you go—even to the market. (An American driver's license is safer to carry on the street than a passport because it is less complicated to replace if a pickpocket lifts it.)

Always keep your visa and residency papers up to date. Leniency, while not an American speciality, is even less likely to be in style overseas.

Always assume that any official who asks to see your papers means business. No jokes, no sarcasm please. In virtually all countries other than ours people can be required, for no apparent reason, to prove who they are and why they are in a certain place. "Innocent until proven guilty" is one of the rights that you leave behind when you go overseas.

SEE IT NOW OR NEVER

Newcomers to the expatriate community are often obsessed with "fitting in" with the other expatriates. For a while, at least, they are willing to forego their ambitions, their curiosities, their dreams— even willing to postpone their major *raison d'etre* in order to "fit in."

For some strange reason, newcomers sometimes assume that to be too "touristy," especially to take an interest in local and regional culture and geography, isn't "cool." They are afraid that mentioning a weekend trip to see the Taj Mahal or the Matterhorn will call attention to their newness, and so they put off doing so until after the "adjustment period."

Putting things off can become a habit. Make the effort to be a tourist now and then, even if it isn't stylish. One reason to be over-

seas is to widen your experience. There are Washingtonians who
have never stood silently gazing into Lincoln's great marble face.
There are Chicagoans who have never been inside the incredible
Field Museum of National History, and Michiganders who have
never spent a day at the marvelous Greenfield Village, old Henry
Ford's incredible plaything. And, believe it or not, there are Americans in Paris who have never been to the top of the Eiffel Tower.

You have to start within the first month if you are going to develop the habit of *seeing* the place. Wherever you are, there are
things to see. Make a list before you go; after you arrive, revise the
list and group the places you want to see according to importance
and convenience. Start with those that are easiest to get to.

The hundreds of chores of settling in are powerful competitors
for the precious hours of "spare time." To assume that there will be
more time available later on is quite reasonable. But before you
know it, you will have fallen into a pattern. The work or the family
will come first. The indispensable "survival chores" will come next.

There are dozens of things taken for granted in America that
take time and effort in almost any overseas situation. These chores
center on the "fetch-it" tasks: daily bread, newspaper, fuel for this
or that, fresh vegetables, fresh fish, and so forth. To get a feeling for
the problem, make an inventory of what you have in your freezer
and what is delivered to your door—including mail. Assume you
have to make a special trip or at least a separate stop for each of
these items, and you begin to see the problem. If you let these
dozens of chores become the center of your life, you will find yourself constantly in the company of other expatriates who are doing
the same thing.

All the while another group of expatriates, whom you will see
only at an occasional party (and maybe at work), have decided to
see the world—and they're doing it! You could have chosen to go
their direction, but you should have made the choice earlier. If,
within the first month in your overseas assignment, you haven't
made a half-day excursion or two—better yet an all-day hiking tour
or train-car-hike combination, you may get stuck for good. Your
motto should be "See it now or never."

Seeing the World

Putting too many cities, towns, and sights-to-see on an itinerary often comes from a sort of Irish Sweepstakes approach to travel. For

many Americans, going to "far-away places with strange sounding names" is a fulfillment of dreams. Even for those who are going overseas to live or for extended business and professional responsibilities, it is unlikely that the fantasy component can be suppressed. Perhaps it *shouldn't* be suppressed—enjoy it. But watch out for the tendency of fantasy to get out of hand.

Travel of any sort is stressful. Living out of a suitcase is annoying after several days. Especially if there are children involved, the breakdown of daily routine and the frustrating unpredictability of life's thousand little things can put travelers into a morose mood in a hurry.

Complicating all of this is the American's bargain-hunting instinct which can overwhelm sane rationality at the time of travel-planning. "Since we're going so near, we surely wouldn't want to miss Venice, and Florence, and Padua, and Rome." "Then why don't we just hop over to Athens for a day or two and see where Paul preached?" "That reminds me, where is Corinth?" "Maybe there are tours of Galatia and Ephesus and Philippi and Colosse and Thessalonika." "And how about Timotheus and Titus, Petra, and Johannesburg and Revelatia?" "Let's do it all. We may never get back." The marvel is that so many live to tell the tale.

Especially beware the while-we're-there-anyway sort of add-on. A stop or two enroute to a major assignment, especially for a *family* moving to an overseas location, can be a delightful treat. Three days in London and three days in Athens can be a great lift for a family moving to Saudi Arabia, Kenya, or Zimbabwe. But never plan a day each in London, Paris, Rome, Athens, Istanbul, and Cairo. Don't try the Grand Tour in a week.

It is false economy to include more stops than are emotionally and intellectually manageable. It is far better to appreciate than merely to see.

STAYING OUT OF PRISON

Ending this chapter on a note of warning is necessary. Not as a threat or to induce fear, but in order to prepare the sojourner for the needed frame of mind, it is important to sound the warning bells about laws and rules. The Islamic countries have strict regulations against possessing or even attempting to make alcoholic drinks. Prohibition, to an American, is a sort of historical bad joke—not to be taken too seriously. Watch out. Your host-country colleagues may be taking it quite seriously. Even a devout household servant may be offended by the bottle on a high shelf or at the back of the refrigerator. Americans have gone to prison here and there over such "trivial" matters. In most of the western world, the only serious hazards are drugs and unregistered firearms or ammunition. But even in the modernized cities of the Orient, it is important to stay out when a sign so directs, to be off the streets by curfew hour, and to carry the required documents.

Most of what you read in the American press about prisons overseas is true. Getting in trouble with the law enforcers or the overseers of political affairs is no laughing matter.

For all of the well-known inadequacies, overcrowding, and bestiality of American jails and prisons, it is far better to take one's chances on being a scofflaw in the United States than to do so while overseas. Matters of black-market money exchange, "removal of national artifacts" (carrying or shipping out of the country souvenirs that were picked up on the grounds of a temple or historical site), and the ubiquitous trafficking in drugs are "little" matters with big consequences. Yes, even highly moral and upstanding people have been known to get into difficulties over drugs. The American habit of carrying a mixture of several types of pills in one container or the practice of carrying pills or other drugs loose, out of their original or pharmaceutical packages, can lead to a dangerous hassle if one is searched carefully, at a border station, for example. Americans also often have the helpful habit of being willing to carry back for a stranger this "little package for my daughter who is a student at the university." The innocent-looking package contains a pen and pencil set or "her aunt's prayer book—please, just drop it in a mailbox when you get back to the U.S." No problem? Gullible Americans can spend some anxious hours, to say nothing of missing the next several planes, if narcotics agents are tracing this package to discover just who the carriers may be.

Several days in Bogota's lock-up can be followed by some unpleasant conversations in Miami. The police of many nations, pushed as they have been by the United States to "cut off the supply," are ever so delighted to turn over to the American authorities any real live nephew or niece of Uncle Sam who seems to be even momentarily affiliated with the drug trade. If they have a strong case, they handle it themselves.

Americans have rights that are virtually unique among the nations. Arguing with police, demanding to see a lawyer and to make a telephone call, demanding an accounting for confiscated prop-

erty, resisting search unless a warrant or court order is in hand—
these are assumed to be part of the American's rights. It is wise to
leave all these assumptions at home. In fact, going to another nation
means you have left the Bill of Rights behind. Don't forget it!

Yes, the American embassy staff or consular office will try to
check on you from time to time, while you sit out your weeks wishing you hadn't been sarcastic to the policeman. And those welcome
faces from the outside world may even be able to visit you occasionally, but be forewarned that one of their first messages will be the
sobering reminder that they—like you—are outsiders and guests of
another sovereign nation; the rules that pertain are not the American rules. Grin and bear it.

Better yet, stay out of trouble. Learn to keep your mouth shut
and pay attention to the local rules of the road. And never carry unknown gifts or "messages" across a border for a stranger.

FOCUS FOR SELF-EVALUATION

The importance of adapting to things that can't be changed suggests all
sorts of preparational steps to take. Patience and skills, in the right combination, will enable the sojourner to make the best of even the most disagreeable realities.

Reflection

When I think back over Chapter 12, these three ideas seem most important
in my situation:

1. _____

2. _____

3. _____

Review

What do I need to take overseas in order to cope with:

1. *Insects.* _____

2. *My need for cleanliness.* _____

3. *Predictable health concerns.* _____

4. *My need for occasional back-home style foods.* _____

Commitment

What mental state do I need: careful, serious, hopeful, patient, happy, conscientious, creative? Select the three terms that best express your commitment and will be most important for you, and describe the importance of each.

1. _____

2. _____

3. _____

13

Come Back Stronger

LOOKING AHEAD TO what it will be like to return to the United States may seem premature. But since the problems associated with repatriation are important, you should take a moment to consider what lies ahead at that distant time.

The problems of returning home are similar in many ways to the problems of going overseas in the first place. Even after a year or two the styles, customs, and patterns of daily life in the United States will have changed. In some respects you will be a newcomer all over again. Whatever your image of "back home again" may be now, it will be different when you get there.

In his last novel, Thomas Wolfe gave a deeper and more poignant meaning to the simple phrase, "You can't go home again." The theme suggested by the title of his novel is that *everything* changes once one's perspective changes. Wolfe's insights are conveyed through the character and experiences of a maturing novelist, George Webber, whose attempt to return to his simple boyhood in an Appalachian mountain town is a deep disappointment. Webber knows that he has changed, but what startles him is that *others* have changed. Things aren't the way he remembers them.

It is clear from Wolfe's telling of this bittersweet story that there are two basic problems, not just one: The changes are real, not just in George Webber's perceptions, and Webber's consciousness has been altered by his experiences in the "outer world." He has concerns and interests that are different from those back home. This dual problem is exactly the same for the expatriate. You can't go home again. It won't be the same.

What drives many people into overseas service is the same little spark of restless curiosity that has motivated the wanderer and the sojourner since the beginning of humankind. Those who leave the status quo and take the big step overseas show a willingness to encounter the unknown. Staying at home is in itself an inadequate proof of rigidity, but it is reasonable to assume that many who restrict themselves to living out their lives in one cultural context do so as a matter of choice.

When the sojourner returns, the contrast between these two levels of risk-taking and the increased differences in values that have developed are likely to result in some unexpected adjustment problems.

REENTRY ORIENTATION

Straight out of the jargon of the Space Age, a new term has entered the literature of intercultural orientation training: reentry orientation. There is a demonstrated need for such programs, and as the demand grows, so grows the knowledge needed for meeting the needs.

In the "old days," reentry was taken for granted. Being back home again, they called it. Those were simpler times; change processes moved more slowly, and three years out of the country then was not apt to span much social change.

Today, anyone who takes a vacation for three or four weeks gets a pretty good idea of the problem. Things change—and not just the length of the grass! Someone has moved from the neighborhood. Eve Smith's apartment was broken into; there's a new foundation already dug on the lot next to the gas station, and the gas station is closed and boarded up. The city changed the garbage pickup day, and the next door neighbors have separated. And all that happened in just one month. Coming home after two or three years will present far more adjustment problems. Move over, Rip Van Winkle!

Instead of being a warm and reassuring experience, homecoming can be a disaster. Events in one nation proceed at a different pace from those of another, and engender different outlooks; even the "world situation" looks different when you go home. In this era of rapid social and moral change, just reconciling one's values to the way things are is a challenge. More and more returning expatriates describe themselves as victims of "reverse culture shock." The phenomenon is real, there's no question about it.

As yet there are few "homecoming orientation" programs. The need hasn't yet been thoroughly recognized; many managers and personnel people still seem to be living in that bygone era when the problems of the returning veteran were not so serious.

More study of the problem is forthcoming. The needs, possibilities, and values of the outcomes of reentry orientation programs are being examined. The returning expatriate's transition can be made much more comfortable. A few pioneering programs have developed ways to help the trainees "find themselves" and adjust to productive fulfillment in the home country.

THE VIEW FROM THERE

Living in another country can give a very different perspective of your own country. Those who live on earth may think of home as "the green planet"; it wasn't until American and Russian astronauts got a new view of earth—from far out in space—that the idea of the *blue* planet caught hold. So it is with cultural perspective: The idiosyncracies of one's own culture are rarely noted until one has found another place to stand—and is able to look back.

Daniel Hess, now a professor of communication at Goshen College in Indiana, has written about the problems and pleasures of the international experience. Reflecting on the several moves he has made over the course of his life, he describes the perspective-building events he has experienced. As a farm boy in Lancaster County, Pennsylvania, his awareness began to enlarge when he started school: "Not until I entered the town's consolidated school did I realize that I was a country boy." Of his move onward to college, he reflects, "Not until I went to Virginia did I realize that I was a Pennsylvania Dutchman." His first professional employment gave him yet another vantage point: "Not until I lived in Indiana did I realize that I was an Easterner." Back in the East for graduate degrees at Syracuse University, his awareness deepened: "Not until I enrolled in graduate school did I realize that I was a Mennonite." This reflection illustrates a deeper concern: the essential meaning of what one claims to be. Finally, of a period of overseas service in Costa Rica, Hess reflects, "Not until I left the United States did I realize that I was a citizen of the United States, and depending where I was, a yankee, a gringo, an Anglo-Saxon, a capitalist, an imperialist, or a rich man."[1]

THE CHOICE

You do have a choice. Like many another fork in life's road, coming home again can confront you with a choice for which you have not prepared. The choice is between a repatriation built upon your flexibilities and awareness as an internationalist, or a repatriation with jolt after jolt arising from a return to rigidity and to the worst of the old habits that you had left at home. It is too easy to fall back into old ways.

What makes the difference? The way you relate to the overseas experience will influence what happens when you return. If you don't use the overseas experience to build strength, it will merely intensify your weaknesses. No one comes back unchanged. Unless one is adequately prepared, the overseas experience can be disorienting. Similarly, being prepared makes the major difference in coping with the difficulties of reorientation to the "back home" environment.

The approach that has been encouraged in this book is to see all of life's adjustments to other people's frame of reference in essentially the same way: as cultural matters to be understood, accepted, and willingly undertaken as adaptation or accommodation. The person who has been developing intercultural skills and cultivating an accepting posture toward others during several years of overseas experience should be far more able than before to cope with the adjustment problems of repatriation—*if* the repatriation problems are recognized as cultural problems. But if there has been no serious consideration about what it will be like, the jolts of coming home again will be unexpected and the return can be a huge setback.

JOLTS THAT AWAIT THE RETURNING AMERICAN

Being ready and able to deal with the following discoveries can determine the degree and kind of difficulty at the time of repatriation. Try to imagine how each of these problems could occur within your own situation. Anticipating the problems will make you alert for possible solutions.

People Have Been Able to Get Along Without You

They say they missed you and that things weren't the same without you, but the nagging evidence is right in front of your nose: They made it without you. Your relatives, your friends, your co-workers—they all seem to be doing surprisingly well. How does that make you feel?

Expecting other people to go on "hold" while you do your thing is not realistic. Accepting the fact that each person has a life to lead is basic to any good human relationship. The very idea that other persons, especially close friends, can get along without you is a compliment to the relationship you had established with them. It means that your relationship was free of extreme dependency.

Being missed doesn't always show. Take it at face value when someone says, "It's nice to have you back." Those words of welcome are the foundation for a new phase of life: becoming a vital part of the day to day relationships with those you left behind. It may take time to sort life out, but a healthy attitude will make the process easier.

You Are Far More Interested in What You Were Doing Overseas than Anyone Else Is

"Tell me what it was like!" "Start at the very beginning and tell me everything you did." Now and then you will run into someone who asks you to describe your experiences, but the fun goes out of it when you find the listener's attention wandering after only five minutes. Though it shouldn't be surprising, it always hurts when your exciting moments, your marvelous discoveries, your new insights, and the everyday things that gave your life meaning overseas are of relatively little interest to anyone else.

Like an actor on a stage who is blinded by the footlights, you start to tell your stories: "There is a great big world out there. And the people—so strange yet so much at home with themselves. How much we can learn when we look and listen! How much we can learn when we begin to break free of a view of the human race being centered in people like us. We are only some among many. . . ."

There are no murmurs, no sounds of deepened breathing, no signs of increased interest. Look into that darkened hall more carefully. Your eyes are beginning to adjust. Take a breath and make your next point: "Those human beings over there are just as important as you and I. . . ."

Wait now. Can you see the truth? The auditorium is empty. There is no audience. You are alone on the stage.

Not everyone can handle this. When it finally comes through to you that the difference in your life for the past several years has produced so little interest for those at home, you tend to feel rejected. And this rejection is deeper and hurts more than the rejections you felt while overseas. Even those closest to you—parents, brothers, sisters, neighbors—may sit patiently, even curiously through one showing of your slides, but then they change the subject.

If you are a good storyteller and can dramatize things a little, you will find children to be an interested audience. Senior citizen groups will show interest—will even invite you back. But the problem remains: the experiences and insights of overseas living are hard to share. At home, as elsewhere in the world, people tend to be locked into their own preoccupations. Insights from elsewhere are easy to ignore.

Missionaries, of course, will find that their supporting churches and individual contributors will show more interest than most. But even those experiences can be depressing. The presuppositions of such people are often so loaded with half-truths and imaginings that they seem to pay attention only to that which conforms to their stereotypes.

Is this lack of interest predictable? Yes, loneliness, in the sense of a lack of someone with whom to share deep and sobering thoughts, is one of the most commonly reported problems of the returned sojourner.

Your overseas years will have done more than provide a supply of tales to be told, and it is at this deeper level that even more troubling encounters may occur. Traces of both jealousy and threat can be noted, perhaps because overseas experiences may be seen by some as challenges to the standards held at home. For example, "You had to eat with your fingers? Yuk." The American who has learned to live competently and happily with people of another nation finds that the experience has broadened and deepened his or her perspectives. The sensitive returnee is more apt to see racism and chauvinism for what they are—more apt to react critically to the shortsighted selfishness that goes along with some forms of patriotism.

Preparation for this apparent lack of interest might well be centered on the stories you plan to tell and how you plan to tell them. While you are living through an experience, it is inevitable to see it as something to share with others who are near and dear. "Wait until they hear about this!" By the time you get back to tell the tale, it has probably faded a bit even in your own recollection. Maybe some events are best left in this sort of shrinking limbo—don't try too hard to recreate the significance of a past episode that cannot be shared in the present.

When the expatriate returns, the best course of action is to make the very most of the *now*. The "overseas stories" that make the biggest hits are those you took time to write about while they were still fresh. Don't live in the past after you get home. Be responsive to genuine interest, of course, but be prepared for an early point of satiation (enough is enough, already) when you recount this or that story.

As was true of Scheherazade's retelling of the travels of Sinbad, the entertainment value of these tales depends much on one's skills as a storyteller. It is an art to cultivate. Keep in mind a few basic rules:

- Make the story simple. Extra details can confuse the hearer.
- Get to the point before your hearer's attention wanders.
- Keep the cast of characters small. Nothing confuses the hearer more than a string of names of unknown people.
- Use the names rather than pronouns. Talking in terms of he, him, his and she, her, hers is sure to be confusing if there is more than one person of each gender in the story.
- Don't follow one story with another. Let the hearer ask for more or wait until another time.

Much of What Has Become Important to You Is Hard to Put into Words

The deeper the feeling, the harder its expression. So much of what makes the overseas experience profound is in the realm of feelings. You will find it difficult to tell folks back home about your changed outlook, you deeper appreciations, and your new sense of priorities. What makes it even worse is the apparent breakdown of communication which all of this suggests. All communication depends on shared experiences; when crucial experiences have not been shared with another person, appropriate words are especially hard to find.

The tendency is to quit trying. Since this difficulty can be an especially profound disappointment, many an expatriate will simply bottle up the feelings that emerged during the intercultural experience along with the additional insights gained during repatriation and put the whole thing to rest on some closet shelf of the mind. Thus much of the value of the intercultural experience is denied. "Since it is hard to share, maybe it isn't important after all."

The solution lies in part in a realistic expectation about the individuals with whom one *can* share. Rather than trying to share the deeper and more abstract meaning of your experience with anyone and everyone, be selective. Then take it slow and easy. Don't try to dump a complex thought in one mad burst of words. The sharing of more worthwhile experiences deserves time and care.

Your Interests and Concerns Have Diverged from Those of the "Folks Back Home"

Of all the problems that can disorient the returning sojourner, this one should be the most easily anticipated. Most expatriates know that it is happening; they know that the intercultural encounters have aroused new and deeper consciousness; they know that certain things which once were very important are now fading or being replaced by other interests and concerns. In sum, they know that being overseas has changed them.

Knowing in the intellectual sense and *feeling* are often quite different. The shock that can disorient the returning sojourner is a matter of feeling. Yes, he or she knew all these shifts were taking place and, for the most part, felt rather good about it. But now the emotional reaction to discovering that one has learned to hear Thoreau's "different drummer" can be quite hard to handle. Rarely does a person intend to get out of touch with the "old folks at home." But when repatriates find themselves once again side by side in Mom's kitchen, across the desk from Frank and Meg at the office, the differences are all too real.

Be careful to keep alive your new horizons and deepened consciousness. I have known people whose racist tendencies and jingoism went with them overseas, where their new experiences served to liberate and reorient them toward a more humane outlook, only to fall back into their old patterns when they returned to the United States and their home communities. The pressures to conform to the norms and values they had once left behind were strong enough to cause them to deny and ultimately to reject the broader perspective they had developed overseas.

The solution for this moral dilemma is not easy. Does one stay faithful to ideals and values which have arisen from experiences in a foreign culture in preference to returning to the expectations and standards of one's compatriots? The advice Polonius gave to his son is sound, if not easy to follow—even for Polonius.

> *This above all: to thine own self be true,*
> *And it must follow, as the night the day,*
> *Thou canst not then be false to any man.*
>
> *Hamlet*, Act I, Scene 3

The ideals are in place—but what of the strains on relationships? If there is any intercultural skill that is important to bring home, it is the capacity to work effectively—in trust and honest commitment—with those whose values and world view are different. Even as it was not necessary to agree and to conform on every matter in order to work well overseas, it is not necessary in order to relate well with others back home. Integrity, respect, and trust should not be left overseas!

Dissonances May Exist Between Your Values and Those of "Other Americans"

Partly because the situation has actually changed while you were gone and partly because you are more aware than before of the values that Americans tend to hold, the dissonances are becoming clearer. If your overseas service was in a less materialistic society, and especially if you were engaged in some sort of humanitarian service that brought you face to face with some of the really difficult circumstances in which people live, you have a new appreciation for the things many Americans take for granted. You see more and you appreciate more of what you see.

An expatriate who has been oriented well for the overseas experience is likely to gain a sense of political perspective that makes for uneasiness when back home again. When you have lived in another political context for a while, you see that political matters are really quite vital. But you aren't sure what to do about it when you are back in America. On the one hand, you are aware as never before that Americans are very privileged not to live in a totalitarian or anarchic state, and you fret because so few people talk about the blessings of democracy. You feel like getting out the flag and saying, "Do you realize what you have here? Wake up!"

On the other hand, you see the potentialities for a twist toward the extreme—either of the right or of the left—and you wonder if flag-waving is really justified among people whose values are so chauvinistic and self-serving. Thus you fret. What can you do?

You wonder how Americans can be so unaware of the heartbeat of humankind—how they can be so uninterested in events elsewhere, so ignorant of the world as an integrated stage. They seem so content with playing out the little, petty events of one place in one state in one nation.

The repatriated American is apt to be a more zealous American, but is also likely to be confused about what to do about the social and political problems at home. Your experiences have given you a different way of looking at things. To some extent these ways are "foreign" to your fellow Americans. They can't see things through your eyes.

The American Lifestyle Has Changed While You Were Away

Two things work together to create a real headache: nostalgia and the reality of change.

Nostalgia plays strange tricks. "How good it was. . . ." Was it really as it seems now in memory? The good ol' days—a stereotype created by fond remembrance. How thankful we can be that the human memory is selective. The flow of time washes away the silt of discomfort, anxiety, and unpleasantness, leaving exposed in the stream bed those jewels and nuggets that form the substance of warm memories. The problem is more one of selective memory than of actual distortion. The result, however, is a kind of bias that can set up false comparisons.

"I don't remember that people were so impersonal." "Before I went overseas the city took much better care of the streets." "How different—we never even used to lock our doors." Perhaps each of these recollections is true in some objective sense, but they are more easily explained in terms of the three tricks played by time and space:

1. *The tendency to remember selectively.* Whether one tends to remember the good or the bad depends on personality and habits, and on one's overall assessment of the object of those memories. Perhaps people at home are no more impersonal now than they were before, but the recollection of "how things were" can play strange tricks. A sojourn in Switzerland or Japan may have made one nostalgic for the greater overt friendliness and emotional openness of the people in one's home town. In fact, it can cause the sojourner to forget that not everyone in Akron is open and friendly. Thus, the effect is to distort or exaggerate the recollection.

2. *Sensitization to realities previously ignored.* Living in a place where streets and spare lots are virtually public dumping grounds can cause a person to think about such matters for the first time. Whether or not one ever really notices the matter of neatness "back home," it now seems certain that things weren't this bad. By comparison, an image of immaculate streets and vacant lots back home emerges. When one returns from overseas, that image, rather than any previous *reality*, is the basis of comparison.

The opposite can also operate to create new sensitivities. Consider the possibility of becoming thoroughly attuned to a slower pace of life. In a Latin American country, for example, the rush of life seems largely confined to a small minority of urban folks who seem to be out of tune with the national standard of never doing today what can be put off until tomorrow. After becoming attuned to the tranquility of a small town or quiet neighborhood in such a region, returning to the United States will result in a predictable reaction: "How much more frantic and compulsive life has become since we left for Ecuador!" Maybe. But more to the point is the comparison of the United States as you thought it was with the United States as it is—and maybe always has been.

3. *Comparison of yesterday's apples with today's oranges.* The places where most of us grew up are changing, whether or not we go overseas. The fact that we can recall a time when the neighborhood was more intimate and caring, a time when neighbors looked after each other's homes, kids, and property suggests an awareness of an early stage in the "maturing" of a neighborhood. Going home again inevitably finds the neighborhood changed. Some of the original families remain, some are gone, replaced by "new" neighbors.

The mix is different, and the relationships are different. Doubtless these are losses. The fact that a returnee doesn't know all the newer arrivals is itself a distance-producing factor, at least until acquaintance and friendship can be developed.

In general this sense of alarm ("we never used to lock our doors") will settle back to a sense of confidence as soon as the returning sojourner fits back in again.

TECHNOLOGY AND SHOPPING CENTERS

The telephone store, the video arcade (today's pool hall), the dealer in personal computers—these and other additions await the returning sojourner of today. What will it be in another five years? When I left the little town where we lived for many years, the closest things to nationally advertised merchandising were a small Western Auto store and a Rexall drugstore. Returning after several years, I found that a J.C. Penney's had come in with a small version of the company's big-time merchandising. A few years later another return revealed that the impossible dream was being fulfilled: McDonald's, Burger King, Radio Shack, and a Pizza Hut. So much change on Main Street in a small American town can lead to reverse cultural shock!

EVEN SHOCK TEACHES

Coming home can be seen as a harvesting of what has been learned overseas. Peter Adler's research suggests that even culture shock isn't all bad—it can play a positive and motivating part in your social development that will become part of the strengths that you bring home. Adler proposes seven ways that culture shock can have positive benefits:

1. Sojourners become better learners. Since learning always involves some form of change, the different situations sojourners have to face provide opportunities that demand new responses, thus stimulating a *learning* approach to life.
2. Culture shock leads to individualized motivation. No two people are affected in the same way. Most people enjoy feeling unique or special, and past encounters with culture shock contribute a motivational force to new experiences.

3. The feelings arising from cultural change are provocative. Effective handling of cultural differences encourages people to analyze the reasons for their feelings.

4. Anxiety, at some levels, encourages learning. At low levels, there is no reason for people to work on learning new materials or ideas. The frustration, anxiety, and personal pain stemming from culture shock can bring the level of anxiety to the optimal level. Then people will be motivated to learn so that they will acquire new knowledge and skills which can be used to reduce the anxiety. However, when the anxiety level is too high, people may be so upset that they will be unable to focus on new learning possibilities.

5. Culture shock arises, in part, from differences in presuppositions and background. People who cope well with these differences become good users of feedback. The unique role of the sojourner as outsider encourages the perception of ideas which are taken for granted by hosts.

6. The shock effect of cultural difference can lead to experimentation. Sojourners can engage in trial and error to discover ways to meet a situation; thus they learn a great deal in the process about experimental inquiry methods, often experiencing the elation of success through the discovery of appropriate behaviors.

7. The new ideas learned during experimentation are frequently based on comparisons and contrasts. Given the motivation provided by culture shock, sojourners can relate the new ideas to the functioning of various societies. The motivation to learn also encourages a confrontation with, and a greater understanding of, one's own culture.[2]

CHANGED FOR THE BETTER

It is never too soon to think about what you will be like when you come home again. Your home away from home occupies your thoughts and keeps you busy now. But when it is time for you to return, will you come back stronger?

The overseas experience will change your life in many ways. Whether it is a month, a year, or ten years, the effects will be felt. Your broadened cultural perspective, your acquaintance with a wider variety of people, your having learned to accept and even to appreciate their lifestyles—these things will make you different.

If you prepare yourself for this return—as a changed person—and make preparations for that time, just as surely as you are making preparations now, you can regain your stability and composure with relatively little stress. But if you neglect these preparations, your homecoming can be disorienting. In my own experiences what makes the disorientation more severe is not just the length of time overseas, but the emotional intensity of the activities and events.

Returning home can be seen as just one more cultural adjustment. Whether you handle it well or badly depends largely on how well prepared you were to go overseas in the first place. Prepare to go, learn while you are overseas, and when you come home again, bring all your new skills with you. Follow these suggestions and you will come back stronger.

FOCUS FOR SELF-EVALUATION

The overseas experience can be a significant period of personal and professional development. This final chapter has suggested many possibilities for bringing home more mature and refined interpersonal skills, a more holistic perspective, and a higher degree of social responsibility.

Reflection

Through the overseas experience my viewpoint on certain issues might

change, such as the following: _____

_____

_____

_____

Review

1. Name four "jolts" that await me when I am a returning sojourner.

    a. _____

    b. _____

    c. _____

    d. _____

2. Why is "homecoming orientation" important?

_____

Commitment

I intend to take advantage of overseas opportunities that will make me stronger in the following ways: _____

_____

_____

_____

_____

APPENDIX A

Games for Culture Learning

The exercises that follow illustrate and assist the development of particular skills needed for overseas living. Each exercise is presented here in a format for small-group experience—as it might be used in an orientation training program. With a little imagination, these exercises can be turned into useful experiences for a family group. Most of the exercises will also work as "solitaire" games, but they are more fun and provide a greater possibility for new learning if at least two people share the activities and discussions.

1. The View from Outside

This exercise will encourage participants to see themselves as people from another culture might see them. Technically, it is an exercise in perspectivism, called by some social psychologists "role reversal." The exercise may be conducted as follows:

• Organize groups of four people each. (If extra persons, some groups will need to consist of five people.)

• Distribute copies of "Body Ritual Among the Nacirema" by Horace Miner.

• Read or explain the following to the whole group:

This article is a classic. It has been published and reprinted in many forms and in various anthologies. The reasons for its popularity are easy to guess: Miner has a sense of humor and he knows how to get people to see themselves from another viewpoint, not viciously as if cut down by some superior morality, but brightly and cheerfully. All it takes to enjoy Miner's article is a little imagination and a willingness to laugh at oneself.

As you read the article note each detail and try to think about what it symbolizes. Start with the name: "Body Ritual Among the Nacirema." What sort of a society has "body ritual" as part of its culture? Surely not ours. Oh? The idea here is that some things are so much taken for granted that their structure is only apparent from some other viewpoint. Miner's humor is built on the fact that in every society "common" things are taken for granted. If you take something for granted, you don't "notice" it.

Consider Nacirema as a country or society—who might this be? Read on, and interpret the symbolism.

• Read Miner's article silently.
• When all participants have read the article, the work really starts. Each work team should identify a list of features or aspects of take-it-for-granted American life that might look very different to an outsider, especially if the outsider were completely unfamiliar with American habits, tasks, attitudes, and outlooks.

Each team is to decide upon and write down at least one good example for each of the listed categories on the form "The Strange People of Asu." *Avoid using any of Miner's points*; think of new ideas. Remember, select things that are "commonplace" to insiders.

The first team to fill in all nine examples is judged the winner in the "speed" category. Other teams can stop writing at this point or continue until until each team has identified something for at least six of the categories on the form. (The form should be reproduced on paper or on a chalkboard in preparation for the exercise.)

THE STRANGE PEOPLE OF ASU

Relationships of the people of Asu to other living creatures:_____

_____

Movement of people and things in Asu:_____

_____

Things eaten in Asu:_____

_____

Evidences of honesty or dishonesty in Asu:_____

_____

Political tolerance in Asu:_____

_____

Attitudes toward life and death in Asu:_____

_____

Use of water or waterways in Asu:_____

_____

Attitudes toward outsiders and foreign observers in Asu:_____

_____

The most confusing characteristics of the Asu:_____

_____

• Sharing: The winning team in the "Speed" category is now expected to read and explain each of its listed items to the whole group.

The facilitator should then write on the board two items from this list as entries for the "Horace Miner Award," given for examples of comparable merit to the "sacred vessel." The speed-winners team can recommend the nominees or the facilitator can choose them.

Each of the other teams then must put two items from its list on the list of nominations.

The winning entry can be determined by show of hands and the Horace Miner Award is then presented to the team sponsoring the winning entry. Judgments should be based upon the following: (1) appropriate contrast of insider's view and outsider's view, and (2) humor or cleverness of thought.

Body Ritual Among the Nacirema
Horace M. Miner

The anthropologist has become so familiar with the diversity of ways in which different peoples behave in similar situations that he is not apt to be surprised by even the most exotic customs. In fact, if all of the logically possible combinations of behavior have not been found somewhere in the world, he is apt to suspect that they must be present in some yet undescribed tribe. The point has, in fact, been expressed with respect to clan organization by Murdock (1949:71). In this light, the magical beliefs and practices of the Nacirema present such unusual aspects that it seems desirable to describe them as an example of the extremes to which human behavior can go.

Professor Linton first brought the ritual of the Nacirema to the attention of anthropologists twenty years ago (1936:326), but the culture of this

Reproduced by permission of the American Anthropological Association from the *American Anthropologist* 58 (3), 1956, pp. 503–507.

people is still very poorly understood. They are a North American group living in the territory between the Canadian Cree, the Yaqui and Tarahumare of Mexico, and the Carib and Arawak of the Antilles. Little is known of their origin, although tradition states that they came from the east. According to Nacirema mythology, their nation was originated by a culture hero, Notgnihsaw, who is otherwise known for two great feats of strength—the throwing of a piece of wampum across the river Pa-To-Mac and the chopping down of a cherry tree in which the Spirit of Truth resided.

Nacirema culture is characterized by a highly developed market economy which has evolved in a rich natural habitat. While much of the people's time is devoted to economic pursuits, a large part of the fruits of these labors and a considerable portion of the day are spent in ritual activity. The focus of this activity is the human body, the appearance and health of which loom as a dominant concern in the ethos of the people. While such a concern is certainly not unusual, its ceremonial aspects and associated philosophy are unique.

The fundamental belief underlying the whole system appears to be that the human body is ugly and that its natural tendency is to debility and disease. Incarcerated in such a body, man's only hope is to avert these characteristics through the use of the powerful influences of ritual and ceremony. Every household has one or more shrines devoted to this purpose. The more powerful individuals in the society have several shrines in their houses and, in fact, the opulence of a house is often referred to in terms of the number of such ritual centers it possesses. Most houses are of wattle and daub construction, but the shrine rooms of the more wealthy are walled with stone. Poorer families imitate the rich by applying pottery plaques to their shrine walls.

While each family has at least one such shrine, the rituals associated with it are not family ceremonies but are private and secret. The rites are normally only discussed with children, and then only during the period when they are being initiated into these mysteries. I was able, however, to establish sufficient rapport with the natives to examine these shrines and to have the rituals described to me.

The focal point of the shrine is a box or chest which is built into the wall. In this chest are kept the many charms and magical potions without which no native believes he could live. These preparations are secured from a variety of specialized practitioners. The most powerful of these are the medicine men, whose assistance must be rewarded with substantial gifts. However, the medicine men do not provide the curative potions for their clients, but decide what the ingredients should be and then write them down in an ancient and secret language. This writing is understood only by the medicine men and by the herbalists who, for another gift, provide the required charm.

The charm is not disposed of after it has served its purpose, but is placed in the charm-box of the household shrine. As these magical materials are specific for certain ills, and the real or imagined maladies of the people are many, the charm-box is usually full to overflowing. The magical packets are so numerous that people forget what their purposes were and fear to use them again. While the natives are very vague on this point, we can only assume that the idea in retaining all the old magical materials is that their presence in the charm-box, before which the body rituals are conducted, will in some way protect the worshipper.

Beneath the charm-box is a small font. Each day every member of the family, in succession, enters the shrine room, bows his head before the charm-box, mingles different sorts of holy water in the font, and proceeds with a brief rite of ablution. The holy waters are secured from the Water Temple of the community, where the priests conduct elaborate ceremonies to make the liquid ritually pure.

In the hierarchy of magical practitioners, and below the medicine men in prestige, are specialists whose designation is best translated "holy-mouth-men." The Nacirema have an almost pathological horror of and fascination with the mouth, the condition of which is believed to have a supernatural influence on all social relationships. Were it not for the rituals of the mouth, they believe that their teeth would fall out, their gums bleed, their jaws shrink, their friends desert them, and their lovers reject them. They also believe that a strong relationship exists between oral and moral characteristics. For example, there is a ritual ablution of the mouth for children which is supposed to improve their moral fiber.

The daily body ritual performed by everyone includes a mouth-rite. Despite the fact that these people are so punctilious about care of the mouth, this rite involves a practice which strikes the uninitiated stranger as revolting. It was reported to me that the ritual consists of inserting a small bundle of hog hairs into the mouth, along with certain magical powders, and then moving the bundle in a highly formalized series of gestures.

In addition to the private mouth-rite, the people seek out a holy-mouth-man once or twice a year. These practitioners have an impressive set of paraphernalia, consisting of a variety of augers, awls, probes, and prods. The use of these objects in the exorcism of the evils of the mouth involves almost unbelievable ritual torture of the client. The holy-mouth-man opens the client's mouth and, using the above mentioned tools, enlarges any holes which decay may have created in the teeth. Magical materials are put into these holes. If there are no naturally occurring holes in the teeth, large sections of one or more teeth are gouged out so that the supernatural substance can be applied. In the client's view, the purpose of these ministrations is to arrest decay and to draw friends. The extremely sacred and traditional character of the rite is evident in the fact that the natives return to the holy-mouth-men year after year, despite the fact that their teeth continue to decay.

It is to be hoped that, when a thorough study of the Nacirema is made, there will be careful inquiry into the personality structure of these people. One has but to watch the gleam in the eye of a holy-mouth-man, as he jabs an awl into an exposed nerve, to suspect that a certain amount of sadism is involved. If this can be established, a very interesting pattern emerges, for most of the population shows definite masochistic tendencies. It was to these that Professor Linton referred in discussing a distinctive part of the daily body ritual which is performed only by men. This part of the rite involves scraping and lacerating the surface of the face with a sharp instrument. Special women's rites are performed only four times during each lunar month, but what they lack in frequency is made up in barbarity. As part of this ceremony, women bake their heads in small ovens for about an hour. The theoretically interesting point is that what seems to be a preponderantly masochistic people have developed sadistic specialists.

The medicine men have an imposing temple, or *latipso*, in every community of any size. The more elaborate ceremonies required to treat very sick patients can only be performed at this temple. These ceremonies involve not only the thaumaturge but a permanent group of vestal maidens who move sedately about the temple chambers in distinctive costume and headdress.

The *latipso* ceremonies are so harsh that it is phenomenal that a fair proportion of the really sick natives who enter the temple ever recover. Small children whose indoctrination is still incomplete have been known to resist attempts to take them to the temple because "that is where you go to die." Despite this fact, sick adults are not only willing but eager to undergo the protracted ritual purification, if they can afford to do so. No matter how ill the supplicant or how grave the emergency, the guardians of many temples will not admit a client if he cannot give a rich gift to the custodian. Even after one has gained admission and survived the ceremonies, the guardians will not permit the neophyte to leave until he makes still another gift.

The supplicant entering the temple is first stripped of all his or her clothes. In everyday life the Nacirema avoids exposure of his body and its natural functions. Bathing and excretory acts are performed only in the secrecy of the household shrine, where they are ritualized as part of the body-rites. Psychological shock results from the fact that body secrecy is suddenly lost upon entry into the *latipso*. A man, whose own wife has never seen him in an excretory act, suddenly finds himself naked and assisted by a vestal maiden while he performs his natural functions into a sacred vessel. This sort of ceremonial treatment is necessitated by the fact that the excreta are used by a diviner to ascertain the course and nature of the client's sickness. Female clients, on the other hand, find their naked bodies are subjected to the scrutiny, manipulation, and prodding of the medicine men.

Few supplicants in the temple are well enough to do anything but lie on their hard beds. The daily ceremonies, like the rites of the holy-mouth-men, involve discomfort and torture. With ritual precision, the vestals awaken their miserable charges each dawn and roll them about on their beds of pain while performing ablutions, in the formal movements of which the maidens are highly trained. At other times they insert magic wands in the supplicant's mouth or force him to eat substances which are supposed to be healing. From time to time the medicine men come to their clients and jab magically treated needles into their flesh. The fact that these temple ceremonies may not cure, and may even kill the neophyte, in no way decreases the people's faith in the medicine men.

There remains one other kind of practitioner, known as a "listener." This witch-doctor has the power to exorcise the devils that lodge in the heads of people who have been bewitched. The Nacirema believe that parents bewitch their own children. Mothers are particularly suspected of putting a curse on children while teaching them the secret body rituals. The counter-magic of the witch-doctor is unusual in its lack of ritual. The patient simply tells the "listener" all his troubles and fears, beginning with the earliest difficulties he can remember. The memory displayed by the Nacirema in these exorcism sessions is truly remarkable. It is not uncommon for the patient to bemoan the rejection he felt upon being weaned as a babe, and a few individuals even see their troubles going back to the traumatic effects of their own birth.

In conclusion, mention must be made of certain practices which have their base in native aesthetics but which depend upon the pervasive aversion to the natural body and its functions. There are ritual fasts to make fat people thin and ceremonial feasts to make thin people fat. Still other rites are used to make women's breasts larger if they are small, and smaller if they are large. General dissatisfaction with breast shape is symbolized in the fact that the ideal form is virtually outside the range of human variation. A few women afflicted with almost inhuman hypermammary development are so idolized that they make a handsome living by simply going from village to village and permitting the natives to stare at them for a fee.

Reference has already been made to the fact that excretory functions are ritualized, routinized, and relegated to secrecy. Natural reproductive functions are similarly distorted. Intercourse is taboo as a topic and scheduled as an act. Efforts are made to avoid pregnancy by the use of magical materials or by limiting intercourse to certain phases of the moon. Conception is actually very infrequent. When pregnant, women dress so as to hide their condition. Parturition takes place in secret, without friends or relatives to assist, and the majority of women do not nurse their infants.

Our review of the ritual life of the Nacirema has certainly shown them to be a magic-ridden people. It is hard to understand how they have managed to exist so long under the burdens which they have imposed upon themselves. But even such exotic customs as these take on real meaning when they are viewed with the insight provided by Malinowski when he wrote (1948:70):

> Looking from far and above, from our high places of safety in the developed civilization, it is easy to see all the crudity and irrelevance of magic. But without its power and guidance early man could not have mastered his practical difficulties as he has done, nor could man have advanced to the higher stages of civilization.

References Cited

RALPH LINTON, *The Study of Man*, D. Appleton-Century Co., New York, 1936.
BRONISLAW MALINOWSKI, *Magic, Science, and Religion*, The Free Press, Glencoe, 1948.
GEORGE P. MURDOCK, *Social Structure*, The Macmillan Co., New York, 1949.

2. Baggage Check

This exercise provides an opportunity for people to take a look at their "cultural baggage." In this context, cultural baggage refers to the values, habits, lifestyle, and expectations that the sojourner takes along into the overseas assignment.

Individuals will prepare their own responses to a list of self-perception and self-assessment questions. Then small groups of two to four people each will be formed to compare and discuss the items.

• Individuals should write their responses to the items on the "Baggage Declaration." (The two forms should be reproduced to provide copies for each participant.)

BAGGAGE DECLARATION

I. *Personal characteristics*

    A. In your own country, what do people notice when they see you coming?

        1. _____

        2. _____

        3. _____

    B. In the country where you are planning to go, what will people notice when they see you coming?

        1. _____

        2. _____

        3. _____

    C. What do you try to avoid?

        1. _____

        2. _____

        3. _____

        4. _____

    D. What do you most enjoy?

        1. _____

        2. _____

        3. _____

        4. _____

II. *Relational style*

    A. What sort of people do you prefer to work with? Indicate major characteristics, traits or qualities:

        1. _____

        2. _____

        3. _____

    B. What sort of people do you prefer to be with for social and recreational activities? Indicate major characteristics, traits or qualities:

        1. _____

        2. _____

        3. _____

    C. How you feel about *authority*?_____

    _____

    _____

    D. How do you feel about *equality*?___ _____

    _____

    _____

    E. How do you relate to beggars and panhandlers when they confront you on the street?_____

    _____

    _____

    F. How do you react when invited to a formal or prestigious event?

    _____

    _____

    _____

• As each individual completes the "Baggage Declaration," ask him or her to pair up with another person who is done to compare and discuss their Baggage Declarations while waiting for the others to finish. When everyone has finished writing, go to the next step, the "Baggage Checklist."

• Explain or read aloud to everyone:

As we all know, when you enter any country, there are some items that you are not allowed to bring in. At the level of personal judgment, there are things you know that you should leave home. The next part of this exercise asks for some careful judgments about what you carry into the country and what you leave home.

BAGGAGE CHECKLIST

Make a list of your cultural baggage and indicate items that fall into each of the three categories.

1. *Must carry.* My professional or career role absolutely requires that I not leave these items behind—whether or not I might want to.

   Give one example here: _____

2. *Would like to leave behind but probably can't.* My judgment is probably better than my capability of following through. I will try not to take these things, but they may show up as embarrassing "stowaways."

   Give one example here: _____

3. *Must be left behind.* My overseas assignment will be a new page in my life as far as these items are concerned. I will not take them along.

   Give one example here: _____

• Discuss the meanings and share a few examples of each of these items as individuals suggest them.
   • Next, each individual should fill in the "Baggage Check" form.
   • Share by grouping people in sets of two or four as they complete the writing. Put the following questions on the chalkboard or a poster to guide the discussion:

What "baggage" might embarrass you if you take it overseas?
What can you do about things you should leave at home? (Be specific—discuss particular items.)
What sort of help will you need to follow through on your good intentions? (Again, be specific—talk about particular items.)
Find examples of each of the following (if they are on your lists) and discuss what can be done:

1. Matters that might give offense
2. Sources of "personality clash"
3. Matters that will interfere with one's major purposes in being overseas

Baggage Check

Categories of Cultural Baggage	Must Carry	Would Like to Leave Behind	Must Be Left Behind
Appetites (for foods and *other!*)			
Attitudes toward other people			
Feelings about myself			
Feelings about my country and other countries			
Habits (especially things I do without thinking)			
Things (yes, *things*—for example, your microwave oven)			

3. Postcard Tour

The purpose of this exercise is to develop the habit of linking *disciplined* inferences to observations. More simply, the intention is to encourage careful
observation and to guide the participant into a conscious drawing-out of
reasonable meaning.

• At least one day before the exercise begins all participants should be
organized into "country teams" of two to ten persons each. Each team will
collect, pool, and organize a display of ten to twenty pictures which together provide a glimpse of life and experience in the country to which
they are preparing to go. (More than one team per country should be organized if there are more than ten persons intending to go to that country.)

Any sort of picture (color or black and white, photograph, sketch, car-
toon) is allowable if it is 4″ × 6″ or smaller. Postcards are ideal. Travel
folder pictures and magazine clippings are also useful. (Warn the neighborhood collectors of *National Geographic* to bar their doors!) Participants
should be aware that only one side of back-to-back pictures can be used.
Each picture should be cut and ready to mount on a 4″ × 6″ index card.

• On the day of the exercise, distribute white glue and twenty 4″ × 6″
index cards to each team.

• Each team will select ten to twenty of the pictures according to the
following criteria:

1. Each picture should contain at least one clear indication that it
   could have been taken in the country the team is illustrating.
2. Each picture must have at least two possible interpretations, not
   necessarily contradictory. To test this criterion see if there are at
   least two somewhat different answers to this question: *What impression about the country or its people does the picture suggest?*
3. The collection as a whole should present an impression of the country that is not essentially misleading.
4. The collection should represent some of the contrasts and ambiguities of the country. Test this by asking: *What conflict, tension, or
   potential misunderstanding could be inferred from these pictures as
   a whole?*

• Each team should predict the reaction of other teams to its collection
of pictures. Each team should use the "Postcard Tour Report" to record
the anticipated reaction of the other viewers of its collection of pictures.

(Note that each team should be given two additional blank copies of
the "Postcard Tour Report," for the two "tours" to follow.)

Throughout the whole exercise the emphasis should be on the following
points. (This list should be written on the chalkboard while the groups are
taking their Postcard Tours).

POSTCARD TOUR REPORT

Assume that you know nothing about this country other than what this "Postcard Tour" is showing you. Respond as a team.

A. What emotions do you feel as you see this country "for the first time"?

    1. _____

    2. _____

    3. _____

B. What do you notice from the pictures as major features of this country?

    1. _____

    2. _____

    3. _____

    4. _____

C. What temptations to form judgmental conclusions do you experience?

    1. _____

    2. _____

D. What specific information would you want in order to form a more responsible opinion about this country?

    1. _____

    2. _____

    3. _____

    4. _____

    1. Observe carefully—Consider even what small details might mean.
    2. Look into your emotional reactions—What triggers them?
    3. Be slow to come to judgmental conclusions.

    • Explain that each team's pictured experiences are a simulation of a newcomer's brief introductory tour of a given country. As a team look at the pictures provided by another team and talk about the experiences they suggest. How does this picture make you feel? What do you see? What does it mean? What impressions does the collection give to you? After a five-minute conversation, each team should take ten minutes to write its responses on the "Postcard Tour Report." After 15 minutes, each picture collection should be passed to the next team in the cycle and the Postcard

Tour experience will begin again in another country. Each group will report on two countries in addition to its original prediction.

• Share by asking each originating group to read its *predictions* of reactions. Encourage discussion based on contrasting or fulfilling reactions experienced by the other teams that took each respective Postcard Tour.

4. Strange Customs

Some of the "strange customs" encountered in another culture leave the newcomer gasping. Unusual ways of doing things always tend to catch our attention and quite often add to our discomfort simply because they don't seem to make sense. This exercise is concerned with the attempt to imagine, grasp, and accept the logic of particular customs. The purpose is to encourage the habit of looking for the underlying reasons which could explain how the custom got started or what function it still serves.

The exercise provides an opportunity for participants to "open up" and talk about some of the less understandable things that they have heard about. Among these matters will be some which are, indeed, matters of anxiety, fear, or aversion. To discuss and create constructive speculations about such matters is a useful habit. The exercise puts the participants into a simulation of the deliberative process wherein the mystified newcomer tries to "make sense" of the clues in the "strange" environment.

• Organize teams of four or five persons each. One person in each team should take notes and be prepared to speak for the group during the sharing time.

• Write on a chalkboard or poster: "NO SHOES IN THE HOUSE"

• Read or explain to the whole group:

The custom of taking off shoes at the door and wearing slippers (or less) in the house is still a common custom in various places in the Orient, especially in Japan. There are several practical advantages of this custom. Americans find it difficult to remember at first, and for some it just seems to be nothing more than an annoyance.

• Ask each team to discuss the question: What practical and esthetic purposes are served by this custom? Allow ten minutes for this activity.

• The teams then share the ideas that have emerged in each team. Each team's recorder can read notes to the whole group, and others should be encouraged to add to the explanations.

• List other "strange customs" on the chalkboard. Everyone in the group should be encouraged to add to the list. Some of the customs suggested will be less appropriate for this exercise than others, but a list of ten or more customs should encourage enough lively discussion. To get the list started, try "Sleeping on mats on the floor;" or "Shutting down all commerce at noon for a two-hour siesta." (Stop after five or ten minutes or when the list gets to twenty items.)

• Each team (as organized earlier) may select for itself any one or two customs from the list and follow the procedure used in the original example: What practical and esthetic purposes are served by this custom? Allow about fifteen minutes for this discussion.

• Ask the teams to share highlights only. Each team should have a few minutes to tell how it attempted to understand the custom or customs selected.

5. Converting "Don't" to "Do"

The common forms of advice, especially from well-meaning friends, tend toward "don't." The all-time classic is "Whatever you do, don't drink the water."

This exercise is concerned with the practical problem of turning negative advice into positive or action-oriented guidelines.

The teams are to engage in two speed contests in which they compete to draw up lists. These contests are followed by a more serious sorting out of important advice.

• Organize teams of two to five persons each. These teams can be chosen on a random basis or by clustering people as they are seated. The exercise will work best if each team is mixed on the matter of country of assignment—in other words, more than one country should be represented in each team. Each team selects as its scribe one person who is able to write very quickly. Give each scribe a blank sheet of 8½" × 11" paper.

Contest I

In a four-minute time period, each team should write down as many items of specific "don't" advice as possible. To get ready and before the timing starts, each recorder is to write: "Don't drink the water." This item is "free"; it is the starting item for each list. From here on, each team thinks of as many such "don't" items as possible in four minutes.

The winning team will be the one with the most pieces of advice listed. In order to count, a piece of advice must be *reasonable*, in the sense that it deals with a matter of some value for intercultural sojourners or international travelers.

• Identify the winning team. Its scribe should read that team's list aloud, slowly. Other teams should check items against their lists. After the winning team's list is read aloud, *other items* should be contributed by each other team.

Challenges may be made only on the grounds of irrelevancy—if an item relates in no way to the intercultural or traveler issues. The importance or worth of the item is not to be challenged at this time. By majority opinion an item can be disqualified if it is irrelevant.

Contest II

Each team is to transform its list of "don't" items into a parallel list of "do" items. Give each scribe another piece of paper. For each "don't," teams should try to find *one or more* items for positive, specific advice. Provide two "free" items as starters before the time starts: "Carry safe water when going to a region of unknown water," and "Drink bottled drinks or boiled drinks." Allow ten minutes for this contest.

• Identify the winning team. The scribe should read the list slowly. Other teams should check off their items as before, adding any items not already mentioned.

After a general discussion of all the items, the group as a whole is to make a list of the most valuable pieces of "do" advice for each of the following categories. Try to write three items for each category. Allow 30 to 45 minutes.

Advice for Intercultural Sojourners

A. *Health-related*

    1. _____

    2. _____

    3. _____

B. *Family-related*

    1. _____

    2. _____

    3. _____

C. *Job-related*

    1. _____

    2. _____

    3. _____

D. *Religion-related*

    1. _____

    2. _____

3. _____

E. *Relationships-related (with host-country persons)*

   1. _____

   2. _____

   3. _____

F. *Relationships-related (with Americans and other expatriates)*

   1. _____

   2. _____

   3. _____

G. *Other*

   1. _____

   2. _____

   3. _____

6. The Walking Tour

Knowing how to learn on one's feet is an important skill. Cultural clues are all around us, but we must learn to notice them and convert them into ideas and meanings. And this requires slowing down. It's hard to do from a car seat at 55 miles per hour!

The exercise described here is in the form of a semistructured walking tour through a familiar or unfamiliar neighborhood. As a prefield exercise, it may be done in relatively familiar surroundings; if used in this way it will have value both now and as a practice experience for carrying out the same exercise in the future in an "other-culture" neighborhood.

The walking tour can be done as an impromptu "wandering tour" or the facilitator can scout the vicinity ahead of time and plan the itinerary. The trip should *not* be destination-oriented. The walk itself is to be more important than any particular destination. The major value of the experience comes from observing the unexpected. Think of it as an invitation to serendipity.

• Organize "touring squads" of four persons each.

• Guidance: In general, the path chosen should be zig-zag, neither straight-line nor circular.

• Procedural rules:

1. Walk in pairs. Stay near the other pair in your squad. Keep the rest of the group in sight.

2. (Not applicable if there is a set itinerary.) The squad that arrives first at a corner or other intersection is to decide whether a turn is taken or not; all squads must abide by that decision. After a squad makes such a choice, it must drop back to the last-squad position. In other words, the decision-making is to be rotated. (A decision *not* to turn is a decision—drop back.) This will have the desirable effect of keeping everything at a relatively slow pace.

3. Each squad is to stop to converse after every five minutes of walking. Conversing time should last from one to three minutes. Each group should keep track of its own time so that the group can find a relatively convenient spot to stand (or sit) for its periodic talks.

4. The entire group should be reorganized after 30 to 45 minutes. At some convenient place the facilitator should call everyone together and new squads should be formed with all-new combinations of people. The facilitator's squad will then lead out from this reorganization and activity will continue as before.

• The ideal walking tour lasts from two to three hours, depending on the physical condition of the participants.

Cards should be prepared, each listing all the following questions:

What have you seen that you didn't expect to see?

What have you noticed many times before but today you are thinking about for the first time or in a new way?

What "unusual" uses of artifacts have come to your attention?

What have you seen being undervalued or treated with less respect than you would give it?

A card should be issued to each squad before the walk begins, and these questions should be constantly on the minds of the participants. They should try to answer some of the questions on each of the five-minute interval stops.

Variation on the Walking Tour

Prepare and use this card to guide squad discussions:

What is there that . . .

Makes me curious?
Mystifies me?
Threatens me?
Frightens me?
Amuses me?
Saddens me?

APPENDIX B

Added Advice

1. Health on Your Own

Health supplies as we know them can be very expensive or completely unavailable in certain overseas situations. Especially for those whose assignments will be in remote rural locations, it makes good sense to make room in your suitcase for an initial supply of the following items:

Prescription drugs
Water purification materials
Tylenol, aspirin (headache, fever remedies)
Pepto-Bismol, Kaopectate (antidiarrheal medicine)
Sunscreen (especially important for high altitude or the tropics)
Insect repellent
Band-Aids (adhesive bandages)
Gauze, adhesive tape
First aid cream or other antibacterial cream
Fever thermometer
Ace bandage (elastic bandages for twisted ankles and knees)
Tinactin or other antifungal cream, for skin fungus, especially for toes
    in the tropics
Tampons
Easily laundered handkerchiefs

In some of the more underdeveloped areas, bar soap and toilet paper can be hard to find and an initial supply should be carried with you. They can be obtained in regional cities, however. Mosquito netting to sleep under is necessary in some areas; if you are going to such a region, ask what is needed and how to use it.

Check medical records to see that *all* family members are currently immunized against tetanus, polio, and measles and that your children have had all other shots recommended by their pediatrician. In some parts of the world it will be necessary to be immunized against other diseases, such as typhoid and cholera. Your county health department will have a listing of the specific immunizations required or recommended for individual countries. Be sure to check requirements for countries you may be expected to visit on short-term assignments or side trips. Get an international certificate of vaccination (yellow health card) for each family member from your travel agent and take it with you to the county health department because certain immunizations must be officially recorded when you get them. Call the health department for an appointment at least six weeks before your departure for two reasons: some vaccines are given only one or two days a month and several require a series of shots. Get it all done early to avoid the "last-minute shot syndrome." After an immunization you may feel sick for a day or two; it can be a real nuisance to feel less than your very best those last few days before departure when you are certain to be very busy.

In areas where malaria is endemic, it is essential that you take medication to prevent this very serious disease. A form of chloroquine is usually taken by Americans, and it must be prescribed by a physician. You must take it orally, beginning two weeks before arriving in the area where you might contract malaria and continuing *all* the time you are there and for several weeks *after* you leave the area. Unfortunately, some people get malaria despite such precautions.

Following good practices of basic personal hygiene can be even more important in helping to keep you healthy overseas than at home, although it can be more difficult. A few specific suggestions may be helpful. Bathroom facilities may be very good in some places overseas, but in some parts of the world they may be very dirty or nonexistent. Keeping free from infections may require vigilance. Some simple precautions will help: Always wear shoes or sandals, resist the urge to scratch insect bites, and keep your fingers away from your face.

When overseas you must always assume that tap water (or any other water) is unsafe to drink unless you know otherwise. In cities and more developed areas, bottled water may be readily available for drinking and cooking. Even then, boiling is the simplest and safest way to purify water: a full rolling boil for ten minutes. If boiling is impractical, then chemical treatment must be used, usually iodine tablets. These are available at specialty camping shops. There are drawbacks to chemical water purification: thyroid patients should check with their doctors before using iodine preparations, and most people dislike the taste of chemically purified water.

One of the great delights of overseas living is the sampling of new foods and different methods of food preparation. A few words of caution are in order before you begin to eat as the local people do.

Milk and milk products have not necessarily been pasteurized or tested. If you are uncertain, boil the milk or use canned or powdered milk that has been reconstituted with purified water.

Even if you enjoy it rare at home, meat should always be cooked very thoroughly and served hot. In Japan, as an exception, the raw fish served at sushi bars may be safe; make your decisions about them case-by-case, preferably on the basis of recommendations of other expatriates. Under-cooked meat, fish, and seafood are high-risk sources of hepatitis and parasites. In impoverished rural areas, be alert to the sources of meat. To avoid waste, an animal that has died of "natural" causes may be cooked. Sometimes people who eat the meat of such animals also die "natural" deaths.

There are places where it pays to be a "short-term vegetarian" and eat *cooked* vegetables. In some regions vegetables are raised with raw sewage as fertilizer. Regardless of washing techniques, such vegetables should not be eaten raw. Even diluted chlorine bleach may not kill all the baddies. In fact, "if *you* don't peel it, don't eat it" is the best rule for fruits and vegetables.

These precautions are not meant to frighten nor do they need to prevent you from having some wonderful culinary experiences overseas. Every nation has its special foods, and the more you try them, the more you will appreciate the culture. As you travel to various places overseas, you may enjoy comparing cuisines and finding the similarities among eating habits. For example, whether we call them *ngau yuk mai*, *empanadas*, *somozas*, or pasties, everyone seems to have some form of meat pie. Living to eat is not particularly healthful advice; but when you are overseas, try not to limit yourself to eating only to live.

2. A Note for Single Women

The topic of "special problems of the single woman" smacks of prejudice and inequality. For some women it is sufficiently offensive to make them reject certain overseas assignments. It is important to learn from knowledgeable people and to reflect carefully on one's willingness to live within different constraints. Men, as well, need to reflect and plan with respect to these matters, but the injustice of this fallen world decrees that women are under stricter constraints and will pay more severely for violating norms and expectations. And make no mistake about it, the single woman is apt to be the most rigorously and narrowly restricted.

Everyone must draw the line somewhere. No one—woman or man, single or married—can do anything and everything that strikes the fancy without paying a price. Wisdom calls for discretion, and discretion usually requires that the line be drawn carefully in the interest of one's own welfare and credibility.

One can learn to accept disagreeable tasks and situations, and perhaps grow thereby, but risks to health and safety must be approached with caution. This advice underlies parents' relationships with children in almost every culture. Although easy to resent, this advice needs to be given. The American tendency to prove adulthood through rejection of parental influences can get the young sojourner into great danger. To the extent possible, rebelliousness should be left at home.

Walking to the corner store alone after dark may be unwise anywhere. The forms of danger differ from one place to another, but the need to consider danger is always part of life. Life would be dull if there were no risks to take, no reason to take precautions.

In a new culture, just as in a new neighborhood in an American community, there are new dangers to assess, new precautions to take. This fact is not, in itself, either a menace or a handicap: becoming adjusted is a matter of learning the new realities and accepting responsibility for one's wellbeing and happiness. The degree of risk one chooses to take is a matter of lifestyle and personal choice. The tasks one must undertake to become oriented are getting knowledge of the realities and developing a lifestyle that will bring risks within acceptable limits.

Orientation, then, provides an alternative to the less liberating lists of *don'ts* and *nevers*. Such lists are valuable if developed for oneself based on a knowledgeable grasp of the situation. Old-timers, of course, will suggest items for your lists but no two people can follow exactly the same set of self-imposed restrictions.

One firm rule of competent coping with a new culture is that one cannot transplant habits, expectations, and standards intact. There are limitations on personal freedom everywhere. The strictures one finds overseas will be different but no less real than those one has learned to live with "back home." The greatest tensions arise from personal regressions encountered in the move; for example, an ardent advocate of women's rights would find an assignment in an Arab country almost unbearable. A person who has worked diligently toward cultural change in her or his own country feels an almost overwhelming temptation to continue or even to redouble the efforts in the new, "less free" culture.

Behavior in Context

The most perplexing problem facing the single woman overseas is to learn the new set of meanings attached to the behaviors she has come to take for granted in the home country. What do *these* people read into a smile? What does it mean to them when a single woman walks alone here or there, by daylight, at night, with a shopping bag, without a shopping bag? What message do these people read from visits to or from single persons of the opposite sex? What do these people assume to be the moral standards of an American? Of an American woman? Of an American woman who lives alone? What does it mean when a woman enters a bar or a restaurant alone?

Behavioral standards for women are somewhat more conservative in America than in western Europe. To Africans and Orientals, westerners "all look alike"; thus an American woman may be surprised at their tendency to read "looseness" into her appearance and manners.

The very presence of a woman in certain places and situations communicates a message. In addition, in every society sexual meanings are associated with certain gestures and postures—even with certain styles of conversation and humor. That these meanings differ from place to place can be unnerving to the unprepared person.

Clothing in Context

Although it could represent avant garde fashion, a super-short skirt communicates at least one other strong message in Times Square in New York City. Even in smalltown America, beachwear is not for the supermarket. The meanings communicated by clothing almost always relate to context. In every society these rules of relationship are somewhat different, and in every case the rules are applied more rigorously to women than to men.

What do these people read into clothing types and styles? All sorts of local notions about what is appropriate and inappropriate are based on these readings. The sojourner never grasps all the subtleties of these readings; even trying hard to learn them is sure to be frustrating. But to ignore the differences between such meanings at home and in the new culture is to court disaster.

When is an occasion or context formal? What is the appropriate clothing for the given degree of formality? Learning the answers to these questions and dressing accordingly will go a long way toward gaining acceptance in the society. It may be inconvenient or tiresome, but it pays well!

APPENDIX C

Sources of Practical Information*

Health

HUCKINS, ANNE, ed. *Staying Healthy in Asia*. Volunteers in Asia, Box 4543, Stanford, CA 94305. Most advice also pertains to Africa and Latin America. Inexpensive paperback to carry.

FRAME, JOHN, M.D. *Health Common Sense*. Associated Medical Mission Office, 475 Riverside Drive, New York, NY 10027. Inexpensive paperback especially written for missionaries; one of the best for any sojourner.

JACOBSON, HELEN SALTZ. *The Special Diet Foreign Phrase Book*. Emmaus, Pa.: Rodale Press. Primarily a tourist's manual, but because of its concern for matters of health, diet, and handicap, can be a substantial help and reassurance.

LONDON, MEL. *Easy Going—A Guide to Traveling in Good Health and Good Spirits*. Emmaus, Pa.: Rodale Press. A book of practical hints, centered on health maintenance and conservative advice by an experienced world traveler.

General Information

PIERCE, ELEANOR R., for Pan American Airways. *All You Need to Know about Living Abroad*. Garden City, NY: Doubleday and Company.

*Sources are listed in order of usefulness in each category.

The Center for Area and Country Studies, Foreign Service Institute, U.S. Department of State, 1400 Key Boulevard, Arlington, VA 22209. Country-specific bibliographies and compilations of up-to-date information.

Consumer Information Center. *Your Trip Abroad*. Dept. 128, Pueblo, CO 81009. Price: $1.

Taxes

Price Waterhouse and Co., 1251 Avenue of the Americas, New York, NY 10020. Brochures and tax information on nearly one hundred specific countries.

Business Consultation

U.S. Department of Commerce, 14th Street and Constitution Avenue, N.W., Washington, DC 20230. Country-by-country consultants and documentary materials.

Office of Commercial Affairs, U.S. Department of State, 2101 C Street, N.W., Washington, DC 20520. Consultation in international business and industry matters.

Center for International Business, Suite 105, 4600 Post Oak Place Drive, Houston, TX 77027. Conference, consultation, and special briefings for members.

Overseas Jobs

Transcultural Services, 59 Rogers Street, San Francisco, CA 94103. Information and assistance for overseas assignments and family relocation services.

"Opportunities Abroad for Educators, 1983–1984 Teaching, Seminars." Document ED 1.19:983–84 S/N 065-000-00141-1. U.S. Government Printing Office, Superintendent of Documents, Washington, DC 20402.

Business Council for International Understanding, American University, Washington, DC 20016. Foreign deployment service, brochures, catalogs.

Overseas Assignment Directory Service, Knowledge Industry Publications, 2 Corporate Park Drive, White Plains, NY 10604. Country-specific information available to companies.

Price Waterhouse and Co., 1251 Avenue of the Americas, New York, NY 10020. Series of publications: "Information Guide for Doing Business in ___" (cite the country).

KUCHER, ERIC. *International Jobs—Where They Are and How to Get Them*. Reading, Mass.: Addison-Wesley, 1984.

International Exchange Experiences

Experiment in International Living, Brattleboro, VT 05301. International exchange organizations; training and assignments for students and professionals.

Intensive Training Services

Family Relocation Services, Inc., P.O. Box 10797, Stamford, CT 06904. Orientation and preparation resources for overseas assignments.

Language and Intercultural Research Center, Brigham Young University, 240, B–34, Provo, UT 84502. Orientation, training, evaluation services available for all fields.

Intercom, American Graduate School of International Management, Glendale, AZ 85306. Language and intercultural preparation for executives and spouses.

Intercultural Communication, Inc., P.O. Box 14358, University Station, Minneapolis, MN 55414. Culture-specific orientation programs for families and managers; language training, assessment, and counseling.

Missionary Internship, Inc., Box 457, Farmington, MI 48024. Short and longer development programs and counseling services, especially for religious missionaries and church-related relief and development professionals and volunteers.

Overseas Briefing Associates, 355 Lexington Avenue, New York, NY 10016. Training materials and briefings for managers and families.

Wayne Shabaz Associates, International Personnel Consultants, 16705 Chandler Park Drive, Detroit, MI 48224 Telephone: 313-343-0987. Specialized training and consultations for employees and families preparing for overseas assignments in business and industry.

Other

Diplomatic services of most nations are able to provide information and limited assistance in matters related to an international move. To start, a letter addressed to the Embassy of _____, Washington, D.C., will elicit more detailed information. Many nations maintain consular offices in major cities around the United States.

Remember: When overseas, the *consular* office, *consulate*, or other designation of a *consul*, rather than the *embassy* or ambassador's offices, will be the major contact point for most of what an expatriate needs.

One of the finest topical bibliographies of resources and helpful literature is George W. Renwick's *The Management of Intercultural Relations in International Business* (Chicago: Intercultural Press, 1981).

Films and Videotaping

For its thorough coverage of the variations in the conditions of human life in Asia, Africa, or Latin America, one collection of 16 mm films and videotapes is remarkable. The collection, "Habitat: Improving Human Settlements," offers many materials suitable for group use in orientation training programs. Discussions of vital matters of human understanding are stimulated by virtually every film in the collection.

The core of the collection is about 100 films on international development and human settlement developed by the United Nations Centre on Human Settlements, Nairobi, Kenya.

The University of Illinois has the exclusive distribution and sales rights in the United States. Their catalog of this collection is well organized and provides explicit detail on each of the titles. These materials are readily available for rental or purchase at reasonable rates.

The catalog, entitled "Habitat: Improving Human Settlements" is available at no cost upon request from
University of Illinois Film Center
1325 South Oak Street
Champaign, IL 61820
Telephone: 1-800-FOR-FILM (1-800-367-3456)
            1-800-252-1357 (within Illinois)
The University of Illinois catalog also includes numerous films and videotapes from Britain's Thames Television International, a collection of great acclaim in its own right.

APPENDIX D

Country-Specific Descriptions and Guidebooks

Human Relations Area Files

For highly informative materials on particular countries, the exhaustively detailed collections in the Human Relations Area Files (HRAF) should be noted. No finer source exists for the contemporary and historical study of cultures and subcultures of the world. The "home base" is at 755 Prospect Street, New Haven, Connecticut, but the collection is made available through the cooperation of a selected group of university libraries.

University of Colorado
University of the District of
Columbia, Mt. Vernon
University of Illinois
Indiana University
University of Iowa
University of Massachusetts,
Boston

University of Michigan
City University of New York
State University of New York at
Buffalo
University of Pennsylvania
University of Pittsburgh
University of Southern California
University of Washington

In addition, microform copies of the file are held at many other major libraries and are available through
HRAF, Inc.
P.O. Box 2054, Yale Station
New Haven, CT 06520

Country Studies

Formerly entitled *Foreign Area Studies* and *Area Handbooks*, each of these studies describes one country's social, economic, political, and military organization. They are designed for the nonspecialist. The cultural and historical origins and the role these play in the country's present institutional organization and functioning are researched by an interdisciplinary team, in order to describe a coherent dynamic system of relationships and interactions. Page counts run from 200 to 800. All volumes are clothbound. The dates shown here are of the most recent revision. Order by number from

> Superintendent of Documents
> U.S. Government Printing Office
> Washington, DC 20402

Afghanistan	S/N 008-020-00461-8	$13.00	1973
Albania	S/N 008-020-00362-0	10.00	1971
Algeria	S/N 008-020-00791-9	11.00	1979
Angola	S/N 008-020-00816-8	11.00	1979
Argentina	S/N 008-020-00536-3	12.00	1974
Australia	S/N 008-020-00540-1	13.00	1974
Austria	S/N 008-020-00598-3	11.00	1976
Bangladesh	S/N 008-020-00591-6	11.00	1976
Belgium	S/N 008-020-00544-4	10.00	1974
Bolivia	S/N 008-020-00506-1	12.00	1974
Brazil	S/N 008-020-00564-9	13.00	1975
Bulgaria	S/N 008-020-00528-2	11.00	1974
Burma	S/N 008-020-00391-3	11.00	1971
Burundi	S/N 008-020-00219-4	9.50	1975
Cambodia (Khmer Republic)	S/N 008-020-00445-6	12.00	1972
Cameroon, United Republic of	S/N 008-020-00488-0	11.00	1974
Ceylon	S/N 008-020-00366-2	13.00	1971
Chad	S/N 008-020-00423-5	10.00	1972
Chile	S/N 008-020-00495-2	13.00	1969
China, People's Republic of	S/N 008-020-00888-5	12.00	1969
China, Republic of	S/N 008-020-00437-5	12.00	1972
Colombia	S/N 008-020-00647-5	13.00	1977
Congo, People's Republic of (Congo Brazzaville)	S/N 008-020-00346-8	10.00	1971
Costa Rica	S/N 008-020-00340-9	10.00	1970
Cuba	S/N 008-020-00626-2	13.00	1976
Cyprus	S/N 008-020-00831-1	11.00	1980

Czechoslovakia	S/N 008-020-00408-1	11.00	1972
Dominican Republic	S/N 008-020-00484-7	11.00	1973
Ecuador	S/N 008-020-00449-9	12.00	1973
Egypt	S/N 008-020-00605-0	12.00	1976
El Salvador	S/N 008-020-00367-1	10.00	1971
Ethiopia	S/N 008-020-00870-2	12.00	1980
Finland	S/N 008-020-00514-2	10.00	1974
Germany	S/N 008-020-00186-4	20.00	1960
Germany, East	S/N 008-020-00421-9	11.00	1972
Germany, Federal Republic of	S/N 008-020-00578-9	12.00	1975
Ghana	S/N 008-020-00382-4	12.00	1971
Greece	S/N 008-020-00718-8	11.00	1977
Guatemala	S/N 008-020-00215-1	11.00	1970
Guinea	S/N 008-020-00587-8	12.00	1975
Guyana	S/N 008-020-00218-6	11.00	1969
Haiti	S/N 008-020-00486-3	9.50	1973
Honduras	S/N 008-020-00368-9	10.00	1971
Hungary	S/N 008-020-00485-5	11.00	1973
India	S/N 008-020-00572-0	15.00	1975
Indian Ocean Territories	S/N 008-020-00393-0	10.00	1971
Indonesia	S/N 008-020-00508-8	13.00	1975
Iran	S/N 008-020-00761-7	13.00	1978
Iraq	S/N 008-020-00818-4	11.00	1979
Israel	S/N 008-020-00790-1	12.00	1979
Italy	S/N 008-020-00648-3	11.00	1977
Ivory Coast	S/N 008-020-00481-2	13.00	1973
Jamaica	S/N 008-020-00604-1	11.00	1976
Japan	S/N 008-020-00520-7	15.00	1974
Jordan	S/N 008-020-00839-7	11.00	1980
Kenya	S/N 008-020-00614-9	13.00	1976
Korea, North	S/N 008-020-00606-8	12.00	1976
Korea, South	S/N 008-020-00592-4	12.00	1975
Laos	S/N 008-020-00467-7	11.00	1972
Lebanon	S/N 008-020-00553-3	12.00	1974
Liberia	S/N 008-020-00414-6	12.00	1972
Libya	S/N 008-020-00817-6	11.00	1979
Malagasy Republic	S/N 008-020-00453-7	11.00	1973
Malawi	S/N 008-020-00567-3	12.00	1975
Malaysia	S/N 008-020-00637-8	12.00	1977
Mauritania	S/N 008-020-00438-3	9.50	1972
Mexico	S/N 008-020-00585-1	12.00	1975
Mongolia	S/N 008-020-00509-6	13.00	1970
Morocco	S/N 008-020-00762-5	12.00	1978
Mozambique	S/N 008-020-00716-1	10.00	1977
Nepal, Bhutan, and Sikkim	S/N 008-020-00480-4	13.00	1973
Nicaragua	S/N 008-020-00327-1	12.00	1970

Nigeria	S/N 008-020-00404-9	14.00	1972
Oceania	S/N 008-020-00307-7	13.00	1971
Pakistan	S/N 008-020-00573-8	12.00	1975
Panama	S/N 008-020-00868-1	11.00	1981
Paraguay	S/N 008-020-00402-2	11.00	1972
Peripheral States of the Arabian Peninsula	S/N 008-020-00347-6	9.50	1971
Peru	S/N 008-020-00869-9	11.00	1981
Persian Gulf States	S/N 008-020-00682-3	12.00	1977
Philippines	S/N 008-020-00619-0	13.50	1980
Poland	S/N 008-020-00450-2	11.00	1973
Portugal	S/N 008-020-00630-1	12.00	1977
Romania	S/N 008-020-00433-2	11.00	1972
Rwanda	S/N 008-020-00220-8	9.50	1969
Saudi Arabia	S/N 008-020-00628-9	12.00	1977
Senegal	S/N 008-020-00521-5	11.00	1974
Sierra Leone	S/N 008-020-00625-4	12.00	1976
Singapore	S/N 008-020-00651-3	10.00	1977
Somalia	S/N 008-020-00646-7	12.00	1977
South Africa, Republic of	S/N 008-020-00892-3	12.00	1981
Southern Rhodesia (Zimbabwe)	S/N 008-020-00552-5	12.00	1975
Soviet Union	S/N 008-020-00335-2	17.00	1971
Spain	S/N 008-020-00611-4	13.00	1976
Sudan, Democratic Republic of	S/N 008-020-00440-5	11.00	1973
Syria	S/N 008-020-00813-3	11.00	1979
Tanzania	S/N 008-020-00767-6	11.00	1978
Thailand	S/N 008-020-00859-1	11.00	1980
Trinidad and Tobago	S/N 008-020-00610-6	11.00	1976
Tunisia	S/N 008-020-00792-7	11.00	1979
Turkey	S/N 008-020-00832-0	12.00	1980
Uganda	S/N 008-020-00212-7	12.00	1971
Uruguay	S/N 008-020-00361-1	12.00	1971
Venezuela	S/N 008-020-00676-9	11.00	1977
Vietnam, North	S/N 008-020-00202-0	13.00	1967
Vietnam, South	S/N 008-020-00333-6	13.00	1976
Yemen	S/N 008-020-00650-5	10.00	1977
Yugoslavia	S/N 008-020-00490-1	15.00	1973
Zaire	S/N 008-020-00776-5	11.00	1979
Zambia	S/N 008-020-00814-1	11.00	1979

Background Notes

Background Notes of the Countries of the World is a series of 160 short, factual pamphlets written by officers in the Department of State's geographic bureaus, providing information on the country's land, people, history, government, political conditions, economy, foreign relations, and U.S. policy. Included also are a profile, brief travel notes, map, list of government officials, and a reading list. Each booklet is $2.00. A complete set of all currently available *Background Notes* is $34.00 post-paid. Order by number from

> Superintendent of Documents
> U.S. Government Printing Office
> Washington, DC 20402

Afghanistan, Democratic Republic of	S/N 044-000-92556-7
Albania, People's Socialist Republic of	S/N 044-000-92606-7
Algeria, Democratic and Popular Republic of	S/N 044-000-92617-2
Andorra, Principality of	S/N 044-000-92669-5
Angola, People's Republic of	S/N 044-000-91288-1
Argentina, Republic of	S/N 044-000-92574-5
Australia, Commonwealth of	S/N 044-000-92686-5
Austria, Republic of	S/N 044-000-92632-6
Bahamas, Commonwealth of the	S/N 044-000-92718-7
Bahrain, State of	S/N 044-000-92710-1
Bangladesh, People's Republic of	S/N 044-000-92639-3
Barbados	S/N 044-000-92681-4
Belgium, Kingdom of	S/N 044-000-92595-8
Belize, Colony of	S/N 044-000-92693-8
Benin, People's Republic of	S/N 044-000-92694-6
Bermuda	S/N 044-000-92618-1
Bhutan, Kingdom of	S/N 044-000-91295-3
Bolivia, Republic of	S/N 044-000-92644-0
Botswana, Republic of	S/N 044-000-92600-8
Brazil, Federative Republic of	S/N 044-000-92732-2
Bulgaria, People's Republic of	S/N 044-000-91203-1
Burma, Socialist Republic of the Union of	S/N 044-000-92672-5
Burundi, Republic of	S/N 044-000-92591-5
Cambodia (Democratic Kampuchea)	S/N 044-000-91136-1
Cameroon, United Republic of	S/N 044-000-92736-5
Canada	S/N 044-000-92625-3
Cape Verde, Republic of	S/N 044-000-92633-4
Central African Republic	S/N 044-000-92601-6
Chad, Republic of	S/N 044-000-91191-4
Chile, Republic of	S/N 044-000-92586-9
China, People's Republic of	S/N 044-000-92634-2
China, Republic of (Taiwan)	S/N 044-000-92584-2
Colombia, Republic of	S/N 044-000-92723-3
Comoros, Federal Islamic Republic of the	S/N 044-000-92728-4

Congo, People's Republic of	S/N 044-000-92580-0
Costa Rica, Republic of	S/N 044-000-92724-1
Cuba, Republic of	S/N 044-000-91200-7
Cyprus, Republic of	S/N 044-000-92676-8
Czechoslovakia, Socialist Republic of	S/N 044-000-92635-1
Denmark, Kingdom of	S/N 044-000-92659-8
Djibouti, Republic of	S/N 044-000-92705-5
Dominica, Commonwealth of	S/N 044-000-92663-6
Dominican Republic	S/N 044-000-92660-1
Ecuador, Republic of	S/N 044-000-92682-2
Egypt, Arab Republic of	S/N 044-000-92695-4
El Salvador, Republic of	S/N 044-000-92619-9
Equatorial Guinea, Republic of	S/N 044-000-91155-8
Ethiopia, Socialist	S/N 044-000-92645-8
European Communities	S/N 044-000-92596-6
Fiji, Dominion of	S/N 044-000-91240-6
Finland, Republic of	S/N 044-000-92698-9
France (French Republic)	S/N 044-000-92673-3
French Antilles and Guiana	S/N 044-000-91236-8
Gabon (Gabonese Republic)	S/N 044-000-92607-5
Gambia, Republic of the	S/N 044-000-92725-0
Germany, Democratic Republic of (East Germany)	S/N 044-000-92664-4
Germany, Federal Republic of (West Germany)	S/N 044-000-92696-2
Ghana, Republic of	S/N 044-000-92620-2
Greece (Hellenic Republic)	S/N 044-000-92677-6
Grenada	S/N 044-000-92571-1
Guatemala, Republic of	S/N 044-000-92640-7
Guinea, Republic of	S/N 044-000-92602-4
Guinea-Bissau, Republic of	S/N 044-000-92706-3
Guyana, Cooperative Republic of	S/N 044-000-92729-2
Haiti, Republic of	S/N 044-000-92621-1
Honduras, Republic of	S/N 044-000-92697-1
Hong Kong	S/N 044-000-92608-3
Hungarian People's Republic	S/N 044-000-92611-3
Iceland, Republic of	S/N 044-000-92641-5
India, Republic of	S/N 044-000-92699-7
Indonesia, Republic of	S/N 044-000-92636-9
Iran, Islamic Republic of	S/N 044-000-92700-4
Iraq, Republic of	S/N 044-000-92714-4
Ireland	S/N 044-000-92683-1
Israel, State of	S/N 044-000-91281-3
Italy	S/N 044-000-92684-9
Ivory Coast, Republic of	S/N 044-000-92737-3
Jamaica	S/N 044-000-92685-7
Japan	S/N 044-000-92582-6

Jordan, Hashemite Kingdom of	S/N 044-000-92637-7
Kenya, Republic of	S/N 044-000-92715-2
Korea, Democratic People's Republic of (North)	S/N 044-000-92588-5
Korea, Republic of (South)	S/N 044-000-92666-1
Kuwait, State of	S/N 044-000-92638-5
Laos, People's Democratic Republic	S/N 044-000-91277-5
Lebanon, Republic of	S/N 044-000-92707-1
Lesotho, Kingdom of	S/N 044-000-92674-1
Liberia, Republic of	S/N 044-000-92670-9
Libya	S/N 044-000-91149-3
Liechtenstein, Principality of	S/N 044-000-92627-0
Luxembourg, Grand Duchy of	S/N 044-000-92716-1
Macao	S/N 044-000-92719-5
Madagascar, Democratic Republic of	S/N 044-000-92687-3
Malawi, Republic of	S/N 044-000-92605-9
Maldives, Republic of	S/N 044-000-92628-8
Mali, Republic of	S/N 044-000-92646-6
Malta	S/N 044-000-92624-5
Mauritania, Islamic Republic of	S/N 044-000-92647-4
Mauritius	S/N 044-000-92730-6
Mexico	S/N 044-000-92629-6
Monaco, Principality of	S/N 044-000-91296-1
Mongolian People's Republic	S/N 044-000-91070-5
Morocco, Kingdom of	S/N 044-000-92688-1
Mozambique, People's Republic of	S/N 044-000-92733-1
Nauru, Republic of	S/N 044-000-92671-7
Nepal, Kingdom of	S/N 044-000-92701-2
Netherlands Antilles	S/N 044-000-92609-1
Netherlands, Kingdom of	S/N 044-000-92689-0
New Zealand	S/N 044-000-92690-3
Nicaragua, Republic of	S/N 044-000-92735-7
Niger, Republic of	S/N 044-000-92727-6
Nigeria, Federal Republic of	S/N 044-000-92711-0
Norway, Kingdom of	S/N 044-000-92661-0
Oman	S/N 044-000-92648-2
Pakistan, Islamic Republic of	S/N 044-000-92630-0
Panama, Republic of	S/N 044-000-92678-4
Papua New Guinea	S/N 044-000-92564-8
Paraguay, Republic of	S/N 044-000-92708-0
Peru, Republic of	S/N 044-000-92720-9
Philippines, Republic of	S/N 044-000-92649-1
Polish People's Republic	S/N 044-000-91297-0
Portugal, Republic of	S/N 044-000-92631-8
Qatar, State of	S/N 044-000-92712-8
Romania, Socialist Republic of	S/N 044-000-92583-4
Rwanda, Republic of	S/N 044-000-92594-0
Saint Lucia	S/N 044-000-92665-2

San Marino, Most Serene Republic of	S/N 044-000-92652-1
Sao Tome and Principe, Democratic Republic of	S/N 044-000-91238-4
Saudi Arabia, Kingdom of	S/N 044-000-92738-1
Senegal, Republic of	S/N 044-000-92668-7
Seychelles	S/N 044-000-92626-1
Sierra Leone, Republic of	S/N 044-000-92604-1
Singapore, Republic of	S/N 044-000-92691-1
Solomon Islands	S/N 044-000-92662-8
Somali Democratic Republic	S/N 044-000-92613-0
South Africa, Republic of	S/N 044-000-92709-8
South West Africa (Namibia)	S/N 044-000-92734-9
Spain (Spanish State)	S/N 044-000-92573-7
Sri Lanka (Ceylon), Democratic Socialist Republic of	S/N 044-000-92561-3
Sudan, Democratic Republic of the	S/N 044-000-92726-8
Surinam, Republic of	S/N 044-000-92702-1
Swaziland, Kingdom of	S/N 044-000-92610-5
Sweden, Kingdom of	S/N 044-000-92721-7
Switzerland (Swiss Confederation)	S/N 044-000-92713-6
Syrian Arab Republic	S/N 044-000-91129-9
Tanzania, United Republic of	S/N 044-000-92653-9
Thailand, Kingdom of	S/N 044-000-92739-0
Togo, Republic of	S/N 044-000-92623-7
Tonga, Kingdom of	S/N 044-000-91299-6
Trinidad and Tobago, Republic of	S/N 044-000-92675-0
Tunisia, Republic of	S/N 044-000-92692-0
Turkey, Republic of	S/N 044-000-91293-7
Uganda, Republic of	S/N 044-000-92679-2
United Arab Emirates	S/N 044-000-92717-9
United Kingdom of Great Britain and Northern Ireland	S/N 044-000-92642-3
United Nations	S/N 044-000-91232-5
Upper Volta, Republic of	S/N 044-000-92654-7
Uruguay, Oriental Republic of	S/N 044-000-92731-4
USSR	S/N 044-000-92655-5
Vatican City, State of	S/N 044-000-92656-3
Venezuela, Republic of	S/N 044-000-92667-9
Vietnam, Socialist Republic of	S/N 044-000-92622-9
Western Samoa	S/N 044-000-91276-7
Yemen Arab Republic (North)	S/N 044-000-92614-8
Yemen, People's Democratic Republic of (South)	S/N 044-000-92615-6
Yugoslavia, Socialist Federal Republic of	S/N 044-000-92579-6
Zaire, Republic of	S/N 044-000-92643-1
Zambia, Republic of	S/N 044-000-92703-9
Zimbabwe	S/N 044-000-92722-5

The Culturgram

Of the many country-specific materials available, the *Culturgram Communication Aid* is one of the most useful. Costing as little as 20¢ in quantity purchases and 35¢ in single copy, the individual issues of *Culturgram* are a bargain.

Brevity is their major characteristic, with significance of the chosen information running a close second. The concept is simple: put in one folded sheet the most important things an outsider should know before entering the country. Whereas the tendency of most country-specific sources is to run toward overwhelming detail, the *Culturgram* gives the reader no such excuse for putting it in the whenever-I-get-time stack. The information is so well-selected that it is worthwhile to memorize.

The *Culturgram* series now includes the following countries:

Argentina	France
Australia	Germany, West
Austria	Ghana
Belgium (Flemish)	Greece
Belgium (French)	Guatemala
Bolivia	Honduras
Brazil	Hong Kong
Bulgaria	Hungary
Canada (Atlantic)	Iceland
Canada (French)	India
Canada (Western and Ontario)	Indonesia
Chile	Iran
China, People's Republic of	Ireland, Northern
Colombia	Ireland, Republic of
Costa Rica	Israel (Jewish)
Czechoslovakia	Israel (Palestinian Arab)
Denmark	Italy
Ecuador	Japan
Egypt	Kenya
El Salvador	Korea, South
England	Lebanon
Fiji	Lesotho
Finland	Luxembourg

Malaysia	Scotland
Mexico	Singapore
Netherlands	South Africa
New Zealand	Spain
Nicaragua	Sri Lanka
Nigeria	Sweden
Norway	Switzerland
Pakistan	Tahiti
Panama	Taiwan (Republic of China)
Paraguay	Thailand
Peru	Tonga
Philippines	Uruguay
Poland	USSR
Portugal	Venezuela
Puerto Rico	Wales
Romania	Yugoslavia
Samoa	Zimbabwe
Saudi Arabia	

A complete set, including postage, is $19.00. A sample *Culturgram* appears on pages 332–333.

In addition to the *Culturgram* series, intercultural preparation materials are available under the general heading "Building Bridges," including Charles Vetter's valuable *Citizen Ambassadors: Guidelines for Responding to Questions Asked About America*. For further information, write or call

Center for International and Area Studies
Publication Services
Brigham Young University
Box 61, Faculty Office Building
Provo, UT 84602
Telephone: 801-378-6528

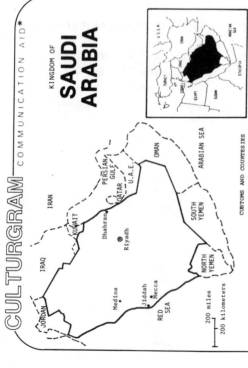

CULTURGRAM COMMUNICATION AID*

KINGDOM OF
**SAUDI
ARABIA**

CUSTOMS AND COURTESIES

<u>Greetings:</u> There are several forms of greeting in Saudi Arabia. The most common is a handshake with the right hand and the phrase "Assalaamu alaykum" (Peace be upon you). Frequently males will follow up by extending the left hand to each other's right shoulder and kiss the right and left cheeks. The greeting used depends on the relationship of the individuals to each other and their status in Saudi Arabian society. When accompanied by a veiled woman, the man will normally not introduce her.

<u>Visiting:</u> Invitations to a Saudi Arabian home are often given to the man alone. If his wife is invited, she may be separated and sent to eat with the other women. Do not bring a gift for the woman of the house. Gifts should normally be given and received with the right hand. Tea or coffee will be served at any meeting. It is best to put a hand over the cup or tilt it several times and say "bes" (enough) to indicate when one has had enough. Drinking of alcoholic beverages is prohibited, and it is best to refrain from smoking in the presence of Saudi Arabians. Coffee is served and incense is passed around at the end of a gathering as a signal that it is time to leave. At the end of a meeting, Saudi Arabians may lose interest and prefer to redirect the conversation.

<u>Eating:</u> Western dining etiquette is normally observed only in more Westernized circles. Finger food must be eaten with the right hand only. However, bread may be torn with the left hand. The Saudi Arabians delight in preparing an abundance of food for their guests, and it is proper to take a second serving. Though hosts often strongly urge their guests to eat more, one may graciously decline. In restaurants, the bill is presented at the table and paid to either the waiter or cashier.

*CULTURGRAMS ARE BRIEFINGS TO AID UNDERSTANDING OF FEELING FOR, AND COMMUNICATION WITH OTHER PEOPLE. CULTURGRAMS ARE CONDENSATIONS OF THE BEST INFORMATION AVAILABLE. YOUR INSIGHTS WILL BE APPRECIATED. IF YOU HAVE SUGGESTIONS OR CORRECTIONS, PLEASE CONTACT: BRIGHAM YOUNG UNIVERSITY CENTER FOR INTERNATIONAL AND AREA STUDIES, PUBLICATION SERVICES, BOX 61 FOB, PROVO, UTAH 84602 (801) 378-6528. COPYRIGHT © 1983 ALL RIGHTS RESERVED. PRINTED IN USA.

<u>Gestures:</u> Do not point at Saudi Arabians or signal them with the hand. Avoid using the left hand for eating, gesturing, and sending items in the presence of the Saudi Arabians. Avoid pointing the soles of your shoes towards Saudi Arabians. Crossing your legs in the company of non-westernized Saudi Arabians may be taken as a sign of disrespect.

<u>Personal Appearance:</u> Saudi Arabian men and women still wear traditional Arab dress. The men wear the ghutra (head cloth) and thobe (white flowing robes). The women wear the veil and abaya (black robe that covers from head to foot, often over long dresses tailored from beautiful, imported fabrics.) Do not ask the Saudi Arabians to remove their head coverings. Visitors should dress conservatively, and women should especially avoid wearing shorts, short sleeves, low necklines, and tight-fitting clothing. Otherwise women may be subjected to misconceptions that could lead to harrassment.

THE PEOPLE

<u>General Attitudes:</u> Life in Saudi Arabia is relaxed and slow paced, and this pace often grates on the rushed American lifestyle. Saudi Arabians like to establish trust and confidence with the people they deal with before proceeding with any business at hand. They are very conscious of personal and family honor and can be easily offended by any perceived insult of that honor. Saudi Arabians are generous and hospitable, and greatly concerned with the welfare of their guests.

<u>Population:</u> Figures estimating the size of the population range from 4 to 9 million. About 75% of the 3 million labor force are foreign workers, mainly from Yemen, Egypt and Palestine. Also, other nationalities include Indians, Pakistanis, Koreans, and Americans. The Saudis consider this large foreign population to be a serious threat to future stability. The indigenous population is fairly homogeneous nomadic tribes. The population density rate is only about 10 people per square mile (58 in U.S.).

<u>Language:</u> Arabic is the official language of the Kingdom. It is the language of the Koran and considered to be the language of God. Some English is spoken in urban markets and is widely spoken in businesses and among educated circles.

<u>Religion:</u> Islam is the only legally and officially recognized religion. Arabia is the birthplace of the prophet, Mohammad, and Saudi Arabia is the home of Islam's two most important shrines: Mecca and Medina. Non-Muslims are not admitted to these sacred cities. The Islamic scripture, the Koran, is the basis for daily life, and Islamic law and tradition form the constitution of the Kingdom. Muslims believe that Moses, Abraham, and Jesus are also prophets, but see no need for an atonement and do not accept Jesus as the Son of God. Saudi Arabians are not allowed to join Christian churches. Foreigners are allowed freedom of religion but proselyting is illegal.

<u>Holidays:</u> The Islamic calendar is based on the lunar month of 29 1/2 days, thus making the year 10 to 11 days shorter than the Western year. For this reason, holidays vary from year to year, with the exception of September 23, National Day. The calendar starts at the year of the Hegira (flight of Mohammad from Mecca to Medina) in the seventh century A.D. During the month of Ramadan, all Muslims abstain from food, drink, and smoking during the daylight hours. Visitors are required by law to observe the fast of Ramadan while in public.

LIFESTYLE

<u>The Family:</u> Although the Saudi Arabian family is traditionally a strong, male dominated unit, with the families of several generations living under the same roof, women exercise considerable influence within the home. More families are moving to the city and living in single family homes. Sons generally live in a neighborhood close to their father's home.

332

Separation of male and female is a way of life in Saudi Arabia. Rules governing the actions of women are based on Saudi Arabian law and custom, and are designed to respect and protect their femininity. A woman's behavior reflects on her family's honor and reputation. Women are not allowed to interact with men outside of their family and are forbidden to drive a car or bicycle. Many of these laws also apply to women visitors.

Dating and Marriage: Marriages are often arranged. Among a growing minority, young men and women are allowed to choose their mates. Currently, non-Saudi wives of Saudi Arabian men need a special permit to be allowed in the Kingdom. A traditional Saudi Arabian wedding is an Islamic civil ceremony followed by separate parties for the men and women. Traditionally, men pay dowries for their brides. Although Islamic law allows a man to have up to four wives at the same time as long as he treats them equally, most Saudi Arabian men have only one wife.

Social and Economic Levels: Since the 1930s, a major goal of the Saudi regime has been to centralize governmental power. To this end, the formerly nomadic tribes have been encouraged to settle in the cities and reorient themselves to a centralized society and economy. The government subsidizes housing projects with oil revenues, and will provide land and the equivalent of a $90,000 no-interest loan to any Saudi Arabian desiring to build. Apartments are available in Western style apartment buildings, but are expensive and in short supply.

Business Hours: The work week runs from Saturday to Wednesday, with Thursday and Friday being the week-end. Friday is the Muslim day of rest and worship. Government offices are open from 9 a.m. to 2 p.m., while non-government shops are open from 8 a.m. to 12, and again from 4 p.m. to 8:30. During Ramadan, working hours are adjusted and many offices are closed by noon.

Recreation: Soccer is the national sport, but only men are permitted to play or watch at the stadium. Saudi Arabian men also enjoy horse and camel races, hunting and hawking. Women enjoy visiting with other women, collecting jewelry, and caring for their own and extended family members' children.

Diet: Saudi dishes are composed mainly of rice with lamb or chicken, and are usually mildly spicey. Saudi Arabians serve coffee and tea with all their meals. Buttermilk and camel's milk are also popular. The Koran forbids the consumption of pork and alcoholic beverages.

THE NATION

Land and Climate: Saudi Arabia is the twelfth largest country in the world. It is one-fourth the size of the U.S. and comprises 1.4% of the world land total. Saudi Arabia is a vast arid plain of sand and rock, with rugged mountains in the west. Rainfall is slight, and only approximately 1% of the land can be cultivated. Another 1% of the land is forest and the remaining 98% is desert. Most cities are built on the coast or in the oases that dot the face of the desert.

History and Government: Arabia possesses a rich and colorful history. Starting in the 7th century A.D., the Prophet Mohammad proclaimed from the centers of Mecca and Medina the message of Islam, which soon spread as far as North Africa and central Asia. The history of present day Saudi Arabia begins in 1902, when Abdulaziz ibn Saud recaptured his ancestral home in Riyadh. After thirty years of fighting, Abdulaziz united the major rival factions and declared himself King of Saudi Arabia. After World War II, the vast oil reserves of the Kingdom were opened, and Abdulaziz began to use the oil revenue to speed the process of modernization. This process has been carried onward by the succeeding Kings Faisal and Khalid. Saudi Arabia is an absolute monarchy and is governed by the Saudi family, descendants of Abdulaziz. The leaders of the family appoint the king. Islamic laws and practices form the basis for modern Saudi law.

Economy: Saudi Arabia has one of the strongest economies in the world. Gross national product (GNP) per capita is nearly $10,000 ($10,470 in U.S.). Although only 3% of the population is involved in oil related industries, oil is the most important part of the economy. Saudi Arabia has the world's largest petroleum reserves (one-fourth of the world total) and the fifth largest natural gas reserves. It is the second largest petroleum producer and the third largest energy producer in the world. Oil accounts for 99% of the country's exports, giving the country the world's most favorable balance of trade. ARAMCO (Arab American Oil Co.) is the major energy producing organization, and came completely under Saudi Arabian control in 1980. Revenue from the oil is rapidly being invested in modernization and in expanding the industrial base. Because of the inhospitable climate and terrain, the nation must import the majority of its food. Dates, grains and livestock are produced. The unit of currency is the riyal, and is considered an internationally solid currency. The inflation rate is over 25% (6-7% in U.S.).

Education: The government finances education through the university level. Saudi Arabia spends a larger percentage of its GNP on education than any other country in the world. Although enrollment in the past has been low, the trend is reversing. Men and women attend separate schools, but more women are getting university degrees and entering the work force. Generous support is provided for vocational training in order to decrease the amount of skilled workers that must be imported from abroad. The literacy rate is over 15 and 25%.

Health: Although standards of health are not yet up to par with the West, the country is rapidly progressing. Medical facilities are improving, and many doctors have been trained in America. Drinking water may need to be boiled or filtered in some places, and fruits and vegetables may need to be soaked in a chlorine solution before eating.

Transportation and Communications: The Kingdom is continually expanding its system of roads and telephones. The most convenient mode of transportation between cities, however, is via airplane. Daily flights link up to twenty cities in the kingdom. Travel in the city is best done by taxi or bus. The telephone system, when completed, will be one of the most modern in the world. International telephone, telegraph, and telex services are available.

USEFUL WORDS AND PHRASES

Salaam alaykum	Peace upon you
Wa alaykum essalaam	And upon you, peace
Keyf haalik	How is your condition? (How are you?)
Shukran	Thank you
Af'wan	You're welcome
Ana aasif	I'm sorry
Maalish	Never mind
Tayyib	Very well or O.K.
Min faddlak	Please

SUGGESTED READING

Hobday, Peter. *Saudi Arabia Today.* New York: St. Martin's Press, 1978.

Lanier, Alison. *Update: Saudi Arabia.* New York: Overseas Briefing Association, 1978.

Lee, Eve. "Saudis as We, Americans as They." *The Bridge* (Fall, 1980), pp. 6-9.

Nyrop, Richard K., et al. *Area Handbook for Saudi Arabia.* Washington, D.C.: U.S. Government Printing Office, 1977.

Pendleton, M. *The Green Book: A Guide to Living in Saudi Arabia.* Washington, D.C.: Middie East Editorial Services, 1978.

"Saudi Arabian" *Overseas Assignment Directory Service.* New York: Knowledge Industry Publications, 1978.

For further information contact: Embassy of the Kingdom of Saudi Arabia, 1520 18th St., N.W., Washington, D.C. 20036.
Special thanks to Jeanne Morris for the initial draft.

Rev. 3/83

This 3/83 version of the Culturgram on Saudi Arabia is reprinted by permission of the Center for International and Area Studies, Brigham Young University. It is one of a series of 81 Culturgrams that may be obtained by writing to the Center for International and Area Studies.

Fodor's Travel Guides (World Series)

Country Guides

Australia	India
Austria	Ireland
Belgium	Israel
Bermuda	Italy
Brazil	Japan
Canada	Mexico
China (People's Republic)	Portugual
Egypt	Soviet Union
France	Spain
Germany	Switzerland
Great Britain	Turkey
Greece	Yugoslavia
Holland	

Regional Guides

Caribbean	Scandinavia
Eastern Europe	Southeastern Asia
Europe	South America
North Africa	

City Guides

London	Rome
Paris	

Guidebooks

Of the many materials available, two series stand out for their thoroughness, detail, and accuracy. The *Fodor's* series is time-honored and well-worn, though frequently updated and organized efficiently for use by tourists and newcomers.

Insight Guides

Somewhat more difficult to find, but very much worth the effort are the *Insight Guides*, a series produced by a group of brilliant young journalists and photojournalists. This production group, based in Singapore, has concentrated so far primarily on Asian nations where most of their members are currently assigned. One might fervently hope that their efforts will be widely appreciated and rewarded and that their catalog of available titles will steadily increase. The increase may be slow, however, because of the care for graphic and textual detail lavished on each book. The books resemble the finest of the National Geographic Society's books, reflecting similarily high standards for expressive text and attractiveness of layout and color photography. Each is organized into a systematic guide to people, places, history and cultural context of a given country or region.

Currently Available

Bali (Indonesia)	Mexico
Burma	Nepal
Jamaica	Philippines
Java (Indonesia)	Singapore
Korea	Sri Lanka
Malaysia	Thailand

In Production

Australia	Indonesia
Bahamas	Taiwan
Caribbean	

Booksellers in the United States and Canada can order *Insight Guides* from

Prentice-Hall, Inc.
Englewood Cliffs, NJ 07632

APPENDIX E

Professional Resources

The Society for Intercultural Education, Training and Research (SIETAR) is the major international affiliation of professionals in the field of intercultural preparation. Regional and international meetings are held annually. A publication series is actively developed by the society in order to encourage the exchange of ideas, materials, and evidences about the skills and understandings required for intercultural competency. SIETAR is affiliated with Georgetown University. Its periodic workshops for practitioners and researchers are usually held on the Georgetown campus. The society's address is

The Society for Intercultural Education, Training and Research
1414 Twenty-Second Street, N.W.
Suite 102
Washington, DC 20037

The Publication Division of SIETAR provides a small but authoritative catalog of materials especially of interest to intercultural trainers and "trainers of trainers." SIETAR membership provides a substantial discount on purchases. Of particular interest are Pierre Casse's *Training for the Cross-Cultural Mind* (1981) and *Intercultural Theory and Practice, A Case Method Approach*, edited by William G. Davey (1981). The address is the same as for SIETAR.

Many of the persons most active in SIETAR have published through the Intercultural Press in Chicago. The SIETAR Publications titles from Intercultural Press are available at the SIETAR membership discount. The

Press's catalog is specifically focused on matters of intercultural preparation.

Titles include such materials as Glen Fisher's *International Negotiations: A Cross-Cultural Perspective*; Joan Rubin and Irene Thompson's *How to Be a Successful Language Learner; Communicating With China* (edited by Robert A. Kapp), and the invaluable *Intercultural Sourcebook: Cross-Cultural Training Methodologies* (edited by David S. Hooper and Paul Ventura).

Intercultural Press, Inc.
70 West Hubbard Street
Chicago, IL 60610

Another of the specialized academic publishers with a substantial catalog in this field is SAGE Publications. Their *Handbook of Intercultural Communications* (1979) has become a definitive reference book. Also through SAGE, the Speech Communication Association's Commission on International and Intercultural Communication publishes a series, the *International and Intercultural Communication Annual*. The 1983 Annual, for example is devoted to "International Communication Theory." Lists of other titles in this field are also available from

SAGE Publications, Inc.
P.O. Box 5024
Beverly Hills, CA 90210

Academic Press's catalog has a subdivision in intercultural communication. Its materials tend toward scholarly and research-oriented titles such as *Cross-Cultural Research at Issue*, edited by Lenore Loeb Adler.

Academic Press, Inc. Publishers
111 Fifth Avenue
New York, NY 10003

Among the sources of the "heaviest" academic literature is the Pergamon International Library of Science, Technology, Engineering and Social Studies. Pergamon is the publisher of the prestigious *International Journal of Intercultural Relations*, as well as textbooks of special merit such as Richard Brislin's *Cross-Cultural Encounters*, which has provided much of the research base for *Living Overseas*. It also publishes the important book by Anthony Marsella and Paul Pedersen, *Cross Cultural Counseling and Psychotherapy*.

Pergamon Press, Inc.
Maxwell House, Fairview Park
Elmsford, NY 10523

The publications of the University Press of Hawaii for the East-West Center include a substantial list of intercultural materials including *Culture Learning: Concepts, Applications, and Research*, edited by Richard W. Brislin (1977), and *Counseling Across Cultures*, edited by Paul Pedersen and others (1976).

East-West Center Publications
1777 East-West Road
Honolulu, HI 96848

In the expanding literature of adult learning and intercultural compe-
tencies for international business and industry, Gulf Publishing Company
has developed a series of books and videotapes entitled "Building Blocks of
Human Potential." Included are two useful books by Philip A. Harris and
Robert T. Moran: *Managing Cultural Differences*, (1979) and *Managing
Cultural Synergy* (1982).

Gulf Publishing Company
P.O. Box 2608
Houston, TX 77001

Much of the more stimulating and experience-based literature comes
from small groups which emerge and then disappear, offering for a time
some curious and rich items of what soon becomes "fugitive literature."
Some such groups persist long enough for their work to be noted in such a
place as this book. The *Volunteers in Asia* is a group currently publishing
an interesting small collection of material of substantial merit. Their titles
include the excellent organizing outline for country-specific study, *Trans-
cultural Study Guide*, second edition, edited by Kenneth Darrow and
Bradley Palmquist (1975).

Volunteers in Asia
P.O. Box 4543
Stanford, CA 94305

APPENDIX F

A Prime Bookshelf

A Clearer View of America and Americans

HACKER, ANDREW, ed. *U/S: A Statistical Portrait of the American People.* New York: Viking, 1983. Lively presentation of census data and other quantitative data.

ROBERTSON, JAMES. *American Myth, American Reality.* New York: Hill and Wang, 1980. If there is a unified "American culture," this book accounts for its sources.

STEWART, EDWARD C. *American Cultural Patterns.* Chicago: Intercultural Press, 1972. When others look at us, this is what they see.

WERKMAN, SIDNEY. *Bringing Up Children Overseas—A Guide for Families.* New York: Basic Books, 1977.

Compilation of the Research in Intercultural Relations and Communication

BRISLIN, RICHARD. *Cross-Cultural Encounters.* New York: Pergamon, 1981. Detailed, thorough, thoughtful.

GUDYKUNST, WILLIAM B. and YOUNG YUN KIM. *Communicating with Strangers—An Approach to Intercultural Communication.* Reading, Mass.: Addison-Wesley, 1984. Thorough theoretical and practical review, filled with well-told stories and illustrations.

Review of Intercultural Training Methodologies

HOOPES, DAVID S. and PAUL VENTURA, eds. *Intercultural Sourcebook*. Washington, D.C.: Society for Intercultural Education, Training and Research, 1979. Useful sampling of material and methods.

Reading for Contemporary Perspective

CRITCHFIELD, RICHARD. *Villages*. Garden City, N.Y.: Doubleday, 1981. To comprehend the "little people" of the world.

GHEDDO, PIERO. *Why Is the Third World Poor?* Maryknoll, N.Y.: Orbis, 1973. Economics and beyond; ideologies and theology of development.

HESS, J. DANIEL. *From the Other's Point of View*. Scottdale, Pa.: Herald, 1980. Latin American case studies and sobering view of U.S. role.

LAMB, DAVID. *The Africans*. New York: Random House, 1982. Blunt, probing, thoroughly intriguing.

Understandable Worldwide Comparisons

KIDRON, MICHAEL and RONALD SEGAL. *The State of the World Atlas*. N.Y.: Simon and Schuster, 1981. Color plates of proportioned maps; intriguing, memorable.

Classics

HALL, EDWARD T. *The Silent Language*. Garden City, N.Y.: Doubleday, 1959.

_____. *Beyond Culture*. Garden City, N.Y.: Doubleday, 1976. A pair of winners, eye-opening for hundreds of thousands of people.

Notes

INTRODUCTION

1. The most outstanding single volume reviewing this literature is Richard Brislin, *Cross Cultural Encounters—Face-to-Face Interaction* (New York: Pergamon, 1981).
2. For example, see L. Robert Kohls, *Survival Kit for Cross-Cultural Living* (Chicago: Intercultural Press, 1979).
3. See Appendix E.

CHAPTER 1. AN INVITATION TO EXPERIENCE

1. J. Watson and Ronald Lippitt, *Learning Across Cultures: A Study of Germans Visiting America* (Ann Arbor: Institute for Social Research, University of Michigan, 1955).
2. C. Kagitcibasi, "Cross-National Encounter: Turkish Students in the United States," *International Journal of Intercultural Relations* 2(2), 1978, pp. 141–160.
3. Richard Brislin, *Cross-Cultural Encounters: Face-to-Face Interaction* (New York: Pergamon, 1981), p. 295.
4. O. Klineberg and F. Hull, *At a Foreign University* (New York: Praeger, 1979).
5. C. Alger, "Personal Contact in Intergovernmental Organizations," in H. Kilman (ed.), *International Behavior: A Social Psychological Analysis* (New York: Holt, Rinehart and Winston, 1965).
6. Kagitcibasi, 1978, p. 153.

7. Peter S. Adler, "Beyond Cultural Identity: Reflections upon Cultural and Multicultural Man," in Richard Brislin, ed., *Culture Learning: Concepts, Applications and Research* (Honolulu: East-West Center, 1977), pp. 24–41.

8. Marvin Mayers, *Biculturalism* (Grand Rapids, Mich.: Zondervan, 1973).

9. Adler, "Beyond Cultural Identity," p. 25.

CHAPTER 2. WHO ARE WE?

1. *Summary of Passport Statistics*, U.S. Passport Services, U.S. Department of State, as quoted in *Information Please Almanac* (New York: A & W Publishers, 1982), p. 317.

2. Don't miss out. For Richard Halliburton's first and most youthfully daring book, check with your library for *The Royal Road to Romance* (Indianapolis: Bobbs-Merrill, 1925).

3. For today's parallel, see Ron O'Grady, *Third World Stopover* (Geneva: World Council of Churches, 1981). O'Grady's highly critical assessment of tourism's effects on third world economy and dignity is a profound warning for all overseas personnel.

4. Brazilian spelling. Sounds the same as *ciao*, the Italian informal "see ya."

5. The Philippines is often cited as an example; apparently because of its long period of domination by white outsiders which was followed by a long phase of being a supplier of agricultural raw materials, especially sugar, to be processed elsewhere, it was late to come into its own as a modernized industrial nation. Even its large investment in higher education has produced a brain-drain exportation of its most promising people.

6. "Getting the U.S. to Measure Up," *Time*, 9 May 1983, p. 70.

7. On July 29, 1983, confusion of Air Canada flight ground crews between the metric system, used in Canada, and the old English system, which Boeing uses, was a contributing factor in a serious aviation safety incident near Gimli, Manitoba (*Time*, 8 August 1983), p. 47.

8. As quoted in *Trans-Cultural Study Guide*, Ken Darrow and Brad Palmquist, eds. (Stanford, Calif.: Volunteers in Asia, 1975), p. 4.

9. An Wang, son of a Shanghai school teacher, is listed by *Forbes Magazine* as the fifth most wealthy American today. His Wang Laboratories, Inc., in Lowell, Mass., is said to be worth $1.6 billion! (Associated Press, 29 Sept. 1983.)

10. *The Speeches of the Right Honorable John Philpot Curran* (Dublin: James Duffy, Wellington Quay, 1865), p. 105.

11. Elmer Davis, *But We Were Born Free* (Indianapolis: Bobbs-Merrill, 1954), p. 228.

CHAPTER 3. LEARNING A CULTURE

1. Ralph Linton, *The Tree of Culture* (New York: Vintage, 1955), p. 3.
2. A. L. Kroeber and Clyde Kluckhohn, "Culture: A Critical Review of Concepts and Definitions," in *Papers of the Peabody Museum of American Archaeology and Ethnology* 67 (1), 1952, p. 157.
3. "World is the structure of meaningful relationships in which a person exists and in the design of which he participates. Thus, world includes the past events which condition my existence and all the vast variety of deterministic influences which operate on me. But it is as I relate to them, am aware of them, carry them with me molding, inevitably forming, building them in every minute of relating. For to be aware of the world means at the same time to be designing it. . . . World is not to be limited to the past determining events, but includes also all possibilities which open up before any person and are not simply given in the historical situation. World is thus not to be identified with culture. It includes culture but a good deal more, such as *Eigenweld* (the one-world which cannot be reduced merely to an introjection of the culture) as well as all the individual's future possibilities. . . . The term 'culture' is generally, in common parlance, set over against the individual (e.g., 'the influence of culture upon the individual'). This usage is probably an unavoidable result of the dichotomy between subject and object in which the concepts of 'individual' and 'culture' emerged. It, of course, omits the very significant fact that the individual is, at every moment, also forming his culture . . ." Rollo May, "Contributions of Existential Psychotherapy," in Rollo May, Ernest Angel, and Henri Ellenberger, eds., *Existence* (New York: Touchstone Books, 1958), pp. 59–60.
4. Eric Casino, "Modes and Forms of Culture Learning." Presented at seminar, Education for Cross-Cultural Perspective, Honolulu, June 1982.
5. This reflection on experiences, leading back into improved capacity to deal effectively with experiences is often called *praxis*. The term refers to the importance of doing what one knows, knowing what one does, and continuously cycling one's reflection into action, into reflection, into action. . . .
6. Pragmatic here refers to the contemporary, self-centered preoccupation with "making things work out" which usually implies one's own concerns as the beginning and ending of all human judgments.

CHAPTER 4. ACCOUNTING FOR DIFFERENCES

1. Based on the response of the Samaritan woman at the well of Jacob at Sychar, John 4:20–21. A reference to Deuteronomy 11:29 is also implied.

2. Richard Brislin, *Cross-Cultural Encounters* (New York: Pergamon, 1981).

3. Margaret Mead, *Coming of Age in Samoa* (New York: Morrow, 1928).

4. Derek Freeman, *Margaret Mead and Samoa: The Making and Un-making of an Anthropological Myth* (Cambridge: Harvard University Press, 1983).

5. Thomas Jefferson, in a letter to a friend, 1824. Cited in Roy Harvey Pearce, *The Savages of America—A Study of the Indian and the Idea of Civilization* (Baltimore: The Johns Hopkins Press, 1965), p. 155.

6. I call "saving face" an exaggeration, not in a spirit of criticism, but only to recognize that what is for *all* human beings a matter of discomfort—being reminded or confronted about a weakness, a mistake, or an emotionally difficult experience—is made a matter of social ritual and even a cause for profound disgrace. Thus, something common to all human feelings is given a stylistic exaggeration, and it becomes a cultural peculiarity or so-called uniqueness.

7. David Lamb, *The Africans* (New York: Random House, 1982), pp. 21–22.

8. Arnold C. Mayer, Jr., correspondence with the author, June 1983.

9. Mayer, 1983.

CHAPTER 5. THE SKILLS OF COPING

1. Kalvero Oberg, *Culture Shock and the Problem of Adjustment to New Cultural Environments* (Washington: Department of State, Foreign Service Institute, 1958). Oberg originated the term "culture shock."

2. Based on L. Robert Kohls, *Survival Kit for Overseas Living* (Chicago: Intercultural Press, 1979), p. 63.

3. Based on Kohls, *Survival Kit*, p. 63.

4. Based on Kohls, *Survival Kit*, p. 64.

5. Richard W. Brislin and Paul Pedersen, *Cross-Cultural Orientation Programs* (New York: Gardner, 1976), p. 17.

6. Richard W. Brislin, *Cross Cultural Encounters* (New York: Pergamon, 1981), p. 155.

7. Edward T. Hall, *The Silent Language* (New York: Doubleday, 1959; Fawcett, 1969), p. 156 (Fawcett ed.).

8. Brislin, *Cross-Cultural Encounters*, p. 137.

9. Adapted from Kohls, *Survival Kit*, pp. 69–70.

10. WKAR, East Lansing, Mich., January 20, 1983.

11. Note Deut. 25:4, as cited also in the New Testament: 1 Cor. 9:9 and 1 Tim. 5:18. This premise of the right of the worker to partake of the

goods being handled is a value similarly shared by Jews, Muslims, and Christians.

12. Awa: Africa Wins Again
13. Luke 10:1–12 (TEV). A parallel situation is described in Matt. 10:1–15.

CHAPTER 6. INTERPERSONAL RELATIONSHIPS ARE THE KEY

1. Working elbow to elbow with Russians suggests that they may be even worse, but hardly any research comparing the two is yet available.
2. Gloria Tiede, "With Sympathy," *Wherever* 7 (2), Winter 1983, p. 12.
3. Tiede, p. 12.
4. Based on Ruth 1:16, 17.
5. Laurence J. Peter, *Peter's Quotations: Ideas for Our Time* (New York: Bantam Books, 1977), p. 389.

CHAPTER 7. LANGUAGE CAN BE BARRIER OR BRIDGE

1. Urban France, especially Paris, is one of the notorious exceptions. Unless you can speak French with considerable skill and accuracy, it is best to stick to English. Parisians are especially rude to people who speak French *poorly*. Brislin thinks that it is because they simply don't like to have to listen to people who are learning (Brislin, *Cross-Cultural Encounters*, p. 64).
2. Benjamin Whorf, *Language, Thought and Reality: Selected Writings* (Cambridge, Mass.: MIT Press, 1956). Further developed in G. Miller and D. McNeil, "Psycholinguistics" in G. Lindzey and E. Aronson, eds., *Handbook of Social Psychology*, vol. 3 (Reading, Mass.: Addison-Wesley, 1969).
3. Lacking a language coach, try *How to Be a More Successful Language Learner* by Joan Rubin and Irene Thompson (Boston: Heinle & Heinle, 1982).
4. By no means is *x* limited to adopted Indian words. In Brazilian Portuguese, it appears in these other phonetic uses: "z" sound as in *exemplo* and *exército*; "s" sound as in *experiência*; "ks" sound as in *inexplicável* and *reflexão*.
5. The names for people and places in North America include a curious combination of insensitive *exonyms* (names imposed by outsiders). Consider the commemoration of Christopher Columbus's big mistake: Indians. Or think of this: if the name for what is now the United States had been based on *autonyms* (what people name themselves) as was accepted by the Spanish in Mexico, what would it be? Surely not a

commemoration of the Italian merchant seaman Amerigo Vespucci! Perhaps the United States of Tahiawagi.

6. Dwight Gradin, "Be Swift to Hear, Slow to Speak," *Instructional Paper of Missionary Internship* (Farmington, Mich.: Missionary Internship, Inc., 1983), p. 1.

7. James Nord, "Three Steps Leading to Listening Fluency: A Beginning," in Henry Wintz, ed., *The Comprehensive Approach to Foreign Language Instruction* (New York: Newbury House, 1981).

8. Gradin, "Be Swift to Hear," p. 2.

9. E. Thomas Brewster and Elizabeth S. Brewster, *Language Acquisition Made Practical* (Colorado Springs: Lingua House, 1976).

10. "Language Learning," *World Christian*, January/February 1983, p. 29.

11. "Language Learning," p. 29.

CHAPTER 8. YOUR JOB AND ITS CONTEXT

1. Ingemar Torbiorn, *Living Abroad: Personal Adjustment and Personnel Policy in the Overseas Setting* (Chichester, U.K.: Wiley, 1982), p. x.

2. Frank Hawes and Daniel J. Kealey, "An Empirical Study of Canadian Technical Assistance: Adaptation and Effectiveness on Overseas Assignment," *Journal of Intercultural Relations* 5, 1981, p. 244.

3. Hawes and Kealey, "An Empirical Study," p. 239.

4. Hawes and Kealey, "An Empirical Study," pp. 255–56.

5. Hawes and Kealey, "An Empirical Study," p. 253.

6. J. Daniel Hess, *From the Other's Point of View* (Scottdale, Pa.: Herald Press, 1980), pp. 249, 250.

7. The overseas marketing of agricultural chemicals is a parallel matter. DDT, long outlawed in the United States, is still widely available across the counter in many Third World nations.

8. Laurence J. Peter, *Peter's Quotations: Ideas for Our Time* (New York: Bantam/Morrow, 1977), p. 450.

CHAPTER 9. A CONSUMER'S GUIDE TO ORIENTATION TRAINING

1. Gerd Seidel, "Cross-Cultural Training Procedures: Their Theoretical Framework and Evaluation," in Stephen Bochner, *The Mediating Person: Bridges Between Cultures* (Cambridge, Mass.: Schenkman, 1981), pp. 189–190.

2. Training in the Peace Corps, in turn, can be traced to the carry-over of World War II assumptions about intensive training for rapid mobilization.

3. Seidel, "Cross-Cultural Training," p. 188.

4. Seidel, "Cross-Cultural Training," p. 187.

5. Eugene Lamoureux, "A Perspective on Culture with Implications for the Planning of Culture Learning." Presented to Michigan State University seminar on culture learning, Tokyo, 1982, p. 7.

6. Eugene Lamoureux, "A Perspective on Culture," pp. 15–16. Quotation by Charles Taylor is found in "Interpretation and the Sciences of Man," in Paul Rabinow, ed., *Interpretive Social Science: A Reader* (Berkeley: University of California Press, 1979), p. 35.

7. Here is one of many habits you won't reshape in one weekend. It takes lots of practice. Start early!

8. Suggestions about various specific materials are provided in the appendices of this book.

9. Richard W. Brislin and Paul Pedersen, *Cross-Cultural Orientation Programs* (New York: Gardner Press, 1976), pp. 101–102. The Harrison and Hopkins orientation program was an early example of a series of procedures to achieve these objectives. The trainees were 82 Peace Corps volunteers being prepared for assignments in Chile, Ecuador, and Bolivia. See R. Harrison and R. Hopkins, "The Design of Cross-Cultural Training: An Alternative to the University Model," *The Journal of Applied Behavioral Science* 3, 1967, pp. 431–460.

CHAPTER 10. THE HUMANITARIANS

1. Acts 17:23

2. Acts 17:30–31 (Today's English Version).

3. The "modern missionary movement" refers to the current period of world-wide missions, usually dated from the Moravian outreach of 1732 or, more generally, from the efforts of John Wesley and George Whitefield.

4. The Apostles' Creed: I believe in God the Father Almighty, Maker of heaven and earth; And in Jesus Christ, His only Son, our Lord, Who was conceived by the Holy Ghost, Born of the Virgin Mary, Suffered under Pontius Pilate, Was crucified dead and buried; He descended into hell; the third day He rose again from the dead; He ascended into heaven, And is seated on the right hand of God the Father Almighty; from thence He shall come to judge the quick and the dead. I Believe in the Holy Ghost; The holy Catholic Church, The Communion of

Saints; The Forgiveness of sins; The resurrection of the body: And the Life everlasting. Amen.

5. Acts 4:12.

6. George Marsden, *Fundamentalism and American Culture* (New York: Oxford University Press, 1980).

7. Matt 3:8–12; Luke 3:3–14.

8. Luke 3:10–14

9. Luke 4:16–21.

10. The ancient African empires and nations—Zimbabwe, for one—were usually tribal affiliations, often regional clusterings, whose territorial borders have little congruence with European-drawn boundaries of the colonial nations. Today's African nations take their boundaries and even their population criteria largely from colonial era maps, simply changing the names.

11. See Denis Goulet, *A New Moral Order* (Maryknoll, N.Y.: Orbis, 1974); Paulo Freire, *Education for Critical Consciousness* (New York: Seabury, 1973); Dom Helder Camara, with Gladys Weigner and Bernhard Moosbrugger, *A Voice of the Third World* (New York: Paulist, 1972); and Gustavo Gutierrez, *A Theology of Liberation* (Maryknoll, N.Y.: Orbis, 1973).

CHAPTER 11. PLANNING THE MOVE

1. Adapted from Volunteers in Asia (Ken Darrow and Brad Palmquist, eds.), *Trans-Cultural Study Guide* (Stanford, Calif.: Volunteers in Asia, 1975).

2. John Useem and Ruth Useem, "The Interfaces of a Binational Third Culture. A Study of the American Community in India," *The Journal of Social Issues* 23 (1), 1967, pp. 130–143.

3. Cliff Schimmels, "T.C.K. + T.L.C. = A.O.K.," *Wherever* 7 (2), 1983, p. 8.

4. Schimmels, "T.C.K. + T.L.C.," p. 9

5. The Calvert School, 105 Tuscany Road, Baltimore, Md. 21210.

6. William Redden, *Culture Shock Inventory—Manual* (Frederickton, N.B., Canada: Organizational Tests, Inc., 1975).

CHAPTER 12. LIVING WITH WHAT YOU FIND

1. Pack clean clothes in the cannisters and put them in one of the large suitcases that you carry with you.

2. See Appendix B for suggestions on this matter and other health hints.

3. Check on the price before you order a steak in a Tokyo or Osaka restaurant. Fifty dollars is not unusual—per person.

CHAPTER 13. COME BACK STRONGER

1. J. Daniel Hess, *From the Other's Point of View* (Scottdale, Pa.: Herald Press, 1980), pp. 271–292.
2. Based on Peter S. Adler, "The Transnational Experience: An Alternative View of Culture Shock," *Journal of Humanistic Psychology* 15 (4), 1975, pp. 13–23.

Index